Forging a language

Forging a language
A study of the plays of Eugene O'Neill

JEAN CHOTHIA

Fellow of Selwyn College, Cambridge

CAMBRIDGE UNIVERSITY PRESS

CAMBRIDGE

LONDON   NEW YORK   NEW ROCHELLE

MELBOURNE   SYDNEY

Published by the Press Syndicate of the University of Cambridge
The Pitt Building, Trumpington Street, Cambridge CB2 IRP
32 East 57th Street, New York, NY 10022, USA
296 Beaconsfield Parade, Middle Park, Melbourne 3206, Australia

First published 1979
First paperback edition 1981

Printed in Great Britain at the
University Press, Cambridge

Library of Congress catalogue card number: 78-73239

British Library Cataloguing in Publication Data
Chothia, Jean
Forging a language.
1. O'Neill, Eugene – Language
I. Title
812'.52   PS529.N5
ISBN 0 521 28523 2

For Cyrus

Contents

Illustrations

Illustrations 1, 2a, 3, 4, 5, 6 are reproduced by permission of the
Collection of American Literature, Beinecke Rare Book and Manuscript Library, Yale University. It has not been possible to trace the
owner/copyright owner of Illustration 2b: if he will write to the author
or publisher, suitable acknowledgement will be made at the earliest
opportunity.

Acknowledgements

I am grateful to Professor Muriel Bradbrook, who acted as my thesis adviser and gave time and attention to my work; to John Russell Brown and Raymond Williams who examined a version of this book, as my Ph.D. thesis, and made cogent comments on it; and to Brian Rothwell, Peter Sawkill, Derek Attridge and Andrew Kennedy, who have all read parts of the manuscript and given helpful advice. I am also grateful to my editor at Cambridge University Press and to Mrs Janet Laing who typed what was sometimes a most difficult manuscript. Part of this study was written whilst I was a Calouste Gulbenkian research student at Lucy Cavendish College, Cambridge.

I would particularly like to thank Mrs Dwight Culler, for hospitality in New Haven; my parents, Gordon and Mary Sandham, for vital help in proof-reading and child-minding, and Mrs Freda Hewish and those other people in Cambridge, New Haven, Rehovot and Paris who, giving their time to my children, enabled me to give some of mine to writing this book. My husband knows what the book owes to him.

I also wish to thank Mr Donald Gallup, Curator of the Collection of American Literature, Beinecke Rare Book and Manuscript Library, Yale University, for the assistance I received in New Haven from him and his staff, and for permission to quote from the manuscripts of the published O'Neill material in the Library. The curators of the theatre collections in the Museum of the City of New York and the New York Public Library; the Principal of the C.W Post Centre, New York, and the Accessions Department of Cambridge University Library were all helpful in making O'Neill material available to me, as were the photographic departments of Yale and Cambridge University Libraries.

The author and publisher are grateful to the following for permission to reprint copyright material: for extracts from *Desire Under the Elms*,

Mourning Becomes Electra, and *The Iceman Cometh*, by Eugene O'Neill, to Jonathan Cape Ltd, the Executors of the Eugene O'Neill Estate and Random House, Inc., and for extracts from *Long Day's Journey Into Night* by Eugene O'Neill to Jonathan Cape Ltd, the Executors of the Eugene O'Neill Estate and Yale University Press.

TYRONE. Yes, there's the makings of a poet in you all right . . .

EDMUND. The *makings* of a poet. No, I'm afraid I'm like the guy who is always panhandling for a smoke. He hasn't even got the makings. He's got only the habit.

The linguistic medium of O'Neill's plays

Date	Low-colloquial (NE rustic/Negro/NY urban/immigrant)	Irish dialect/ Broadway slang	General American	
			Idiomatic	Poetic prose
1913–14	'The Web' 'Warnings'		'Lost Plays'	'Lost Plays'
up to 1917	'S.S. Glencairn' plays		Before Breakfast	
1918	The Rope Horizon The Dreamy Kid			
1919	'Chris Christopherson'	The Straw	The Straw	
1920	Gold Anna Christie Jones Diff'rent			
1921	Ape		The First Man	
1922			The Fountain	The Fountain
1923			Welded	
	Chillun			
1924	Desire		Marco Millions	Marco Millions
1925			Brown	Brown
1926–7				Lazarus
1928–9			Interlude	
1929–31			Dynamo	
1932–3			Electra Wilderness Days Without	
1934–9			End 'A Tale of Possessors, Self-Dispossessed' (Destroyed)	
1939	Iceman	Iceman	Iceman	
1940		Journey	Journey	
1941–2		Hughie		
1942		Poet	Poet	
1943		A Moon	A Moon	

EARLY PLAYS — MIDDLE PLAYS — LATE PLAYS

Completion date of each play is given. Up until 1934, the dating is taken from O'Neill's notebook (Beinecke). The dates of the late plays are taken from O'Neill's letters.

Introduction

Serious dramatists during the last hundred years have been acutely conscious of their task as working playwrights. In their notebooks and their letters as well as in the plays they have written and the plays they have abandoned, they have inquired into how the peculiarly dramatic elements of their art could enable them to explore and recreate their experience. They have recognized, as literary dramatists had failed to do in the previous hundred years and more, that drama, being a performing art, has a density that is different from that of the purely literary arts and that the words of the play, uttered by actors on a stage, exist in a context of gesture and movement, of décor, costume, lighting and non-verbal sound. They have recognized, too, that words spoken by a human voice and heard, not by an individual but by an audience, have a sensory immediacy that is different from that of words read on a page in private.[1] They have, therefore, experimented with dramatic language and form in order to discover how to use to the full the particular force which derives from the staging and the sensory immediacy and to discover how to make the non-verbal elements an organic part of the play, implicit in the text: to be interpreted by director and actors, not improvised arbitrarily by them.

The recognition that drama can be both literary and theatrical has meant that serious writers have again written for the living theatre and that, from Ibsen onwards, the European drama, although very different from the Elizabethan and Jacobean, has possessed a comparable vitality and urgency. This being the case, it is extraordinary that academic critics, with a few impressive exceptions,[2] have shown little interest in the shape and the language of contemporary drama. In the great surge of interest in style and linguistic structure which there has been in the last twenty years, for example, there has been almost no discussion of dramatic language. If critical inquiry is impelled, as I believe it is, by our need to find ways of thinking and talking about experiences that are meaningful to us as individuals and as members of human society then, given the liveliness of the theatre, this absence of thought and talk is strange. Indeed, the language of prose drama of the past has been almost as neglected as that of the drama of our own century.[3] There is good reason to share Pierre Larthomas's indignation when he writes:

Il existe des centaines, sinon des milliers d'ouvrages sur la vie de Molière, sur ses idées religieuses, sur la psychologie de ses personnages, etc. En revanche, le nombre de livres, et même d'articles, consacrés à son style, est extraordinairement faible; rien, ou presque rien, sur les qualités de son dialogue et les problèmes stylistiques qu'il pose. Fait scandaleux, si l'on veut bien admettre que seule, en définitive, l'oeuvre compte, et son efficacité, au sens noble du terme.

(*Le Langage dramatique* (Paris, 1972), p. 7)

There exist some hundreds, if not thousands, of works on the life of Molière, on his religious ideas, on the psychology of his characters, and so forth. On the other hand, the number of books, or even of articles, devoted to his style is extraordinarily small. Nothing, or virtually nothing, exists on the achievements of his dialogue, and the stylistic problems posed by it. A scandalous state of affairs, if one is willing to accept that only the work itself and its effectiveness, in the better sense of the term, finally counts. (My translation)

It has, I think, something to do with the institutionalization of literature, which is one of the hazards of academic criticism. We create our categories and our definitions, our means and our ends, and we can easily come to feel comfortable with them, reluctant to depart from them. The theory of realism as spelled out in the nineteenth century can seem limiting, as can some of the writing deriving from it. But, all too readily, when we encounter a play in which the situation, characters and language have something in common with those of everyday life, we pin on the 'realism' label and with it whatever value judgements the term holds for us. Most of the great drama of the past was written in verse and, because of this, we have certain expectations about dramatic language. But since Ibsen decided, quite knowingly, in the 1870s to devote himself not to verse but 'exclusively to the very much more difficult art of writing straightforward, plain language spoken in real life',[4] dramatists, with few exceptions, have chosen to write in prose and critics, rather than investigate why this should be so and whether prose can be dramatically effective, have lamented the choice. Even so discriminating a critic as T. S. Eliot allowed himself to blur the distinctions between the neutral term 'verse' and the value-laden one 'poetic', between the neutral 'prose' and the value-laden 'prosaic', in what, unfortunately, became an influential statement about prose drama. 'It seems to me', he said in his Spencer Memorial Lecture in 1950:

> that beyond the nameable, classifiable emotions and motives of our conscious life when directed towards action – the part of life which prose drama is wholly adequate to express – there is a fringe of indefinite extent, of feeling which we can only detect, so to speak, out of the corner of the eye and can never completely focus; of feeling of which we are only aware in a kind of temporary detachment from action. There are great prose dramatists – such as Ibsen and Chekhov – who have at times done things of which I would not otherwise have supposed prose to be capable, but who seem to me, in spite of their success, to have been hampered in expression by writing in prose.
>
> (Included in *Selected Prose*, p. 80)

The choice of prose as the medium has been a deliberate one. Has it been miscalculated? Has it hampered the achievement or has it been a necessary part of it? If things have been done in prose of which we 'would not otherwise have supposed prose to be capable', are we not obliged to question our own assumptions about prose? Certainly, there has been verse drama written in the past century and some of it might with justice be called 'poetic' drama, but this is true of only a very few verse plays and even they are hedged about with rather special conditions. Yeats's finest plays are chamber plays, small-scale and unashamedly deriving their framework from the Japanese Nōh play; Hugo von Hofmannsthal is known now chiefly as the librettist of 'Strauss's' *Elektra*, *Der Rosenkavalier*, *Ariadne auf Naxos*, and Eliot's own confidence as a dramatist faltered when he tried to move away from the framework of church liturgy and religious festival, which had enabled him to write *Murder in the Cathedral*. Both Synge and Claudel, although commonly described as 'poetic dramatists', wrote in prose, the latter sometimes using verse chants, and even Lorca, outstanding amongst all the dramatists who have used verse in this century, wrote mainly in prose, intertwining verse in choral or frankly symbolic sequences. The other verse dramatists, although repeatedly hailed as offering new hope for the theatre, failed to fulfil their promise.

The pressing question to which Eliot's statement about prose drama gives rise is whether drama couched in prose dialogue, whose figures are dressed in the costume of our own day and whose action is set in rooms similar to those in which we live, can move its audience very deeply, can stir unaccustomed or barely articulated thought, can lead its audience to apprehend areas of experience which otherwise defy definition. The question is pressing because, since virtually all of the drama of the past hundred years has had this in common, it amounts to a question of whether or not the drama in our time has ceased to be a deeply serious art form.

Two kinds of assumption, I think, have inhibited commentary on the language of prose drama, even when experience in the theatre has made it apparent that the drama is, indeed, still one of the lively arts. On the one hand, it is felt that since the dialogue of much prose drama seeks to represent everyday speech then the dramatist's task is to make it as transparent as possible so that nothing shall interfere with our impression that we are viewing a fragment of the real world. Apart from consideration of how well the dramatist achieves verisimilitude, therefore, our concern cannot be with the style of saying since this must be inconspicuous – styleless – but with the effect of what is said, as though form and content were not as inseparably intertwined in prose writing as they are in verse. On the other hand, dramatic language is sometimes felt, by the fact of performance, to involve too many artifices and devices of an external kind to allow any commentary on the text to have much authority. For not only do décor, lighting and gesture help to create the scenic image, but the word itself is open to interpretation by the voice of the actor – its timbre, inflection, capacity to emphasize or throw away – and is susceptible, too, to the excising pen of the director. The word is not fixed in drama as it is in the purely literary arts. The second problem is, of course, equally present in any discussion of verse drama but, here, the long-standing habit of regarding verse drama as something to be read has allowed commentators to divorce the play as text from the play as performance.[5] It is, I think, necessary to consider these two problematic areas rather more fully.

Drama and performance

The shifting nature of the dramatic event is clearly a problem in dramatic criticism but, although it should certainly make us wary of what we say about a text, it need not silence us altogether. We must be clear that we are not aiming at theatrical criticism – the description of an individual production of a play – but at dramatic criticism – the description of words written to be spoken in an implicit context of action on a stage. A new production of a play offers new insights and interpretations, but the dramatist's text remains the imaginative core of each realization in the theatre: it is the common factor in each production. In giving the play visual and aural form the director, designer and actor can be more or less true to the 'spirit of the text'. Quite what this is in any particular case is as elusive in the drama as it is in the novel or poem, for there can be no one definitive reading of any complex work of art, but perhaps it could be characterized as the recognition we have of the organizing consciousness of the dramatist as it exists in the words he has written, both in dialogue and in implicit or explicit stage directions. My own experience is that, after seeing a new play of any significance, I am impelled to seek verification of the production in the text. The individual production seems complete in itself and yet, however overwhelming the experience in the theatre, something remains unresolved until I can compare it with the script. This may be a penalty of living in a society in which the printed word is of such importance or it may be because we can expect to see more than one production of any significant play and, inevitably, we find changes from one to the next and want to discover what was intended. Probably not during a production of a play with which we are familiar, but certainly in retrospect, we qualify the production in the light of our own imaginary production and simultaneously extend our own interpretation in the light of the production we have just seen. We will be more or less articulate about this process, depending on our own private experience but it is just such verification which is taking place in familiar comments like: 'That Juliet was wrong for the part'; 'It was exciting but it wasn't *The Cherry Orchard*'; 'I wonder why he emphasized Hedda's pregnancy and changed Ibsen's set so drastically?'; 'I'd never imagined *A Midsummer Night's Dream* in that way – but it worked'.

It is necessary to adapt and extend our critical language, which has been developed, after all, largely in relation to the lyric poem, so that we can take account of the implications about the drama in performance *that are present in the text*. It is the dramatist who establishes the sequence of events; the presence or absence of the characters on the stage at any given moment of the action, and their closeness to or distance from the central action; the mounting towards climax and descent into anticlimax; the acceleration or slowing of tempo and, more often than we might immediately realize, gesture, stance, quality of voice and even lighting and costume. Similarly, we must be alert to ways in which words which in reading may seem neutral can flash into life in performance. A word or phrase can take on significance if it is repeated in changed circumstances, having previously been used at a vital moment in the action. Our ear will catch the echo and the sensory response will create resonance which in reading might have been missed. In commenting on a play we must be alert to the ways in which visual and verbal echo, superimposition and ironic contrast create meaning within the continuing time and space of the action. The member of an audience, unlike the reader, must experience the play in its entirety, at a sitting. He cannot vary the pace, call for a replay or pause to think. If his attention wanders, some of the action will have passed irrevocably. The onus of compelling attention is on the dramatist who must, therefore, create an action which is sufficiently varied to allow his audience to rest actively by being at times less fully or differently engaged with the action. He must encourage and stimulate concentration by rewarding some expectations and introducing surprises which baffle others. As commentators, we must be conscious of whether and how the dramatist is taking account of the concentration limits of his audience and of the way the response to one scene is affected by those preceding and succeeding.

Verisimilitude and dramatic artifice

In the wake of the Brechtian attack on the traditional theatre,[6] it is sometimes claimed that the audience can become so absorbed in the action on the stage or can come to identify so closely with one of the characters that they take what is happening to be real and wholly set aside their private capacities to judge, consider, associate.

How valid is this as the description of the response of members of the audience in a theatre? I think we are more complicated beings than such an account allows. Given that the dramatist has been sufficiently skilful in peopling his stage world with figures that draw our interest or concern, then the action, too, will be sufficiently complex for the audience at any given moment to be faced with mysteries or to be able to make connections that do not face and cannot be made by any character on the stage. We may engage with the emotion Hamlet or Oedipus is represented as experiencing but, at the same time, we retain the capacity to perceive things about Ophelia or Tiresias which the created character cannot. The very construction of the play prevents total identification. At the outset, most characters are assumed to have some experience or information which is gradually revealed to the audience. As the play proceeds, the characters' responses are relevant only to that part of the action in which they are directly involved. The member of the audience, on the other hand, is ignorant at the outset of the play but, by the end, will have an experience composed of everything that has happened on the stage and it is out of this that his response must be ordered.

When we watch a play, by our very act of entering a place set aside for such an activity and by our observation of the appropriate decorum – keeping still, listening, not interrupting the action – we announce that we are prepared to accept the conventions of the stage. Whilst recognizing that we are observers of a fictional action, we allow that action to assume imaginative reality *providing* it does not infringe what we feel to be the limits of the convention. Our awareness of the form and the artifice becomes sharper at the very moment when these limits are overstepped. The performance is as likely to be disrupted if the action becomes too life-like as it is if it becomes too self-consciously rhetorical. Although we have repeatedly adjusted our expectations to allow of previously unacceptable language or kinds of action, the audience is still all too easily distracted from the stage action to the dramatic form in which it is couched by, for example, the frisson attaching to the use of certain words. A familiar example of this is the way in which the use of the word 'bloody', in the first production of Shaw's *Pygmalion*, was sufficient to break the dramatic illusion. Whilst watching *Ghosts*, we might marvel at the 'realism' of the flickering shadows and quicken with Mrs Alving's emotion on seeing the fire but if for a moment we suspected that she was looking out on to a real fire, we would react quite differently. Similarly, however life-like the details, we recognize with part of our minds that any stage death is enacted, even at the very moment of the enactment. Indeed, in a recent London production of *Lady Julie*, the audience's attention was distracted from the stage action to the activities of the actor in the sequence in which Jean kills Julie's bird, since the actor's sleight of hand in substituting a stuffed bird for the evidently live creature that had been on stage until that moment, had been too adroit. The dramatic conventions of our own period may well be different in some ways from those of the past, but they nevertheless exist and we accept them as easily as audiences have ever done.

When we turn our attention to stage dialogue we find that it, too, has its conventions, whether we choose to label it 'realistic' or not. Inquiry into the language of prose drama necessitates some consideration of that largely unexplored area of linguistic activity, actual speech – what a linguist would describe as 'performance' as opposed to 'competence'.

Stage dialogue is different from real speech. It operates by duplicity: it is not spontaneous but must appear to be so. It is permanent but must appear to be as ephemeral as the speech it imitates. The actor must seem to speak what in reality he recites. In sharing the convention, the audience in the theatre has a share in the duplicity. We simultaneously accept the illusion of spontaneity and know that it is a pretence. We can see how true this is in the light of our consciousness of threats to the illusion, such as when an actor's delivery betrays that his part is learned by rote (an experience which is turned to comic use in the Pyramus and Thisbe episode of *A Midsummer Night's Dream*), or when, knowing a text, we recognize that an actor is departing from it and improvising words of his own, or when a pause is miscalculated and we experience embarrassment with the thought that the actor may have forgotten his words.

Whereas everyday speech is a spontaneous exchange between speaker and interlocutor, in dramatic dialogue, whether cast into poetry, into a representation of middle class, or into low-colloquial dialect, words are invented by the dramatist to be spoken by invented characters, created for and existing within a brief and invented action. For it is not the hearing of the words by the interlocutor that completes the exchange, as it is in everyday speech, but the witnessing and interpreting of both the utterance and the response by the audience. Much of the particular effect of drama derives from the gap between two ways of hearing, that of the interlocutor on stage and that of the audience, and from the audience's consciousness of the gap. The audience sets each utterance beside each previous utterance made within the limited time span of the play and, in doing so, catches implications beyond those immediately relevant to speaker and interlocutor: it responds, in Stanislavskian language, to the subtextual as well as to the surface meaning – to the 'web of innumerable, varied inner patterns inside the play'.[7] If the dramatist is to create an action of significance in the brief three or four hours of performance time his dialogue, however natural it may appear, must be most *un*naturally resonant with meaning and implication.

Accurate reproduction of everyday speech is scarcely possible in the theatre, even were it attempted. Even at the most obvious level of the mechanics of the language, the gap between the most natural sounding dialogue and real speech is vast. So little recording and description of speech has been undertaken by linguists that we are largely ignorant of how we do speak. Information so far published by the Survey of English Usage at present in progress at University College in London, has demonstrated how prolix and, by written standards, how incomplete and non-grammatical most educated speech is, how much information has to be supplied by the context and by the shared experience and assumptions of the speakers.[8] It has shown, too, that 'within any given stretch of conversation very little occurs'.[9] The dramatist must compress, must make much more happen, verbally, than would happen in a comparable stretch of real speech.

And yet, dramatic dialogue does have some direct association with everyday speech. If the dramatist's task is not to reproduce speech, it is to make us believe that what we hear is a natural utterance between the characters on the stage. We do find some dialogue 'life-like' and some stilted, or not lively, even though the forms of dialogue to which we respond in this way may be very different from each other. When we find that the dialogue of *Hamlet*, of Strindberg's *The Father*, or of Pinter's *The Birthday Party*, sounds natural, what we are in fact responding to in each very different case are echoes of the living language caught by the writer and arranged, patterned, elaborated into the ordered utterance of that particular play. Indeed, it is frequently those elements which we would regard as substandard in writing which draw and hold our attention when they occur in speech. Hesitation, pause, repetition, unfinished sentences, a sudden change of direction, a lively confusion of metaphors, the rushing of one thought in upon another, the cutting in of one speaker on another's words, as well as certain shared or fashionable idioms, certain idiosyncracies of construction: these are vital, if shifting, elements in the grammar of the language as it is actually spoken.[10] The writer 'with an ear' is one who is consistently able to incorporate appropriate elements of the living language – 'speech markers', we might call them – which enable the actors to utter the dialogue easily and the audience to listen intently to it.

In whatever form it might be cast, then, dramatic dialogue does not reproduce: it represents speech. It is an artificial construct created by the dramatist with more or less skill so that, within the given convention, it sounds natural when spoken whilst incorporating into itself a patterned subtext of such density that a complex action can take place within the fixed performance time. The questions, therefore, that we ask about the language of the drama of the past hundred years are essentially those that we ask about the poetic language of Elizabethan drama: what devices and markers are used to create the effect of the living language? How dense is the language? How much meaning is incorporated in it? How fully does it bind its audience; what degree of alert activity does it demand from them?

   Part of our inheritance from nineteenth-century realistic theory is, as I have suggested, the attitude which I would call the 'realistic fallacy': that dramatic dialogue should and could be transparent, and that such transparency would be achieved if the dramatist wrote his dialogue as it came to mind without concern for or, even, with deliberate avoidance of, order and patterning. The fallacy here is that such dialogue would carry conviction as a representation of living speech. It is, in fact, unlikely to do so, as scores of nineteenth-century 'realistic' plays bear witness, because, since the dialogue is composed in writing and not orally, the dramatist will tend to use the habitual grammar and cliché of his written rather than of his spoken form of the language. Such dialogue, therefore, forfeits not only density, operating, as it does, too much at the surface, but also liveliness. Similar assumptions about the relationship between the casual and the realistic by commentators on the drama have meant that, where there has not been an immediately apparent rhetoric in contemporary prose dialogue, as there is in Synge's poetic prose or in the linguistic parody and role-playing of Beckett and of Pinter, we have failed to differentiate between major writers and journeymen playwrights; between the realistic convention and the realistic fallacy. The dramatic language of Chekhov and Ibsen can do extraordinary things because neither dramatist has succumbed to the realistic fallacy but both dramatists have struggled to make their dialogue expressive at the subtextual as well as at the textual level so that their audiences are compelled to be active not passive listeners.

   The discussion of dramatic language in general terms can only take us so far before there is a pressing need for examples and exegesis. One might proceed by comparing the language of a number of dramatists working in the same period or one might proceed historically and, taking certain dramatic devices, explore their role at different times to discover what modifications they have undergone and what seem to be common elements of all dramatic language. My own method is to explore the language of a single dramatist at different periods of his creative activity. This is to lose something in breadth but is perhaps to gain in thoroughness and, indeed, in the case of Eugene O'Neill, because of the unusually prolonged period of experimentation in the struggle to find an expressive language and because of the remarkably erratic nature of his achievement, there is much for comparison and contrast within the work of the individual writer, so that we are constantly led back to the general questions about the nature of dramatic language.

In the exploration of O'Neill's dramatic language which follows, I have been conscious of the linguists' stricture that:

few books written by literary critics which purport to discuss an author's language have achieved anything like the degree of precision required to make their observations meaningful to the linguist – or to anyone who concedes the importance of objective, verifiable descriptive information as a critical tool.
(Crystal and Davy, *Investigating English Style*, p. 81)

But I have also been aware that to make an exhaustive record of the linguistic features of the dialogue would not in itself be very helpful to my purposes. In exploring how the organization of the words of the text has contributed to the meaning and unity of the play under discussion, I have had to be selective in what I discuss and which linguistic features I record. The basis of my selection here has been my own intuitive judgement of which elements seemed significant. This, of course, as in all liberal criticism, is an area of risk but the intuitive judgements of traditional discursive criticism have been underpinned as fully as space and the sharpness of the argument allowed, by systematic linguistic analysis, although often there has been room for only one or two examples where a dozen could have been given. I have attempted to make my choice of scenes and examples reflect the variety of language within the plays. Besides those more obvious areas of syntax, diction and expressive imagery, I have looked at the different kinds of language which compose the dialogue, the most obvious of these being dialect, idiolect and speech register, and the quotation from and echoing of other writers. I have considered what the structural use and emotive effect of these might be. I hope that in developing this rather open method I have conveyed an impression of the intricacy of the language without forfeiting that sense which we have in performance of the coherence and dramatic tension of the plays under discussion.

Dramatic criticism and the paradox of Eugene O'Neill

The posthumous production, in 1956, of *Long Day's Journey Into Night* was followed by a resurgence of interest in O'Neill's drama, which had ebbed since the mid-1930s, and has resulted in four or five major studies of the plays.[11] But, despite this critical activity, there remains a paradox in O'Neill criticism that is closely related to the questions which I have already raised.

Commentators repeatedly testify to the 'power' and 'force' of O'Neill's drama but the consensus, nevertheless, is that the language in which the plays are cast is inadequate. The testimony as to dramatic power is of the strongest. T. S. Eliot, placing O'Neill's work 'very high indeed', described *Long Day's Journey Into Night* as 'one of the most moving plays' he had ever seen,[12] whilst Allardyce Nicoll in his influential *World Drama* wrote:

Eugene O'Neill is not only a symbol of the dramatic movement that flourished so rapidly and with such resultant fruitfulness during the century's third and fourth decades; he also stands, a powerful and vibrant figure, over all his playwriting colleagues throughout the world.   (p. 880)

But O'Neill has also been called 'a tone deaf musician', a 'giant in chains', who 'lacked that basic gift of a major playwright – the ability to write dialogue that was both functional and distinctive', whose style is 'not only strained and turgid, but awkward, inarticulate, banal'.[13] Although the two kinds of assertion, about forcefulness and incompetence, would seem to be mutually exclusive, they are often found together. Nicoll, for example, continues:

With the deepest regret we must confess that O'Neill is not a finished literary artist. No words of rich import and beauty wing themselves from his pages; we remember his scenes but not the language in which they are couched.

Francis Fergusson describes certain scenes as being 'deeply convincing' despite 'inadequate language'; Ronald Peacock groups O'Neill with Shakespeare, Racine, Ibsen for 'sheer genius for drama', but adds the qualification, 'however prosaic his work', and Lionel Trilling, placing O'Neill in comparably high company, has written:

We do not read Sophocles or Aeschylus for the right answer; we read them for the force with which they represent life and attack its moral complexity. In O'Neill, despite the many failures of his art and thought, this force is inescapable.[14]

It is tempting to follow some commentators and explain the paradox by pointing to O'Neill's achievement in creating a 'language of theatre'.[15] Such commentary has been valuable in demonstrating how capable a theatre craftsman O'Neill was but it fails to explain how the audience can bear to listen to so many words, if they really are inert. It fails, too, to explain why certain theatrically complex and spectacular pieces, such as *The Fountain* or *Lazarus Laughed*, do not hold their own in the theatre. Do we, then, simply accept the paradox and continue to worry at the writing of a Fry or a Maxwell Anderson in the hope that their verse will suddenly become fully dramatic? Or do we attempt to develop our critical language until it can cope with stage works, whose style may not accord with our preconceived criteria, but in which, in reading or performance, we have felt the presence of a creative imagination, shaping and controlling the elements of the play in such a way that we have been stirred uncommonly?

It will already be apparent that my central concern in this study is to demonstrate that the language of prose drama can be flexible and complex, can contain a finely patterned organic imagery that might justly be called 'poetic'. I hope, too, to reverse the frequently stated idea that O'Neill is a great dramatist *malheureusement*, whose inadequate language leads to embarrassing incongruities in the work. I hope, at the very least, that my account will lead readers to see and hear that O'Neill's dramatic language is an essential element in the plays: that it is much more varied and dramatically forceful than is commonly acknowledged.

Principles of organization

The sheer amount of O'Neill's writing is, in part, responsible for the critical confusion, as is also the fact that O'Neill is a near contemporary.

O'Neill's reputation was made by his experimental rather than his mature works. The plays which are now acknowledged to be his most important came to public notice only in the mid-1950s, after the publication of certain influential books about the modern Western theatre, and after many eminent critics had passed final judgement on his drama. The result has been that, in many cases, the earlier assessment has been transferred to the later plays.[16] There is a problem when criticizing any contemporary writer, of maintaining openness to work-in-progress. There has not been time for a consensus to have developed which will point us to the most accessible part of the writing first. Indeed, the most rewarding work may be yet to be written when we sample, and judge, and pass on. O'Neill would seem to have reached that point in time when he can re-emerge to startle his old audiences and to draw the interest of those to whom he is little more than a name, with the emotional power of his writing and the unexpected contemporaneity of the matter of his plays.

But we are not dealing with a simple case of critical misjudgement, for O'Neill's writing was remarkably erratic. When we consider the whole of his work we must ask how one dramatist could have written a play as bad as, say, *Dynamo* and one as good as *The Iceman Cometh*. If a new play by O'Neill invariably aroused more interest than one by a contemporary, it was also, frequently, more disappointing. O'Neill was an experimental dramatist but the experimentation itself raises questions. Why was the period of experiment so protracted? Why did he find his own form only, as I shall suggest, at the end of his career? And what did the long period of experimentation contribute to the final form?

Clearly it is important that we find some way of gaining an overview of O'Neill's whole career, and yet the large number of plays involved make this very difficult unless we can group them so that one or two can represent several. If we concentrate on the mature plays, we leave out of account the work which *was* the American drama for many audiences for two formative decades; which has influenced the subsequent development of the American drama, and which provides an essential background against which to view the method of the mature work. If, on the other hand, we attempt to discuss the whole oeuvre we are left with little space to investigate the mature work.

A solution to this problem of grouping is offered when we recognize that different *kinds* of language are used by O'Neill. The table on p. xii shows that O'Neill's plays were written in one of three different linguistic modes and that the three modes were grouped roughly chronologically. I shall suggest in my discussion that they also represent three different kinds of dramatic achievement. The plays written before 1925, which I shall call the 'early' plays, are predominantly cast into one of the forms of American low-colloquial. These, I shall suggest, are the work of a promising dramatist, struggling with his form, developing what amounted to an idiosyncratic poetic diction and, occasionally, achieving dazzling results. The linguistic medium of the 'middle' plays, written between 1924 and 1934, the period in which O'Neill was established as the Great American Dramatist, is Standard American English. The change of mode is accompanied by a sharp break in O'Neill's practice: whereas, in the early plays, the language usage had tended to be over-schematic, it is now loose and unorganized. In the 'late' plays, those written between 1939 and 1943, a strategic use of Irish dialect or Broadway slang is intermingled with the idiomatic mode of Standard American. I shall demonstrate by detailed discussion that the language of these plays is finely achieved.

Not only does it seem essential to be aware of O'Neill's whole oeuvre, but recognition of the nature of the context in which O'Neill worked seems to me to be a necessary basis for an understanding of the various experiments with dramatic form and language that absorbed him during his slow development to his mature style.

It has been suggested in several recent studies that, in an open, mobile and technically advanced society such as ours, newly efficient transport and communications and the invention of machinery to record and reproduce, make accessible the potentially enriching images and forms of the art and ritual of past and present cultures: enriching but also, possibly, confusing.[17] One 'unavoidable consequence', according to Daniel Boorstin, of the gathering of arts and crafts into museums has been that 'all these things were being removed from their context. In a sense, therefore, they were all being misrepresented' (*The Image*, p. 101). At the same time, the new eclecticism means that local traditions lose something of their power and the artist in search of a personally expressive mode may find himself isolated, a prey to panic and confusion, without a firm framework within which to operate, or against which to rebel, whilst the audience, no longer certain how to evaluate the good, reserve their praise for the new and the ingenious.[18] All of which raises fundamental problems of self-knowledge, as Lionel Trilling suggests when he says:

> The individual who lives in this new circumstance is subject to the constant influence, the literal inflowing, of the mental processes of others, which, in the degree that they stimulate and enlarge his consciousness, make it less his own. He finds it ever more difficult to know what his own self is and what being true to it consists in.
>
> (*Sincerity and Authenticity*, p. 61)

For various reasons, deriving from the condition of the American theatre at the beginning of this century, O'Neill faced in a peculiarly acute form the stimulating and confusing effects of the openness of contemporary culture, the breakdown of the authority of tradition and the availability of alternative modes that increasingly face the artist in Western society.

No commentator on O'Neill, indeed, has been as aware as he was himself of the tension between the stimulating and confusing elements in his cultural experience and none has written as sharply about his language as he has himself. His letters and notes show him to have been a self-conscious writer and reinforce the impression we get from a sensitive reading of the plays that O'Neill was a writer who struggled throughout his career to forge a fully achieved language. He was also, and this, too, identifies him as peculiarly of this century, a writer concerned with articulacy: doubt about the reliability of words, and the gap between what is known, or experienced, or hesitatingly apprehended and what can be expressed, were a necessary part of his subject matter. How to give expression to such subject matter without becoming inarticulate himself was one of his central problems.

For these reasons, it has seemed necessary to give an account of O'Neill's literary and theatrical context and to investigate such of his ideas about theatre as have come to light in his non-dramatic writing. This will provide a platform of information for my subsequent discussion of O'Neill's experimentation with realistic and anti-realistic modes, and with his attempts to make his dialogue expressive whether through effects of sound, set and choreography or through the ordering and patterning of the dialogue.

In the first part of the book, then, I set O'Neill's search for form and his twenty years of experimentation, within the context of the American theatre in which he worked, and within the more private context of his literary interests. Then, after an examination of the more specifically linguistic contexts of contemporary interest in the American vernacular, and of the function of the vernacular in the nineteenth-century drama, I enter on the real critical discourse with an examination of the language of selected plays from the early and middle years. I deliberately select *Mourning Becomes Electra* when discussing the language of the middle years, with the hope of making good an imbalance that has arisen in O'Neill criticism. *Electra* and *Strange Interlude* both received popular and critical acclaim when first produced, and they have frequently been studied in isolation from the rest of O'Neill's work. The transferral of stream-of-consciousness technique from the novel to the drama in the one play has meant that it has proved a useful example in general discussions about genre, whilst the modern interpretation of the story of the *Oresteia*, in the other play, has made it an obvious example to use in comparisons of Modern and Greek Tragedy.[19] The result has been that these plays have been taken as satisfactorily representing O'Neill's oeuvre, and not, as I would prefer to see them, as representing a stage in his search for an integrated form. This examination serves as a prelude to the chapter-length studies of *The Iceman Cometh* and *Long Day's Journey Into Night* which make up the substance of the second part of the book.

I

O'Neill and the American theatre

In the fifteen months after O'Neill began to write plays, he wrote eleven one-act and two full-length pieces. His eagerness to experiment was already apparent. *Servitude* is a Shavian discussion play, whose plot offers an epilogue to Ibsen's *The Doll's House; Before Breakfast* is a monologue in imitation of Strindberg's *The Stronger*, and *The Web* is a piece of Zolaesque realism, complete with a squalid murder, a starving child and the ceaseless coughing of a consumptive heroine, and a background whose every detail reveals poverty and oppression. In *Thirst*, O'Neill uses scenic expressionism, presenting a desolate sea, 'the red eye of the sun', and the menace of continually circling sharks as a context within which to figure human madness whilst in *Fog* he introduces a tentative mysticism with an image of a ship's black hulk, which looms out of a fog-bound sea, summoned by the cries of a dead child.

As early as 1918, O'Neill was greeted as America's 'first really important dramatist', by the critic George Jean Nathan.[1] He was fêted by the press after the success, in 1920, of *Beyond the Horizon* which marked him, as the *New York Times'* critic, Alexander Woolcott, wrote, as, 'one of the most spacious men to be both gifted and tempted to write for the theatre in America'.[2] Thomas Wolfe called him 'the beaconlight in our own drama today',[3] and even the doubters acknowledged that his work showed a promise quite different from that of his contemporaries. Robert Benchley, for example, in a largely negative review of *Dynamo*, said, 'If he isn't [America's greatest dramatist] the question arises, "Who is, then?" and we scurry right back to Mr. O'Neill, with apologies.'[4]

O'Neill's letters reveal that he himself was conscious both of his pre-eminence and of the pioneering role which this gave him. In 1926, he said of the theatre he wanted to create, 'It seems to me most emphatically, a case of shooting at a star or being a dud ... I want to howl: Imagination, Beauty and Daring – or bust!'[5] And it was the conviction that he must do his part to establish the high seriousness of European theatre in America that impelled him to enter briefly into theatre management. His letters to his co-director, Kenneth Macgowan, continually stress the importance of breaking new ground and avoiding compromise with the commercial theatre. In one of the fiercest, he writes:

> Your manifesto is too meekly explicit, the plays you list, too much what might be found in the repertoire of a dramatic club. I think you ought to inject a lot of the Kammerny spirit into your statement with the emphasis on imaginative new interpretations, experimentation in production. That's what the theatre ought to mean in New York today, Kenneth! That's what New York lacks right now. That's the gap we ought to fill ... I'm raving because this isn't developing as you, Bobby and I dream – as Bel Geddes and others dream – and unless it's going to be that dream, or at least approximate to it in spirit, then what's the use? ... If it's going to be anything of anything that is or has been in New York, again, what's the use?
>
> ('Summer', 1923)

But O'Neill's very success and aspiration seem to have been a source of internal conflict. A note of dissatisfaction with his achievement and his working method recurs in his letters. After the success of *Beyond the Horizon*, he had written to Nathan acknowledging that his work was 'mere groping', depreciating his past work with the apology, 'it takes time to get over the itch to put everything on paper regardless', and committing himself to 'a struggle ... long enough and hard enough' to enable him to express his 'real significant bit of truth'.[6] Three years later, he suggested to Macgowan that his role in the newly founded Experimental Theatre should be to provide ideas which others could develop into full productions, since:

> All these ideas of mine are being incorporated into my own plays bit by bit as they fit in but I can't write plays fast enough to fit in with the production-imagination section of my 'bean'. It would be suicidal to attempt it ... If I wish my work to grow steadily more comprehensive and deeper in quality, I've got to give it more and more of my possible sum total.
>
> ('Summer', 1923)

In 1926, he reiterated his concern for depth, saying 'The point is, my stuff is much deeper and more complicated now and I'm not so easily satisfied as I was' (to Macgowan, 7 August 1926). But always the depth, the 'real significant bit of truth', seem to have eluded him so that we repeatedly find him promising himself that, at last, the necessary thoroughness is within his grasp. In 1929, he wrote to the stage manager at the Provincetown:

Forty is the right age to learn! And I think my new work is going to show more poise, more patience with itself to reach at perfection, more critical analysis of itself and more contemplation, more time given it for gestation and genuine birth, more pains. I've gone off half-cocked too many times, driven on to drive myself to write at any cost to the writing, then to finish and be done with it and start something new. It's time I achieved a more mature outlook as an artist – and now I know I have. Perhaps a complete upheaval, a total revaluing of all my own values was necessary to gain that attitude. Well I've certainly been through that! Devil a doubt!

(To Eleanor Fitzgerald, 13 May 1929)

And, to another friend, he wrote, 'What I need now is work – damn hard work! at my job of writing plays without giving a thought about production' (to Robert Sisk, 21 August 1929). Even whilst the multiplicity of his ideas and his excitement in his own capacities spurred him on to write, he was haunted by the suspicion that, in his eagerness to explore, he was neglecting perfection, failing to pursue any one dramatic method single-mindedly, and so forgoing real artistic achievement. So many different ways of presenting experience through drama offered themselves to him, each drawing an ·imaginative response, that he seems to have been obliged to write his way through all of them before finding his appropriate form.

I shall suggest, in this chapter, that O'Neill's need to experiment is one of the major reasons why his career developed in the way it did and why he produced fully articulate drama only at the end of his writing life. The origins of this need are to be found, in part, in the literary and theatrical environment in which he worked. They are to be found, too, in his private life, but O'Neill's psychology has aroused a great deal of speculation, and it seems worthwhile to change the emphasis here. Commentators have too often discussed O'Neill's drama as though it existed in a vacuum, as if the term, 'first American dramatist', so frequently, and not unjustly, applied to O'Neill were literally true. This has blunted recognition of the nature of his contribution to American drama and of the particular kind of artistic isolation he did experience.

The nineteenth-century American theatre

O'Neill's theatrical inheritance and the story of his early days in the theatre is familiar: he was born the son of a matinee idol, James O'Neill, who in 1888 was playing the role of Edmond Dantes in the

Fechter version of *The Count of Monte Cristo*, for the fourteen-hundredth time. Revivals continued until 1913. Finding it increasingly hard to succeed in other roles, growing increasingly embittered, James complained that the commercial theatre and the demands of its conservative audience had ossified his talents; enviously, he praised tragedy as the highest form of dramatic art.[7] O'Neill was stage manager with his father's company in 1910, during a run of the melodrama *The White Sister*, and a supporting actor in *The Count of Monte Cristo* the following year.[8] In a tribute paid to George Pierce Baker in 1935, he expressed his bitterness towards the conventions of the old theatre. Looking back two decades to the 'dark age when the American theatre was still, for playwrights, the closed shop, star system, amusement racket', he commented:

It is difficult in these days, when the native playwright can function in comparative freedom, to realise that in that benighted period a play of any imagination, originality or integrity by an American was almost automatically barred from a hearing in our theatre. To write plays of life as one saw and felt it, instead of concocting the conventional theatre drivel of the time, seemed utterly hopeless ... the most vital thing for us as possible future artists and creators, to learn at that time ... was to believe in our work and keep on believing.[9]

Nor did O'Neill overstate his case. In *Democratic Vistas*, in 1871, Walt Whitman had expressed his scorn at least as ferociously:

Of what is called the drama or dramatic presentation in the United States, as now put forth in the theatres, I should say it deserves to be treated with the same gravity, and on a par with the questions of ornamental confectionary at public dinners, or the arrangement of curtains and hangings in a ballroom – nor more, nor less.

It was a theatre of vaudeville, farce and romantic–historical melodrama; of vehicles for star actors and for mechanical ingenuity in set and costume. The dialogue complemented the plot in its unlikeliness, as this extract from the play O'Neill's father's company presented for more than twenty years makes evident:

FERNAND. Answer me a hundred times more, that I may at last believe it. Tell me that you scorn my love – that my life, my death, are nothing to you – that you reject my hand, my heart! Ah, Mercedes, what have I done that you should kill me thus?
MERCEDES. Blame me not, Fernand, blame yourself. From the very first I told you, 'Fernand, I love you as a brother, but ask not, hope not, more, for my heart is given to another.' – Did I say so, Fernand?
FERNAND. Yes, oh, yes. But, you know, Mercedes, it is a sacred law among us Catalans to intermarry.

MERCEDES. Not a law, merely a custom, Fernand, that is all. Fernand, I will never be yours because I love another, and I am his!

(*The Count of Monte Cristo*, act I: James O'Neill's acting version, p. 5)

The villain and the heroine use an identical rhetoric, which does little to convey the essence of the characters. The use of archaisms and convoluted syntax demand a posturing, exclamatory style from the actors, which is emphasized in the rhythm created by repetition and elegant variation: 'my life, my death . . . my hand, my heart!'; 'Blame me not . . . blame yourself . . . ask not, hope not'.

The cynicism underlying much of the writing is expressed in a shameless description of his method by Owen Davies, who had abandoned verse drama for commercial melodrama:

One of the first tricks I learned was that my plays must be written for an audience who, owing to the huge, uncarpeted, noisy theatre, couldn't always hear the words, and who, a large proportion of them, having only recently landed in America, couldn't have understood them in any case. I therefore wrote for the eye rather than the ear and played out each emotion in action, depending on my dialogue only for the robust sentiments so dear to audiences of that class.

(*I'd Like To Do It Again*, p. 37)

In 1896, with the foundation of the Theatrical Syndicate, the domination of the theatre by such plays became even more secure. For the next sixteen years, the Syndicate held a virtual monopoly of the theatres in New York and several other major cities,[10] and resisted all outside influences which might mar the saleability of their product. Frank Rahill has suggested that it was largely because of the power of the Syndicate that melodrama flourished in America for twenty years after the decline in Europe.[11] Certainly, the revolutionary events in European drama and stagecraft in the late nineteenth century were not allowed to impinge seriously on the contemporary American theatre.

Articles sympathetic to Ibsen's drama by Archer and Gosse had been reprinted in America as early as 1889, and Scandinavian-language readers must have been aware of the stir Ibsen's work was causing in Europe, but there were few translations available in America, no Zola to welcome them, no Antoine to promote them and no amateur companies seeking plays with which to found a new theatre. The influential critic, William Winter, attacked Ibsen's work angrily as offensive to public morality. A few productions were staged, but with a drastically cut text, and usually as single matinees before an invited audience. In his chronicle of his visit to America in

1889, Knut Hamsun[12] gives an outraged description of just such a production:

Now and again our newspapers report that on one date Ibsen's *Ghosts* was produced in New York City, and that on another Sardou was performed in one of the Western cities. These are half truths. I speak from personal experience, somewhat from inside knowledge. *Ghosts* has never been staged in New York City and Sardou has never been performed in a single American city. With *Ghosts*, only those scenes which caused no objections were performed in New York; all the 'ghosts' were sifted out of the drama, and it was staged in a form that was totally unrecognizable. To show how brutally the play was distorted from an artistic standpoint, I need only mention that some lines of verse were appended to the final scene, which had already been mutilated – lines with which Mrs. Alving was then supposed to entertain the audience until the curtain fell.

(*The Cultural Life of Modern America*, p. 96)

One of the attractions of the mid-nineteenth-century American stage had been its complicated and ingenious stage effects. Now, the ideas of Antoine and later of Stanislavski were seized upon and adjusted comfortably to the current practice in America. Hamsun decribes having seen live animals on stage and even, once, a steam train. The sets, he added, were mentioned in bold type on the playbill and called 'realistic scenery' (p. 93). The doyen of American scenic realism was David Belasco who, stage manager of the Lyceum in 1884 and of his own Belasco theatre after 1902, displayed remarkable virtuosity in combining the accurate detail of European fourth wall realism with the technical showmanship of the American stage. The exact replica he built on stage of a Child's restaurant, his dismantling and re-erecting of an actual bedroom from a sleazy boarding house, his blizzard in *Tiger Rose*, whose machinery employed thirty-two artisans, were nine days' wonders, and he himself described spending 5,000 dollars to reproduce a sunset and devoting days to the problem of creating on stage 'the ashen hues of death'.[13] But, as Mordecai Gorelik has pointed out:

Belasco used an idiom newer than that of his Romantic predecessors. The acting was believable in comparison with nature; the settings were infinitely more lifelike than in the past. But underneath both, the Romantic stereotype was there for any alert observer to see.[14]

The pattern Belasco established survives today, even more spectacularly mechanized, in filmed versions of stage musicals.

But Belasco was a self-admitted showman. More striking than the distortion of European experiments in stage management was the unwitting distortion of the idea of the play itself by dramatists whose intentions were sincere enough. For America did have its 'Ibsen Movement', but it was a sadly emasculated affair. In an article entitled 'Art for Truth's Sake' published in 1897, James Herne, presenting his manifesto, showed clearly enough where the emphasis was to be put:

I stand for art for truth's sake. It perpetuates the everyday life of its time, because it develops the latent beauty of the so-called commonplaces of life, because it dignifies labour and reveals the dignity of the common man.[15]

Herne's plays and those of a handful of his fellow dramatists were regarded as remarkably lifelike by American commentators. 'Actuality', 'contemporaneous human interest', 'natural' became commonplaces of theatre criticism, and yet, in retrospect, the realism is found to be compounded with conventional method and sentimentality. Romantic melodrama was replaced by social problem melodrama. From Herne's *Margaret Fleming* (1890), the story of a pure woman who faces the knowledge of her husband's faithlessness and adopts his illegitimate child, to Eugene Walter's *The Easiest Way* (1909), in which the reformed prostitute heroine forsakes her true love and new-found respectability under pressure of poverty and isolation, we find a succession of vigorous attacks on public hypocrisy, which is the element of Ibsen's drama most readily communicated in journalistic description. These writers did not attempt to change the theatre fundamentally but merely widened its subject matter. They are in the mould, not of Ibsen, but of the 'realistic' dramatists of the London stage, Tom Robertson, Pinero and Henry Arthur Jones. Their very dialogue, and this was to be particularly important for O'Neill, reveals this. William Dean Howells rejoiced that Clyde Fitch's *Her Own Way* (1903) had put 'the spirit of New York recognizably on the London stage',[16] but although setting and situation might show America, Georgiana, the American rose, speaks standard stage English and her maid Lizzie, sounds like one of Robertson's Cockneys:

Beg pardon, sir, but Moles has been and told me what you was going to do for him, sir. Would you be considering it a great impertinence if I asked you to take six hundred dollars what I've saved, sir, and do things with it?[17]

The New Yorkers of Langdon Mitchell's *The New York Idea* (1906) and the Southerners of Bronson Howard's *Shenandoah* (1888) or William Gillette's civil war play *Secret Service* (1896) use a vocabulary, rhythm and style of speech indistinguishable from any character of Henry Arthur Jones.

Intimations of change

The commercial theatre continued in its moribund state well after the
turn of the century, but the efforts of a few outsiders began to make
European drama more accessible to Americans. The Russian émigré
actress, Alla Nazimova, gave a season of Ibsen's plays in 1907. In
1938, O'Neill recalled:

the impact upon me when I saw an Ibsen play for the first time, a production of
Hedda Gabler at the Bijou theatre in New York – and then went again and
again for ten successive nights. That experience discovered an entire new
world of drama for me. It gave me my first conception of a modern theatre
where truth might live.[18]

Nazimova's success encouraged other Broadway managers to overcome their fear of Ibsen, whose name in the next five years became
familiar on Broadway.[19] If it was the personal enterprise of a foreign
actress which broke the blockade on Ibsen, it was a foreign company
which first showed America the possibility of an alternative theatre in
English. In 1911, the Irish Players visited New York with their
repertory of plays by Synge, Yeats, Lady Gregory and T. C. Murray.
O'Neill is reported as having seen 'everything they did' and having
been particularly impressed by Synge's *Riders to the Sea* (Alexander,
Tempering of Eugene O'Neill, p. 154). The next year, Reinhardt's
production of his wordless play, *Sumurūn*, was presented in New
York, revealing new possibilities in stage design and direction, and
the Manchester Repertory Company, a model of organization for
small independent theatres, toured America.

Events in publishing were equally exciting. Between 1906 and 1912
many of the major texts of the European theatrical revolution were
made available. Archer's eleven-volume revised edition of the collected works of Ibsen was published in London between 1906 and
1908 and a rival version translated by Farquharson Sharp was brought
out by Everyman; then, in New York in 1912, came Scribners' cheap
popular edition of Ibsen; their selection of Strindberg's plays, which
included *The Father, Lady Julie, A Dream Play* and *The Dance of
Death*, and J. D. Luce's selection, which included *Pariah, Comrades*,
and *Easter*. Strindberg's autobiographical novels were published in
1913. Previous to this, there had been, since 1890, occasional single
translations of Ibsen into English but the first Strindberg had come
only in 1906, when three one-act plays were published in the
magazine, *Poet Lore*. Within a period of five years all Strindberg's
major writing, previously unknown in America, became available.[20]
Synge's plays were published in four volumes in 1912.[21]

O'Neill's new community

The revelation in America of the richness of European drama stirred the interest of many Americans besides O'Neill. Within a very few years of the publication of the major texts and the visits of European companies which I have described, an independent theatre movement, reminiscent of that in Paris in the 1880s and the 1890s which gave a stage first to the naturalist and then to the symbolist drama, was flourishing in America.

In 1910, in Chicago, the city that would later see the founding of *Poetry Magazine* (1912) and *The Little Review* (1914), Maurice Brown founded the Chicago Little Theatre with the intention of producing European plays ignored by the commercial managers. In 1912, the Boston Toy Theatre was founded, bringing similar activity to the East Coast, and soon afterwards, the interest spread to New York with the founding of The Washington Square Players (1915), later to become the Theatre Guild, producer of all O'Neill's plays from the late 1920s onwards, The Neighbourhood Playhouse (1915) and then, the following year, The Provincetown Players. By 1924, a multitude of non-commercial theatres was playing to a regular audience of half a million.

The *Theatre Arts Magazine*, founded in 1916 by Sheldon Cheney, in response to the activity of the little theatre companies, is a vital document, not only because in it we can chart O'Neill's rise to prominence amongst the avant-garde before he was known to the general public, but because it gives an insight into the aspects of drama that were of particular interest to the 'new generation of artist-workers – playwrights, actors, directors', in what the first editorial self-consciously labelled the 'formative period' of American drama (vol. I, p.1).

In the first volume, Cheney lamented that in the five years since the first little theatres were founded no 'great creative figure', no 'artist of world measure – No American Shaw or Barker or Yeats' had appeared (p. 48). The second number welcomed the Provincetown Players, despite the primitiveness of their stage because of their policy of producing original plays (p. 91) and, in subsequent issues, O'Neill's name occurred with increasing frequency until, in October 1920, there was a detailed discussion of his work by Walter Pritchard Eaton, who called him 'a rare artist' (vol. IV, p. 289). The magazine published several of O'Neill's plays, including the full text of *The Emperor Jones* (volume V). His wife, Agnes Boulton (volume VIII), and several of his closest associates contributed to it. It carried articles by artists who had made their mark on the European stage: Claudel (volume I), Isadora Duncan (volume II), Gordon Craig (volume III), Yeats (volume VIII). D. H. Lawrence contributed an article on 'The Hopi Snake Dance' (volume VIII). Jacques Copeau's arrival in New York was welcomed as 'a sign of the times – both dramatically and politically – the best sign we know' (volume I, p. 134). Over half the magazine's space was devoted to discussion of the new stagecraft. Appia's ideas, particularly his use of light and of steps with which to create flow and rhythm, were highly regarded (volumes VII and VIII); Reinhardt's productions were followed eagerly, with sketches and photographs as illustration (full study in volume VII), and the workers in the little theatres also became familiar with the work and projected stage sets of native designers, Robert Edmond Jones, Norman Bel Geddes, Sam Hume, Herman Rosse and Lee Simonson.

An astonishingly large number of the men working in the independent theatre wrote books about their experience and these give an impression of the milieu as nothing else can, communicating their authors' consciousness that they were making history and revealing their mental fervour, their practical energy.[22] George Cram Cook, the founder of the Provincetown Players, is a striking example of such men. Himself a playwright, he sought to recreate the spirit of the Greek theatre in America. His literary ability was limited (see p. 97 below) but he seems to have carried conviction when he spoke. In her biography of Cook, his wife, Susan Glaspell, quotes extracts from his notebooks, amongst them a response to Nietzsche's discussion of the Italian Renaissance:

An American Renaissance of the Twentieth Century is not the task of ninety million people, but of one hundred. Does not that stir the blood of those who know they may be of that hundred? Does it not make them feel like reaching out to find each other – for strengthening of heart, for the generation of inter-communicating power, the kindling of communal, intellectual passion? ... I call upon the vital writers of America to attain to a finer culture, to develop in themselves and in each other more depth and fire – truth felt more blazingly; to be finer souls and finer voices, to make themselves strong as caryatides, prepared to bear together each the hundredth part of our Renaissance.

(The Road to the Temple, pp. 172–3)

O'Neill later described Cook, in words equally applicable to himself, as representing the 'spirit of revolt against the old worn-out traditions, the commercial theatre, the tawdry artificialities of the stage' (Alexander, *Tempering of Eugene O'Neill*, p. 224).

Cook's idea that, 'There ought to be one theatre for American writers to play with – one where, if the spirit move them, they can give plays which are not likely to be produced elsewhere' (Glaspell, *Road to the Temple*, p. 202), distinguished the Provincetown Players from other independent companies and made their alliance with O'Neill particularly fortunate for both. When Cook closed the theatre in 1921, because the Players were losing their amateur spirit and their best writer was looking increasingly to professional productions of his plays, ninety-three plays by forty-seven American playwrights had been produced, although Cook was the first to admit that most of these had been mediocre.[23] Susan Glaspell lets us glimpse the kind of freedom and encouragement her husband's theatre must have given O'Neill:

The people who had seen the plays and the people who gave them, were adventurers together. The spectators were part of the Players, for how could it have been done without the feeling that it came from them, without the sense of them there, waiting, ready to share, giving – finding the deep level where audience and writer and player are one.

(p. 195)

James Herne, by contrast, had had to wait four years to find a manager willing to risk a full production of his modest play, *Shore Acres*.[24]

The importance of such freedom to O'Neill cannot be stressed too much. Because of the new environment his plays found an audience, whilst his meeting with others who respected his work and shared his rejection of the commercial theatre, encouraged him to assume a public role as a missionary dramatist. The effect of suddenly finding himself part of a community was personally and artistically invigorating. His enthusiasm often bubbles up in his letters: he expresses his gratitude to Nathan and Mencken for having given him 'many a boost in spirit' (to Clark, 30 April 1919), thanks Macgowan for understanding his work, saying 'you cannot know how much it means to me' (9 August 1921), and tells Clark how eager he is that the critic should read his latest play (8 June 1919). In 1940, he recalled that his own company, The Provincetown Players, had had 'true integrity and courage and high purpose and enthusiasm' and so had been able to give him 'a theatre in which I knew I belonged, one of guts and idealism' (to Macgowan, 29 November 1940). The first two decades of O'Neill's writing life were a period of astonishing fertility in American letters generally, and the independent theatre movement made it possible for changes to take place in the public and collaborative art of theatre as well as in the more private literary forms of poetry and the novel.

But, whilst it might look as though O'Neill's relationship with the Provincetown Players was comparable with that of Chekhov with the Moscow Art Theatre, Strindberg with the Intimate Theatre or Yeats with the Abbey Players, the difference in place and time, in fact, led to somewhat different problems. Because the independent theatres in America grew in response to a wide range of events and ideas from Europe, O'Neill's colleagues – directors, designers, audiences – approached the drama with their own preconceptions of what was needed.

Europe at the turn of the century had experienced a counter-movement to realism. Its authors introduced overt symbolism into set and costume, projected the action by means of type figures rather than characters, sought a more remote and highly structured dialogue and often turned to myths and legends for their subject matter. For many of them, the conscious purpose was the re-establishing of drama on the ground between art and ritual, the creation of a theatre which would be a spiritually regenerative centre for those who came to it from a society that had lost its faith in formal religion. The symbolist writers for Lugné Poe's Théâtre d'Oeuvre, in Paris, wrote in reaction against the realistic plays of Antoine's Théâtre Libre, but they recognized that Antoine and Zola had already fought the essential battle against the flippancy and outworn conventions of the French commercial theatre.[25] There was a comparably gradual development within the individual careers of Ibsen and Strindberg. In his last plays, Ibsen investigated the more numinous realms of man's experience, introducing innovatory plot structure and staging, whilst Strindberg, in the majority of his plays written after 1899, used scenic means to probe man's unconscious and experimented with non-sequential time patterning. But the revolution was a slow one: fifteen years separated *The Dream Play* from Strindberg's first consciously naturalistic play, *The Father*. The almost simultaneous publication in America of revolutionary and counter-revolutionary texts had a curious telescoping effect. Although acting, stage design and playwriting in America in 1910, were comparable with those in Europe in the early 1880s, naturalism was no sooner discovered than it seemed passé and the cry against realism went up before any serious realistic theatre had been established.

O'Neill's idea of theatre

O'Neill's own reading and early theatre experience led him to certain masters: first Shaw and then Zola, Ibsen and Strindberg. No coherent theory of drama is developed in O'Neill's non-dramatic writing, but reference to his letters and notes does show us the tendency of his thought and indicates that there is an underlying direction in his seemingly erratic experiments. The ideas and practice of these nineteenth-century writers, which suggested the possibility of a quite different kind of drama from that with which O'Neill was so familiar seem to have been absorbed by him and to have given shape to his amorphous feelings of discontent and aspiration.

Shaw's *Quintessence of Ibsenism*, one of the first books O'Neill bought, is singled out for praise by the hero of *Ah, Wilderness!* and, although O'Neill rarely marked his books, passages of his copy of Shaw's essay are heavily underlined. Although O'Neill's response to Shaw's ideas was subsequently modified and elaborated by his encounter with Ibsen's work and, later, Zola's and Strindberg's, we often catch direct echoes of Shaw when O'Neill formulates his idea of drama. In 1924, for example, O'Neill talked about the capacity of truthfully depicted life to stir unusual depths of human compassion in the audience:

I do not write with a premeditated purpose. I write of life as I see it ... As it exists for many of us. If people leave the theatre after one of my plays with a feeling of compassion for those less fortunate than they I am satisfied ... There are those who have not been touched by misery. They may well suffer by proxy for a few hours in the theatre. It will do them good. It will have a humanising effect.[26]

The idea recurs in Shaw's Prefaces. It is stated like this in *The Quintessence*:

changes in technique follow inevitably from changes in the subject matter of the play. When a dramatic poet can give you hope and visions, such old maxims as that stagecraft is the art of preparation become boyish, and may be left to those unfortunate playwrights who, being unable to make anything interesting happen on the stage, have to acquire the art of continually persuading the audience that it is going to happen presently. When he can stab people to the heart by showing them the meanness and cruelty of something they did yesterday and intend to do tomorrow, all the old tricks to catch and hold their attention become the silliest superfluities ... The writer who practises the art of Ibsen, therefore, discards all the old tricks of preparation, catastrophe, dénouement and so forth, without thinking about it ... indeed, he does not know the use of them.

(*The Major Critical Essays*, p. 145)

The notion of stylistic purity expressed here by Shaw is reiterated by O'Neill, the notion that if the subject matter is sufficiently pressing and deeply felt by the writer, then, the words will flow into their own form:

> What I seek everywhere in life is drama. It's what I instinctively seek – human beings in conflict with other human beings, with themselves, with fate . . . I just set down what I feel in terms of life and let the facts speak whatever language they may to my audience.
>
> (To Malcolm Mollan, 3 December 1921)

That Shaw's separation of dramatic poets from 'unfortunate playwrights' dependent on 'old tricks' registered particularly deeply, is apparent in O'Neill's letter of application for Professor Baker's 'Drama 47' Playwriting course at Harvard, in which he wrote:

> Although I have read all the modern plays I could lay my hands on and many books on the subject of drama, I realise how inadequate such a haphazard, undirected mode of study must necessarily be. With my present training I might hope to become a mediocre journeyman playwright. It is just because I want to be an artist or nothing that I am writing to you.
>
> (Kinne, *George Pierce Baker and the American Theatre*, p. 193)

Baker's book, *Dramatic Technique* (1919), essentially a collection of his lectures for the Harvard course, offers a clue to why after his initial enthusiasm O'Neill did not complete the course. Baker's watchword is 'plot'; his method, the imitative exercise, and, final sign that the book is aimed at journeymen, he draws his examples indiscriminately from Pinero and Shakespeare, Dumas fils and Ibsen.[27]

O'Neill by-passed the awkward scientific naturalism in Zola's *Le Roman Expérimental*, and responded instead to his passionate rejection of current stage practices; his emphasis on the joy of artistic creation; his rejection of formulaic plays, which make of drama 'une spéculation intellectuelle, un art d'équilibre et de symétrie, réglé d'après un certain code' (p. 155) [an intellectual game, an art of balancing and symmetry, governed by a particular code], and his claim that the use of a priori structures prevents the dramatist from opening his mind to new and unexpected images. Zola writes:

> Je n'ai pas de goût pour l'horlogerie, et j'en ai beaucoup pour la vérité. Oui, en effet, cela est d'un joli mécanisme. Mais je voudrais que cela fût d'une vie superbe, je voudrais la vie, avec son frisson, avec sa largeur, avec sa puissance; je voudrais toute la vie.
>
> (p. 155)

[I have no taste for clockwork, and I do have a great liking for the truth. That machinery is pretty enough, certainly. But what I would like is that it should partake of the magnificence of life itself, life with its quivering excitement, its breadth, its power: I would like it to have the completeness of life.]

The word 'truth' reverberates through O'Neill's commentary as do 'vrai' and 'la vérité' through Zola's. O'Neill admired Gorki's *Night's Lodging* because 'it simply shows humanity as it is – truth in terms of human life';[28] he said that he had sought in *Ah, Wilderness!* 'an *exact* evocation of the mood of the dead past' (my italics);[29] of *Diff'rent* he wrote, 'whatever its faults may be [it] has the virtue of sincerity. It is the truth, the inevitable truth of the lives of the people in it as I see and know them',[30] and he described having rejected a tragic ending to *Anna Christie* in favour of a wry, anti-heroic one because, having 'looked deep into the hearts' of his characters, he had concluded that it 'would not have been true, they were not that kind'.[31]

When O'Neill uses the word 'truth' he seems to mean that general statements about human life can only be made convincingly when they are not made at all but are implicit in the actions of individuals portrayed with as little artifice as possible. 'Life' must be experienced 'in terms of lives'.[32] But lives penetrated, not merely reflected through a detailing of surfaces.

The aim of realism, in so far as it was a movement with identifiable aims in the nineteenth century, was to give an objective representation of real life, through the recording of everyday details. In part, and even by Zola, the term has been used interchangeably with 'naturalism' but it would seem useful to retain that term for the body of ideas, stemming from Zola's newspaper articles but most accessible in his 'Naturalisme au Théâtre', which claimed that literary works, besides being set in our own time and place with characters speaking a dialogue identifiable with our own speech, should have a philosophical basis in Darwinism and demonstrate the evolutionary laws in action: the strong subduing the weak, inherited characteristics showing themselves, genetics dominating the life process. Naturalism was a theory and, as such, was never wholly embodied in any vital work of art, although it underlay a host of minor works played at Antoine's Théâtre Libre in Paris, in the late 1880s, and at the Freie Bühne in Germany, and it was clearly in Strindberg's mind when he wrote *Lady Julie*. 'Realism' is a more chameleon term.

Immediately we must ask what 'real life' is, what 'reality', what the 'telling detail'. Even where the writer eschews overt symbols, mythical figures, otherworldly scenes and happenings, the elements of the visible world must still be selected and the audience will always be aware that an organizing consciousness has put the piece together. Arno Holz' *Die Familie Selicke*, for example, is often taken as a prime piece of objectively observed reality, and yet, even Holz interprets and shapes his material; the extreme sordidness of the setting is deliberately selected by him, and the plot is consciously developed to present man as the toy of circumstance. Even when the subjectivity of any piece of writing is admitted, other questions remain about what the real is. Is it the physical, observable world, or is that appearance which merely masks reality? Or does artistic realism rather lie in recognition of the devices and artifices of the medium itself? Which is the more realistic, Courbet, Manet, or Gauguin? Is the ordered development of the action in the *Rougon-Macquart* novels of Zola more lifelike than the unsequential happenings in a novel by Robbe-Grillet?

O'Neill derived one of his guiding principles from Strindberg. This is the idea that, at certain moments, we experience ourselves and others more sharply and that the dramatist who wants to penetrate human existence should seek out such moments and portray them on the stage. Strindberg wrote in 1889:

In the new naturalistic drama a striving for the significant motif was felt at once. Therefore, the action was usually centred around life's two poles, life and death, the act of birth and the act of death, the fight for the spouse, for the means of subsistence, for honour, all these struggles – with their battlefields, cries of woe, wounded and dead – during which one heard the new philosophy of life conceived as a struggle, blow its fertile winds from the south.[33]

In all O'Neill's discussion of Strindberg's drama, he searches for words to express his sense of its being at once realistic and capable of going more deeply than other contemporary work into the meaning and mystery of life. They were 'behind life' plays, in which Strindberg 'intensified the method of his time', interpreting in dramatic terms the 'characteristic conflicts which constitute the drama – the blood – of our lives today'. If other plays are 'naturalistic', then a play of such 'poignant intensity' as *The Dance of Death* must be classified as 'supernaturalism'.[34] Of his own play, *Welded*, O'Neill said:

I want to write a play that is truly realistic. That term is used loosely on the stage, where most of the so-called realistic plays deal only with the appearance of things, while a truly realistic play deals with what might be called the soul of the character. It deals with a thing which makes the character that person and no other. Strindberg's *Dance of Death* is an example of that real realism.[35]

The term 'supernaturalism', or, more usefully, 'real realism' is one to hold on to in thinking about O'Neill's own method. It proclaims both his dissatisfaction with the mere presentation of the everyday incident – 'naïve realism', perhaps? – and his clear need to root his plays in a recognizable time and place and to create identifiably human characters. It makes a necessary distinction between the plays of the great nineteenth-century dramatists and those of their imitators. The adjectives – 'super'; 'real' – suggest extraordinary intensity: looking at a man's face but seeing his psychological or metaphysical being; hearing his seemingly casual words and understanding their implications for himself and his relationships with his interlocutor.

When we investigate O'Neill's experimentation with a succession of anti-realistic devices, then, we need to recognize that, in part, the experimentation arises from the dramatist's search for ways of creating 'real realism' on the stage. Although, we must recognize, too, that it also arises from O'Neill's sheer excitement about the new theatrical methods, which gave life to the whole independent theatre movement. O'Neill was a questing artist and he was an artist of his time.

The separation of form and content

In a letter which has frequently been quoted as indicating his sureness of purpose, O'Neill wrote:

To be called a 'sordid realist' one day, a 'grim pessimistic Naturalist' the next, a 'lying Moral Romanticist' the next, is quite perplexing ... so I'm longing to complain and try to convince some sympathetic ear that I've tried to make myself a melting pot for all these methods seeing some virtues for my ends in each type of them, and, thereby, if there is any real fire in me, boil down to my own technique.

(To Quinn, published Quinn, *History of American Drama*, p. 199)

The words might equally be taken as an indication of the isolation and rootlessness in face of the rich range of possibilities offered by the European drama, of a writer in that time and place, anxious to find his own voice. This is even more apparent in a comment O'Neill made about *The Hairy Ape*:

I don't think the play as a whole can be fitted into any of the current 'isms'. It seems to run the whole gamut from extreme naturalism to extreme expressionism with more of the latter than the former. I have tried to dig deep in it, to probe in the shadows of the soul of man bewildered by the disharmony of his primitive pride and individualism at war with the mechanistic development of society ... Suffice it to add, the treatment of all the sets should be expressionistic, I think.

(To Macgowan, 24 December 1921)

Seeking for ways of intensifying the effect of his meaning, of creating a 'real realism' of his own, O'Neill looks to the most recent European drama as to a treasure house from which to draw suggestive devices. Each mode, forged by other writers as the only and inevitable means of probing and presenting experience, becomes an 'ism' for O'Neill. But at this stage he rarely manages to fuse the diverse elements of his play into a dramatic unity and often his enthusiasm for a particular device means that his use of it distorts rather than supports his meaning.

An example is O'Neill's use of masks. Symbolic significance accrues to a mask which hangs on the wall in *All God's Chillun Got Wings* and the phantasmagoric witch doctor of *The Emperor Jones* is masked, but O'Neill's real interest in masks comes with the middle plays.[36] There are masked characters in *Lazarus Laughed*, *The Great God Brown* and *Days Without End* and O'Neill chose to discuss masks in the three articles he wrote for *The American Spectator*, of which he was briefly co-editor. Attention had been drawn to the typifying and ritualistic functions of masks in other cultures by the newly fashionable study of anthropology. Masks of the oriental theatre and possible European variations were discussed and illustrated in Craig's publication, *The Mask*, to which O'Neill occasionally subscribed,[37] and in *The Theatre Arts Magazine*. William Zorach, the Provincetown's designer, had 'a rare book ... which contained photographs of African woodcarvings and masks' (Gelbs, p. 439), and Kenneth Macgowan, O'Neill's friend, had collaborated with Herman Rosse on the book *Masks and Demons*. In *The Theatre of Tomorrow*, his first book, Macgowan had written that masks:

> involve a certain strange and enthralling sense of the mystic quality of the theatre, of art commanding life and of life springing from art. They take a more natural place in these theatres, where realistic illusion is of necessity banned. One can conceive of a drama of group beings in which great individuals, around whom these groups coalesce, could be fitly presented only under the impersonal and eternal aspect of the mask.
>
> (p. 275)

O'Neill's articles begin conventionally enough, with a discussion of the masks of the Japanese Nōh, the Chinese theatre and African primitive ritual. After describing Robert Edmond Jones' masks for Stravinski's *Oedipus*, O'Neill suggests a masked *Hamlet*, saying that this would reduce the individuality of the central character and make of him 'a symbolic projection of a fate that is in each of us'. But as soon as he discusses his own use of masks, the emphasis changes. He says: 'One's outer life passes in a solitude haunted by the masks of others; one's inner life passes in a solitude hounded by the masks of oneself', and asks, 'What, at bottom, is the new psychological insight into human cause and effect but a study in masks, an exercise in unmasking?'[38] The masks his characters wear represent the generalization by which other people recognize and misunderstand them, and attention is focused on what lies behind the mask. Their removal signifies the penetration by the audience to a deeper level of reality. The face shows the hidden and often confused self. But, in the plays, this psychological function of masks is overlaid by one which approximates more closely to the traditional one.

In *Lazarus Laughed*, the central figures wear half masks which permit mask and face and the conflict between them to be shown simultaneously, thus avoiding the awkward donning and doffing which had been both irritating and confusing in *The Great God Brown*. But the chorus wear full masks, and speak as Roman Soldiers or Old Men, Bereaved Women or joyful Followers of Dionysus. There are no individuals amongst them. Rather, that they might symbolize all mankind, O'Neill plans that each mask should combine one of seven racial types with one of the seven ages of man and one of seven character types. The table reproduced in illustration 1, in which O'Neill plotted the distribution, shows how complicated his scheme was, and how confusing it would have been for an audience who, without benefit of O'Neill's tables and stage directions, would have been faced with a huge assortment of masks which fulfilled two quite distinct functions. Equally confusing is the method of *The Great God Brown*, where masked characters occasionally become type figures – Dion speaks as The Artist, Cybel as The Prophetess, as their very names imply – and the unmasked face is momentarily less personal than the masked.

The experiment with masks shows how influential the theory of the new stagecraft was on O'Neill but, more importantly, it demonstrates his own underlying, dogged independence. It is the language and the enthusiasm of the new stagecraft and not its theoretical substance which O'Neill takes here. In adopting the accoutrements but not the fundamental ideas of the anti-realistic theatre, O'Neill created problems of coherence for his own plays, even whilst acting as a source of new vigour and openness in American drama, and being himself responsible for the spread of avant-garde ideas beyond Greenwich Village. For the devices and experiments with form were what drew

1. O'Neill's manuscript: table of masks in *Lazarus Laughed*. A page from O'Neill's notes, demonstrating the intricacy of O'Neill's plan for the masks for the play and his inclination towards realism.

excited attention to each new O'Neill play. Looking back to the period, Lionel Trilling has recalled that:

To the audience of the Twenties, however, it was O'Neill's style rather than the content of his plays that was of first importance. Style, indeed, was sufficient content: the language of *Anna Christie*, the crude colour, the drum-beats and the phantasmagoria of *The Emperor Jones*, the engine rhythms, the masks, the ballet movements of *The Hairy Ape*, all constituted a denial of the neat proprieties, all spoke of a life more colourful and terrible than the American theatre had ever thought of representing. It was at first the mere technical inventiveness of Eugene O'Neill, his daring subjects and language which caught the public imagination.[39]

Kenneth Macgowan, in his book *Continental Stagecraft* (1922), welcomed *The Hairy Ape* as a 'star-like gleam' in which O'Neill said 'Nay to realism' (pp. 37–8), even though O'Neill himself always stressed that, in this play, he had sought to probe the human condition through the exploration of an individual soul.[40]

Several commentators have attributed O'Neill's anti-realism in the 1920s to the influence on him of Kenneth Macgowan,[41] but we have seen enough of the milieu to realise that O'Neill's situation was much more complicated than this. Indeed, it seems from Macgowan's early reviews for *The Globe* that he became conscious of new ideas in drama, largely as a result of seeing O'Neill's experimental plays,[42] and throughout their association, it was O'Neill who recommended new plays to Macgowan and insisted on the importance of experiment in their own productions.[43] Certainly, both Macgowan and Robert Edmond Jones, the third co-director of The Experimental Theatre (1923–7), were advocates of the new stagecraft. Jones had created the first expressionist set in America for his production of *He Who Married A Dull Wife* in 1915 and had travelled to Europe to study the experimental theatres there, after which he collaborated with Macgowan on the locally influential book, *Continental Stagecraft* (1922), in which the effects to be achieved by screens, symbolist settings, imaginative lighting and different kinds of stage, were illustrated and discussed. O'Neill wrote to Macgowan of his plans for *The Fountain*:

I have asked Bobby Jones to suggest reading to me . . . He could tell me just how the thing appeared to him from his angle – and we might combine. It would be an intensely interesting experiment, I believe, to work this thing out in harmony from our respective lines in the theatre – one not done before, as far as I know. For my part a clearer understanding of what he is striving for would be of inestimable value.

(18 March 1921)

Macgowan, in his first book, *The Theatre of Tomorrow* (1921), had attacked realism violently, even to the length of praising the historico-costume romances current in the commercial theatre. Ignoring the long record of such works in the American theatre, he greeted them histrionically saying, 'the sun of realism sinks' (p. 235). For most of the discussion he concerns himself with the writing of Fitch, Herne and the like, and gives scant attention to Ibsen, Strindberg or Chekhov. He does nod to 'realism of the higher type' to be found in 'Ibsen at his best ... or our own O'Neill in portions of *Beyond the Horizon*', but adds 'we are rushing off to other lands' in exploration of 'the ultimate spiritual values', forswearing the material and dramaturgy of realism (p. 224). Even realism of 'the higher type' is regarded as less spiritually valid than drama in which the figures are conventionalized and the dramatist thinks 'more in terms of colour, design, movement, music than he does now, and less in words alone' (p. 249). And yet, in O'Neill's own theoretical writing, we find that, while he adopts Macgowan's language, his 'anti-realism' is remarkably close to that 'higher type of realism' Macgowan hoped to see transcended. So, a manuscript note amongst his papers for *The Great God Brown*, which begins:

Life in terms of life cannot reveal more to us than our own bewilderment. Life in terms of the theatre, as an art separate from the simulcra of what we term reality may find expression in the great forces of which that reality is but a doughy symbol. . . . The theatre should be a refuge from the facts of life which we all feel, if we do not think, has nothing to do with the truth,

ends with an assertion of the importance of characterization:

The theatre should reveal to us what we are ... And if we have no Gods or heroes to portray we have the subconscious, the mother of all gods and heroes.

(Beinecke)

There is a striking example of the conflict within O'Neill in *Desire Under the Elms*. O'Neill's sketches for the set are reproduced in illustration 2a beside a sketch by Yegoroff (illustration 2b) for a Moscow Art Theatre production of Maeterlinck's *The Blue Bird*. Consciously or unconsciously, O'Neill must have derived his plan from the sketch which was printed in both *The Theatre Arts Magazine* (volume I) and *The Theatre of Tomorrow*, where Macgowan had noted that, 'In Yegoroff's land of memory ... the overhanging trees above the little cottage [stand] in silhouette like the calmly sorrowing figures

2. (a) From sketches for the set of *Desire Under the Elms* made by O'Neill. (b) Design by Yegoroff for the Moscow Art Theatre's production of *The Blue Bird*. The scene represents 'The Land of Memory' (from Jacques Bouché's 'L'Idée Théâtral Moderne' – the sketch was reproduced in *Theatre Arts Magazine*)

of past generations.'[44] O'Neill replaces Yegoroff's abstract, shadowy shapes with realistic images of trees but in his foreword insists on the anthropomorphic character of the elms:

> Two enormous elms are on each side of the house ... there is a sinister maternity in their aspect, a crushing, jealous absorption. When the wind does not keep them astir, they develop from their intimate contact with the life of man in the house an appalling humaneness. They brood oppressively over the house, they are like exhausted women resting their sagging breasts and hands and hair on its roof, and when it rains their tears trickle down monotonously and rot on the shingles.
>
> (p. 5)

Certain choices must be made by the writer: is the object intended to be taken as it is represented or is it to be taken to represent something else, to be interpreted symbolically? The stage direction here suggests that O'Neill does intend his elms to have symbolic suggestiveness, but he clings to realistic representation, he deliberately removes the overtly symbolic qualities of Yegoroff's design. The stage direction has frequently been quoted as evidence of O'Neill's capacity to write good prose, but its success is entirely literary, not dramatic. As Ruby Cohn has pointed out, there is, for example, no rain in the play, so that what happens to the elms in rain can hardly be part of the audience's imaginative response to the stage picture. O'Neill himself subsequently complained, 'Has it ever been produced as I wrote it? Never! ... There have never been the elm trees of my play, characters almost' (to Macgowan, August 1926), attributing to a failure of the *mise en scène* what was really his own failure to incorporate his idea of the symbolic significance of the elms into the structure of the play. He wants the audience to penetrate the realistic surface and respond to symbolic values but, at this stage in his writing, he gives no help in the dialogue or in the interaction between dialogue and set. The set, therefore, remains inert.

Never wholly at ease with anti-realistic means, O'Neill seems to have been most effective, in the early years, when he did retain the realistic surface, as in the set for *Desire Under the Elms*, but then improvised upon that basis with linguistic and scenic developments to create the necessary extra significance. Having set *All God's Chillun Got Wings* in a realistic room, to give one simple scenic example, he created an impression of emotional claustrophobia by moving in the walls from scene to scene, so reducing the acting space on the stage. In *The Emperor Jones*, similarly, there is a credible reason for the offstage drumbeat, but its insistence and its quickening pace also have a structural significance in creating the emotional tension of the play.

O'Neill seems to have been impelled to try all forms from romance (*The Fountain*), to satire (*Marco Millions*), to the philosophical marionette play (*Lazarus Laughed*), and to attempt all kinds of dialogue from prose poetry to idiomatic speech, from patterned, choric chant to monologue, through which the stream of consciousness of individual characters might be presented. But if he seems sometimes to over-reach himself, sometimes to be confused in idea or method, those letters which I quoted at the beginning of this chapter (pp. 18–19) are a reminder that his ambition to encompass everything was frequently accompanied by scepticism about his achievement, his confusion, by wry self-recognition.

Towards the end of the 1920s, the strain of O'Neill's pioneering role becomes apparent in his letters. He wrote to Robert Sisk about production plans for *Mourning Becomes Electra:*

As for bringing my next play in quietly, you might as well give up that dream. It can't be done. I've had too much notoriety for too many years and *Interlude* topped all that and put me on a par with Peggy Hopkins! If I stopped producing for a number of years that would do it of course, but it's hardly worth that abstinence ... But let's hope they will discover another 'best American dramatist' this season! That would help in more ways than one. I have been setting the pace for the pack for ten years now – artistically speaking – and it's gotten damn wearisome always breaking the wind. But such again is our dear Motherland. She will insist on 'best' this and 'best' thats.

(28 August 1930)

and in reply to praise from Dudley Nichols, he wrote:

one gets weary and bewildered among the broken rhythms of this time. One misses one's beat and line of continuity, one gets the feeling of talking through a disconnected 'phone, foolishly to oneself ... it's the dream that I may sometime say what must be said as it must be said that keeps me going.

(29 May 1932)

Only four years after the letter to Sisk, O'Neill seems to have decided that his work was 'worth that abstinence'. In 1933, after experiencing great difficulties with the writing of *Days Without End*,[45] he wrote in the notebook in which he recorded his yearly work, as though aware that he had reached some kind of turning point: 'Grand total 29 long plays, 24 one acters.' The entry for the following year reads, 'Near Breakdown from overwork ... six months compulsory rest.'[46] Although he continued to work after the production of *Days Without End*, he withdrew from participation in the theatre and no new play was offered for production until 1946, when his health had broken and his writing life had ended.

Until 1924, O'Neill may be characterized as a promising dramatist. The plays contain conflicting elements but, as I shall show in chapter 3, under the imaginative impulse of the discovery and investigation of new methods, O'Neill sometimes fuses form and meaning in exciting ways. After 1924, the effects of his public role are increasingly apparent. As the plays become more ambitious, the internal conflict can no longer be contained within an ingenious structure and an earnest intention, and the work begins to break up. The uncertainty of the art becomes apparent: the conception seems grandiose whilst the language becomes looser and less controlled. What is astonishing is that O'Neill is able to retrench, to struggle with his work in self-imposed silence, until he reaches the point where he is fully in control of the formal elements and has at the same time sifted his subject matter until his meanings are clear and compelling. We can trace many of the devices and themes of the earlier work in the late plays, but find that they are now used with subtlety and are integrated into the play. In performance, the audience, scarcely aware of the many elements composing the play, is gratified by the fullness and complexity of the action.

2

O'Neill's literary biography

Introductory note

O'Neill's library, now shared between Yale University and the C.W. Post Centre in New York, shows that O'Neill's literary interests were wide, but it is evident from his notes and letters, and from allusions in the plays, that a few writers – Nietzsche and Strindberg; Ibsen, Zola, Conrad and Dostoevski, and the *fin de siècle* poets: Swinburne, Dowson, Wilde and Baudelaire in Symons' translation – were read by him in adolescence and then reread, praised and quoted throughout his life. O'Neill was a surprisingly literary writer: in the early years he borrowed widely and diversely and his late plays contain many direct, acknowledged quotations. In this chapter, I shall investigate O'Neill's literary biography and the changes in kind and function of literary echo that we find at different stages in his writing life.

O'Neill's reading has been remarkably well documented. His first biographer, Barrett Clark, deliberately collected information about O'Neill's literary interests, and subsequent biographers have extended this information although the material has not, until now, been collated. A large number of articles investigating the influence of one writer or another on O'Neill have also been published although, again, none of the commentators has attempted to make general statements about the character of O'Neill's borrowing or the astonishing extent of it. In order to make an amount of factual information available in a brief space, and to permit a more comprehensive view of O'Neill's literary background, I have gathered this information into an Appendix (p. 198) and my comments in this chapter will be based on that information.

O'Neill and literary influence

Commentators have dilated upon O'Neill's early wandering life as gold prospector and seaman, news reporter and habitué of Greenwich

Village bars and have praised the realism of his accounts of rough living on the waterfront. St John Ervine's introduction to *Moon of the Caribbees* is representative:

> Nothing is so obvious in his work as this, that he has wrought it out of his own experience even more than he has wrought it out of his imagination, and that the experience has, on the whole, been hard and bitter.

(v. iii)

Such statements need qualifying. Scott Fitzgerald offers a more helpful approach when he comments, in a letter to Mencken, on the effect of Conrad on a generation of American writers, saying:

> By the way, you mention in your review of *Sea Horses* that Conrad had only two imitators. How about, O'Neill in *The Emperor Jones (Heart of Darkness)* Hergesheimer in *Bright Shawl (Java Head)* Me in *Gatsby* (God I've learned a lot from him) Maugham in *The Moon and Sixpence* (You mentioned it in your own review, five years ago). But his (Conrad's) approach and his prose is naturally more imitated than his material, tho' he did send at least Masefield and O'Neill to sea in ships.

(May/June 1925, in Letters, p. 482)

As Fitzgerald suggests, our reading often does more than we realize to shape the very events of our lives and the subsequent 'realistic' accounts we may give of them. O'Neill did certainly experience life at sea (although for only sixteen months compared with Conrad's twenty years); he suffered an attack of tuberculosis and lived for a brief spell wildly, drunkenly and in extreme squalor. It is probable that he perceived these events as they happened to him, or as he sought them out, with an imagination already prepared by his reading, whilst the reading in its turn was shaped because O'Neill turned to books in which he found his own condition figured.[1]

Those works O'Neill particularly valued are confessional. The plays and autobiographical novels of Strindberg depict man persecuted by and persecuting those with whom he lives most closely, feeding them and feeding off them. More specifically, they have central characters who need maternal wives and who are jealous of and unconsciously hostile to their own children or siblings. O'Neill's favoured late-nineteenth-century poets, for their part, project as the personae of their poems men, world-weary and experienced in dissipation, hurt by and cynical about their fellows, but more finely sensitive than they. Even if, for the moment, we leave aside the evidence of the plays, we find that the biographers do portray O'Neill as one whose close relationships followed these patterns and who, at least in adolescence and early manhood, adopted a persona much like those of the poems, to help him cope with the world.

In other words, O'Neill's life and his experience of literature were closely intertwined, each shaping and extending the other. Indeed, O'Neill seems eventually to have perceived this in himself and it is a mark of artistic objectivity eventually attained that he is able, in *Long Day's Journey Into Night*, to project such a relationship with literature on to the stage, and to make it yield a subtle irony. Early in act IV of the play, Edmund Tyrone quotes from Baudelaire and says:

It's a good likeness of Jamie, don't you think, hunted by himself and whiskey, hiding in a Broadway hotel room with some fat tart – he likes them fat – reciting Dowson's *Cynara* to her.

(p. 116)

The audience accept the portrait, until Jamie appears later in the scene and lets them recognize that the quotation has preshaped Edmund's response and distorted the truth. Because it has also preshaped the audience's, the reality that the presence of Jamie reveals strikes them the more forcibly (see chapter 6). Elsewhere, the literary references are used more straightforwardly to make the audience aware of the situation and the characters' feeling for it. Discussing Dowson, Edmund suddenly perceives himself:

(*He laughs – then soberly, with genuine sympathy.*) Poor Dowson. Booze and consumption got him. (*He starts and for a second looks miserable and frightened. Then with defensive irony.*) Perhaps it would be tactful of me to change the subject.

(p. 117)

As we watch a performance of virtually any of the early plays we seem to catch allusions to other works; our memories are stirred by literary echoes.[2] If the notion I have introduced here of a man experiencing the world with a consciousness shaped by his reading is tenable, then it offers an explanation of the fragmentary nature of many of the echoes. Let us look, for example, at the case of *The Emperor Jones*. Since this is one of the outstanding plays of O'Neill's early career, it is the more interesting that the problem occurs here too. Inspired by his reading about Congo ritual and perhaps also by the memory of a similar device in *The Drums of Oude*, a melodrama by Austin Strong, O'Neill uses the rhythm of beating drums, whose pace gradually accelerates from the speed of the human pulse-beat, to present the mounting urgency of Jones's fear by stirring the audience at a preverbal, even preconscious, level, whilst a sequence of images project on to the stage incidents from the individual, historical and atavistic past of the central character. The idea of portraying terror induced by flight through the primeval forest at night, may have been suggested by an incident in Boucicault's *The Octoroon*, in which something, 'a bear or a runaway nigger' is heard forcing its way through the undergrowth. M'Closky, a slave trade profiteer, rushes on to the stage in a state of collapse:

M'CLOSKY. Save me, save me! I can go no farther. I heard voices.
SCUD. Who's after you?
M'CLOSKY. I don't know, but I feel it's death! In some form human, or wild beast, or ghost, it has tracked me through the night. I fled, it followed. Hark! There it comes – it comes – don't you hear a footstep on the dry leaves?
SCUD. Your crime has driven you mad.[3]

(v, iii)

Using scenic effects, O'Neill creates an image of panic fear and, as Fitzgerald suggested, like Conrad in *The Heart of Darkness*, he probes the mind of his central figure to reveal how close civilized man is to primitivism.

These influences and echoes have been successfully absorbed into O'Neill's play, indeed they are structurally essential to it, but at least one other area of influence has not been absorbed. The play form used by O'Neill leads his audience to expect something which he appears not to have had in mind. We accept the fragmentary nature of the various episodes and the somewhat question-begging references to Jungian psychology and to theories about the relationship between social conditions and personal debasement, because the very shape of the play suggests that these are steps to some other question that will be raised finally. The shape, with its episodic structure and its dramatization of different aspects of the mind of Jones, probably derives from *Peer Gynt*. There is a sense of mystery latent in the set, with its balanced usage of black and white, of shadow and moonlight, with its eerie forms and forest background, and the strange half light in which the visions appear. When O'Neill takes the audience into the recesses of Jones's mind the tempo becomes wilder, the hallucinations more strange and, in sound and visual effect, more generally suggestive, as though the audience is being prepared for a movement on to a mystical level. But the play ends without this movement having taken place. Ibsen, in the final moments of his play, in Peer's encounter with the castaway and the Button Moulder, offers a symbolic representation of the mysterious in human existence and allows his audience to absorb suggestions from the shadowy figures. O'Neill does not let his images open in this way. In the end, the audience can find a rational explanation for each of the hallucinatory figures. The content does not wholly fulfil the expectations which the echoing of Ibsen had raised and so the ending of the play, although thoroughly motivated at the realistic level seems premature.

Our sense of O'Neill's literary biography offers an explanation of what has happened here. O'Neill's vision of life is permeated by the literature he has read. He has taken from that literature those ideas and perceptions that meet his own psychological needs: the work as a whole has not been rationally pondered and repatterned in his mind. The echoes we catch are, therefore, sometimes deliberate but more often they are intuitive: the references often have a private significance that is not communicated to the audience. Even the best of the early works, because of this, leave an unsatisfying sense of something not quite complete, of memory stirred, but not to any purpose. The audience catches at a reference and looks for its implications, but is misled in doing so because the reference has been unconscious on the dramatist's part.

In the middle years, literary references intrude into the climactic moments of the plays. O'Neill's admiration for and internal debate about a particular work becomes the half-concealed subtext of the play, at once too obtrusive to be ignored and too cryptic for its significance to be available to many, or any, of the audience. The situation, which might be fraught with meaning for the author, seems thin or bizarre to the audience. References to Nietzsche in *Lazarus Laughed* have frequently been traced by commentators, and provide a useful example.

Several commentators have recorded the particular passages in which O'Neill echoes Nietzsche's *Thus Spake Zarathustra*, in the middle plays, establishing without doubt that it is Nietzsche's idea of eternal recurrence that is the source of O'Neill's affirmative protestations.[4] Don Juan's dying cry in *The Fountain*, Lazarus's cryptic utterances, Kublai Khan's 'eastern' wisdom in *Marco Millions*, and Cybel's pronouncement on life in *The Great God Brown*, which begins, 'Always Spring comes again bearing life' (p. 108), are all restatements of the Nietzschean message:

Everything goeth, everything returneth; eternity rolleth the wheel of existence. Everything dieth, everything blossometh forth again; eternally runneth on the year of existence.

(LVII)[5]

The very germ of the action of *Lazarus Laughed* lies in Nietzsche's riddle of the shepherd and the black snake. The words with which Zarathustra describes the transformation of the shepherd after he has destroyed the snake, are directly applicable to O'Neill's Lazarus:

No longer shepherd, no longer man – a transfigured being, a light-surrounded being that laughed! Never on earth laughed a man as he laughed!

O my brethren, I heard a laughter which was no human laughter, – and now gnaweth a thirst at me, a longing that is never allayed.

(XLVI)

It has been noted, too, that the laughing, dancing chorus which surrounds Lazarus is modelled on Nietzsche's description of the Dionysiac worshippers in *The Birth of Tragedy*, the other work of Nietzsche which O'Neill frequently praised.

By means of such information, the commentators have been able to elucidate the play's meaning. But it is also necessary to face the implications about O'Neill's method that are raised by the need for such scholarship. For, whilst the building of a text on another literary work has sometimes had exciting results, that has been when the new text has fully absorbed the original; has offered a vital interplay with it, or has expanded its meaning. O'Neill, in the middle plays, neither transmutes nor interprets but acts as an illustrator of his sources and, because he is attempting to do several other things simultaneously, he illustrates only a limited portion of the original text.[6]

Nietzsche presents his character, Zarathustra, dramatically. The riddle of the shepherd is the culminating conundrum of Zarathustra's terrifying vision, after which thirst gnaws at him. His racked state of mind is used as the link between one section of the book and the next, which opens with the words, 'With such enigmas and bitterness in his heart did Zarathustra sail o'er the sea' (XLVII). Zarathustra can be joyful, and the book ends on an affirmative note (LXXX), but only after Zarathustra has experienced nightmares (XL and XLII) and has abandoned his followers in a state of deep depression, bordering despair (XLIV). O'Neill's hero, by contrast, is consistently joyful, his one moment of hesitation, at the' death of Miriam, is quickly banished. Nor is the dramatic conflict shifted convincingly to Lazarus's followers, since their joy and grief exists simply as a reflex response to Lazarus's presence or absence. Zarathustra's message is imparted gradually (I–XXX); it is doubted (XLI); it is debated and evaluated (LVI), and, finally, it is embraced in jubilant song (LIX and LX). In

O'Neill's plays it is present only as a joyful exclamation, admitting no doubts.

O'Neill seems to have been so steeped in Nietzsche's text that echoes from it carry a richness of association for him, which is lost to his audience once the ideas and characterizations have been removed from their original context. (See chapter 4 for a discussion of the specific influence of Nietzsche on O'Neill's style.)

The author's spokesman

Many commentators have noticed the presence, throughout O'Neill's opus, of a character who, in appearance and family background, resembles O'Neill himself. Robert C. Lee's article, 'The Lonely Dream', is the fullest of such studies and includes an account of the first draft of the play, *The Straw*, whose stage directions described the background, education, opinions, past life of the hero in such a way as to leave little doubt that these were modelled on the author's own.[7] The figure is a 'poet–rebel': usually an artist or aspiring artist – a painter in *Bread and Butter*, an architect in *The Great God Brown*, a writer in *Fog*, *The Straw*, *Welded*, *Days Without End*; in *Beyond the Horizon* and *Ah, Wilderness!*, a dreamer and a reader. He compels the adoration of women, the fascination of less passionate men. He is a failure because he has refused to compromise with society, but, despite his cynicism which stems from having tasted deep of the sins of the flesh, he retains an unusual sensitivity to life and to other men. The character may be autobiographical, but it is autobiography filtered through the persona of the *fin de siècle* poets. O'Neill's own adolescent poetry, indeed, was a combination of the late romantic pose and the language and rhythm of Masefield's sea ballads. For example:

I have had my dance with folly, nor do I shirk the blame;
I have sipped the so-called wine of life and paid the price of shame;
But I know that I shall find surcease, the rest my spirit craves,
Where the rainbows play in the flying spray,
'Mid the keen salt kiss of the waves.[8]

Unfortunately, the figure is not given a fully dramatic presence. We know of his moral ardour, because the stage directions tell us it exists and describe appropriate gestures and facial expressions; because of the statements of other characters, and because of their gestures of capitulation, but the dialogue itself contributes very little to the charisma, so that the audience do not empathize with those who yield. Because one figure is so clearly the author's spokesman, possible complexity of viewpoint on the action is forfeited: the other characters are judged by the extent of their sympathy towards the central character and, therefore, exist in a single dimension. The central character is never in contact with another figure of equal stature and, although we do not see him in conflict with himself, we are never asked to doubt his judgement, never made conscious of ambiguities in him, of the kind that Conrad or Melville, for example, introduce into their prose fiction, forcing us to ponder the complex role of their narrators.

Objectivity in the late plays

O'Neill's material remains essentially the same in the late plays, but the focus is sharpened, the picture composed, so that the effect of the finished work is quite different. The characterization of Richard Miller, in *Ah, Wilderness!*, the comedy written by O'Neill in 1933, and to a lesser extent, of John Loving in *Days Without End* (1934), help us to see both the connection and the kind of change that has taken place between the early and late work. The devices O'Neill uses in these two final plays of the middle years are similar but clumsier and, therefore, more apparent than those in the late plays.[9]

Ah, Wilderness! is an affectionate, teasing study of adolescence. Richard, an aspiring poet, sees life through the eyes of the writers O'Neill himself admired. Part of the plot turns on the nature of the books he has been reading, quoting and passing on to his sweetheart, and so his relationship with them is part of the material of the play. The comments of other characters about his reading characterize them and help to place Richard. The elder brother is scornful and ignorant; the mother is frightened by the blasphemy and indecency that received opinion tells her such books contain; the father is tolerant and perceptive, saying, 'Can't you see Richard's only a fool kid who's just at the stage when he's out to rebel against all authority, and so he grabs at everything radical to read and wants to pass it on' (p. 34). O'Neill lets Richard reveal his own naïveté through hyperbole – *Dorian Gray* is 'one of the greatest novels ever written!', Shaw is 'the greatest playwright alive today!', Swinburne 'the greatest poet since Shelley!' (p. 28) – and satirizes him in the salesman's comment in act III after one of Richard's more melodramatic quotations, 'What is it – a child poet or a child actor?' (p. 91). Most effectively, O'Neill creates anti-climax by deliberately contrasting the events and characters of *Hedda Gabler* with those of his own play. The drunken Richard suddenly has a vision of himself which he expresses with the quotation, 'And then – at ten o'clock – Eilert Løvborg will come – with vine leaves in his hair' (p. 93), and in a later scene Muriel, a pale shadow of Hedda, listens excitedly to the exploits of her Løvborg. We are led to recall the frustration and demonic passion of Hedda and to perceive, by contrast, how slight are the loving, posing, and squabbling of O'Neill's characters. Such deliberate scaling down of the characters gives the play its peculiar tone of humorous affection. The bringing of the literary biography into the open, the conscious use of it in characterization and the gentle mockery of the poet–rebel figure, who is clearly no longer to be directly associated with the dramatist, signifies a new and important self-consciousness in O'Neill.

We find the poet–rebel figure in the late plays but O'Neill no longer asks us to empathize with him or to take him as the author's spokesman. The figure is now a fully dramatic character: he engages our interest equally with the other characters, is subjected to the same modifications as they and, like them, is given occasional moments of contact and comprehension, and others of misunderstanding. Moreover, instead of setting a businessman, a dull representative of the material world, in simple opposition to the artist, as he often did in the earlier plays, leaving us in no doubt as to where our sympathy should be, O'Neill now juxtaposes two characters who are at once similar and intriguingly different from each other. Jamie Tyrone, in *Long Day's Journey Into Night*, is a poet–rebel but so is Edmund and each provides a commentary on the other, most notably, perhaps, in the sequence in which Edmund burlesques Jamie's self-pity through references to the late Victorian poets and in so doing casts doubt on his own self-indulgent quotation of the same writers. In *A Touch of the Poet*, Simon, off-stage, and Melody, in the foreground, are variations of the same figure. One is ingenuous, delighting in his first experience of Romantic-Primitivism, the other, an older and more self-conscious man, exults in his image of himself as Byronic hero, but, in flashes, recognizes that he is a poseur and despises himself. Sara, the perceptive daughter who mocks Melody's self-image in her turn is as blind to the posing of her own lover as the mother she criticizes has been to hers. The division in *The Iceman Cometh* is of a slightly different kind. Here, the autobiographical figure, the one who most resembles, in situation and status, the O'Neill of 1912 is Willie Oban, the student. He is a minor character, creative only in inventing variations on a bawdy song, who, younger than the other bums in Hope's bar, is also clumsier, sometimes contravening the etiquette, disturbing the peace of the roomers, by miscalculating the effect of his boisterousness.

Larry Slade, modelled not on O'Neill but on an old anarchist friend, is given some of the attributes of the earlier autobiographical figure and is a kind of vestigial poet–rebel, who quotes Nietzsche but does so wryly and whose judgements are undercut by his own enacted response to events.

What we are identifying here, is a movement to a state of creative objectivity in which O'Neill was able to dramatize his own early condition. O'Neill borrowed widely and diversely in the early years from the books he enthusiastically praised and recommended to his friends. Although his growing library suggests that he continued to read, he wrote and talked much less about his reading after the mid-1930s. When literary echoes occur in the later work, they have been carefully selected and are presented in the form of purposive allusion or direct, acknowledged quotation. This controlled use of literary reference is an essential and effective element in O'Neill's mature style and demands more extensive discussion than has been possible in this chapter. I shall discuss it at greater length when I comment on O'Neill's dramatic language in the mature plays later in the book.

3

The American vernacular in the early plays

At the outset of his career, O'Neill was searching for alternative theatrical modes. Dialogue in the contemporary theatre was exclamatory or flippant, and little attempt was made to create character through speech. The vernacular was used entirely for comic purposes although, by 1914, enthusiasm for American English as a medium for serious literature had become widespread amongst poets and novelists. When O'Neill reproduced the speech of uneducated men, he found a fluency that failed him when he used Standard English for his dialogue. The idea of the American vernacular as an appropriate literary medium, which O'Neill's facility must have encouraged, was reinforced on the one hand by the precepts of what I shall call the American Language Movement and, on the other, by the negative example of the American stage. Before looking at O'Neill's use of the vernacular, I shall briefly discuss the development of the language movement and the situation of the American drama in the years before O'Neill began to write.

The American Language Movement

Many American writers and thinkers in the nineteenth century became convinced that the local form of English was the only possible medium for an American writer who sought to create literature rooted in his own perception of the world. The idea was most coherently stated by Whitman and by Twain, and had reached its moment of greatest urgency when O'Neill was writing his first plays. The culminating work of the movement was Mencken's mammoth study. In the first edition of *The American Language* (1919) Mencken wrote:

As yet, American suffers from the lack of a poet bold enough to venture into it as Chaucer ventured into the despised English of his day, and Dante into the Tuscan dialect, and Luther, in his translation of the Bible, into peasant

German. Walt Whitman made a half attempt and then drew back; Lowell,
perhaps, also heard the call, but too soon.

(p. 385)

There had begun to be discussion of the American idiom as a separate
branch of the English Language, as early as the 1780s. In 1781, the
Reverend John Witherspoon listed neologisms coined to meet needs
not encountered in Europe[1] and, in 1783, Noah Webster published
his *American Spelling Book*. Throughout the nineteenth century,
commentators continued to be fascinated by the multitude of neologisms which some denounced as barbaric and debasing, whilst
others rejoiced to find that the human imagination could still produce
words as apt and pungent as in earlier periods of expansion. The
Philological Society of America, founded in 1788 with the express aim
of 'ascertaining and propagating the American tongue', made the
language question into a political and patriotic cause.[2]

Although scholars and politicians might make the American Language their cause, writers clung to Standard English. Tocqueville,
accusing American literature of being parasitic on Europe, said in
1835:

So the Americans have not yet, properly speaking, got any literature. Only the
journalists strike me as truly American. They certainly are not great writers,
but they speak their country's language and they make themselves heard. I
should class the others as foreigners. They stand to the Americans much as the
imitators of the Greeks and Romans stood to ourselves at the time of the
Renaissance – objects of curiosity, but not of general sympathy. They are
entertaining, but they do not affect mores.

(*Democracy in America*, vol. II. part I, ch. 13, translated George Lawrence)

The majority of writers in the nineteenth century continued to look to
England for their literary models, and even such admirers of the
American Wild and of the vision of the untutored countryman as
Emerson and Thoreau wrote as rigorously pure an English as they
could command. But a minority did experiment with native forms.
They attempted to 'speak their country's language and make themselves heard' when dealing with themes more serious than those of
popular journalism. Fenimore Cooper, Hawthorne and Melville set
their novels in America or amongst Americans and, whilst continuing
to use Standard English for narration, introduced colloquial American into their dialogue. Even Poe, so absorbed in the European Gothic
revival, had his American stories, most notably 'The Goldbug', with
its vernacular-speaking character.

But other writers were introducing the colloquial idiom into narrative, too. Aphorisms and homilies in New England dialect, ballads from the Appalachians and tall tales from Kentucky and the West were published. These were invariably regarded as light reading and did not appear in book form until two writers insisted that such work could be more serious. In 1848, James Russell Lowell's *Biglow Papers*, using a version of New England dialect, presented, in Hosea Biglow, the archetype of the shrewd Yankee. In 1867, Mark Twain's *Celebrated Jumping Frog* was published: a collection of tall tales, recounted in hyperbolic Western slang. In the narration of subsequent books, *The Innocents Abroad, Life on the Mississippi, Tom Sawyer*, Twain's own colloquial voice flavoured the style and then, in *The Adventures of Huckleberry Finn* (1884), the character Huck is presented as the first person narrator and the narrative medium of the whole novel is a form of Mid-West dialect which, in Twain's hands, proves itself capable of expressing a full range of events, emotions and themes, besides bringing, through the boy narrator, a remarkable sharpness of vision.

In the 1880s, the movement became a campaign, with Whitman as its fiercest champion. In *Leaves of Grass*, he had explored what it meant to him to be an American, adopting a nonchalant stance as 'one of the roughs' and seeking a style freed from European models, concrete and bold, using the 'limber, lasting and fierce words'[3] coined on the American continent to describe 'the wonders that fill each minute of time forever and each acre of surface and space forever'.[4] Subsequently, he published two stirring articles in *The North American Review*. In 1881, he quoted from an article in *The Times*, to shame American writers and to make more dramatic his plea for honesty of style. The *Times* writer had said:

They talk of the primeval forest but it would generally be very hard from internal evidence to detect that they were writing on the banks of the Hudson rather than on those of the Thames ... In fact, they have caught the English tone and air and mood only too faithfully ... A nation of readers has required of its poets a diction and symmetry of form equal to that of an old literature like that of Great Britain, which is also theirs. No ruggedness, however racy, would be tolerated by circles which, however superficial their culture, read Byron and Tennyson.

Rejecting the finished style of the English literati, which seemed to him effete and dishonest in the context of American institutions and *mores*, Whitman demanded of his contemporaries a new stylistic robustness which would shift the centre to America.[5] In his second article, *Slang in America*, he looked at the nature of language itself, saying:

Language, let it be remembered, is not an abstract construction of the learned, or of the dictionary makers, but is something arising out of the work, needs, ties, joys, affections, tastes of long generations of humanity, and has its bases broad and low, close to the ground. Its final decisions are made by the masses, people nearest to the concrete, having most to do with the actual land and sea.

(vol. CXLI (November 1884), p. 432)

He praised the liveliness and the rough, natural poetry of the common speech:

The wit, the flashes of humor and genius and poetry – darting out often from a gang of laborers, railroad men, miners, drivers, or boatmen! How often I have hovered at the edge of a crowd to hear their impromptus!

(p. 434)

The spoken language, he wrote, is continually being enlivened by slang inventions which exist briefly and then are discarded or, occasionally, absorbed into the language, contributing to its growth. Their metaphor is fresh, whereas the metaphor in the body of the language has become obscured by usage and so slang acts as a revivifier. From here, it was one step to claiming the validity of slang in literary writing.

After Whitman's battle, 'natural poetry', 'metaphor', 'linguistic regeneration' and, above all, 'honesty', were the watchwords of those championing the American language.[6] Howells cited 'its daring, its savour, its ready metaphor', likening it to the English of Elizabethan England.[7] The comparison was reiterated by Mencken, by Virginia Woolf, in an article on the American Language written in 1929,[8] and, as recently as 1958, by Max Lerner in his study, *America as a Civilization* (p. 805). Such comments are so widespread that they become the rule. Let this by William Archer summarize the many equivalent statements:

New words are begotten by new conditions of life, and as American life is far more fertile of new conditions than ours, the tendency towards neologism cannot but be stronger in America than in England. America has enormously enriched the language, not only with new words, but (since the American mind is, on the whole, quicker and wittier than the English) with apt and humorous colloquial metaphors.[9]

To its advocates, the vernacular represents what is honest, unselfconscious and free in American democracy. Henry James might claim that Americans are 'conscious of being placed on the circumference of civilization rather than at the centre',[10] but others would claim that that depended on the definition of civilization. The movement, indeed, made moral claims. In his Nobel prize address in December 1930, Sinclair Lewis recognized that the prize was awarded as much to emergent American literature as to himself. Of Dreiser he said, 'He has cleared the trail from Victorian and Howellsian timidity and gentility in American Fiction, to honesty, boldness and passion of life',[11] and with Dreiser he grouped O'Neill, Cabell, Willa Cather, Mencken, Anderson, Upton Sinclair, Hergesheimer and Hemingway.

At the same time, the study of the American Language had become a respectable branch of scholarship. Collections of slang, argot and dialect were made and the many articles analysing the divergence of American from British English, published in *Dialect Notes, Modern Language Notes, The Atlantic Monthly, The American Mercury* and *The Bookman*, led to the foundation of the specialist magazine, *American Speech*, in 1925. In 1913, *Harper's* ran a series by Thomas Lounsbury on Americanisms and articles appeared in the popular press with such titles as 'Is there really such a thing as the American Language?' (*New York Sun*, 10 March 1918); 'The Two Englishes' (this by Mencken in *The Baltimore Sun*, 15 September 1910). There were books, too: R. H. Thornton's *American Glossary* (1912), Tucker's *American English* (1921), and the two authoritative general surveys, Mencken's *American Language* (1919) and G. P. Krapp's *The English Language in America* (1925).

The confidence of Twain and Whitman that there was something to be said and that they had the equipment with which to say it was now suddenly present in dozens of writers. The interesting American poets of the first two decades of this century experimented with speech rhythms. This is true not only of Pound and Eliot, but of Frost and Sandburg, William Carlos Williams and Masters and, in prose fiction, of Dreiser and Sherwood Anderson as well as of Gertrude Stein. O'Neill, so often regarded as an isolated giant, was at the outset of his career, as we have seen, part of a theatrical community. His conscious exploration of the possibilities of the American vernacular in his genre, placed him within a wider literary community. In a review of the fourth edition of *The American Language*, in 1936, Edmund Wilson, like Sinclair Lewis before him, grouped O'Neill with other writers whose work seemed specifically American in form. 'Sinclair Lewis and Eugene O'Neill, Sherwood Anderson and Carl Sandburg, Hemingway and Dos Passos, Ring Lardner and Mencken himself in his more colloquial work.'[12] And some of the links were direct. Anderson, Williams and Dreiser were all occasional members of the

Provincetown Players, and their names appear in the magazines which published O'Neill's plays. *Smart Set*, edited by Mencken, published stories by Anderson and Dreiser, poems by Masters and three of O'Neill's early plays (*Long Voyage Home, Moon of the Caribbees* and *Ile*, 1918); James Oppenheim's *Seven Arts Magazine* (October 1916–November 1917), whose aim was, 'to be a channel for these new tendencies, an expression of our American arts, which shall be fundamentally an expression of our American life',[13] published O'Neill's short story, *Tomorrow*, as well as stories by Anderson and Dos Passos, essays by Mencken, and verse by Frost.

What I have said so far has been descriptive. Those who advocated the use of the vernacular stressed its vitality, and emphasized the need for artistic integrity and for writers to respond to what was American in themselves. Before going any further, I want to look rather more closely at the assumptions about the vernacular which have, so far, been accepted at face value. All the writers I have mentioned, including O'Neill, seek a mode of expression different from the mandarin language and all use speech rhythms as the basis of their style. To this extent they are indeed, part of a movement in American literature. Beyond this, in Twain and Whitman, in the writers included in Lewis's or Wilson's lists, we find different ideas of what the vernacular actually is.

'The American Language' and 'the vernacular' are sometimes used as generic terms which include the regional dialects, the slang spoken on the continent and the colloquial speech of the literati. Sometimes they are applied to only one of these forms of the vernacular. The relaxed American colloquial style that Whitman writes reflects his own idiom and enables him to write of what he experiences, uninhibited by English models. His listening to 'impromptus', his avoidance of abstract language, is reminiscent of Wordsworth's position, stated in the *Preface to the Second Edition of the Lyrical Ballads*, where he proposes to use 'a selection of the language really used by men ... with simple and unelaborated expressions ... a more permanent and far more philosophic language than that which is frequently substituted by poets'. Wordsworth admires the peasant but avoids 'meanness' and purifies his language of 'lasting and rational causes of dislike and disgust'.[14] Unlike Tennyson, he does not write poems in dialect, any more than Whitman writes the slang he admires. Both use language germane to their thought processes, and in doing so, widen the range available for poetry.

When he prefaces *Huckleberry Finn* with an author's note about the dialects used, Twain silently acknowledges that these are neither his own nor his audience's habitual idiom. He writes:

> In this book a number of dialects are used, to wit: the Missouri negro dialect; the extremest form of the backwoods South-Western dialect; the ordinary Pike-Country dialect; and four modified varieties of this last. The shadings have not been done in a haphazard fashion, or by guess-work; but painstakingly, and with trustworthy guidance and support of personal familiarity with these several forms of speech.

His attestation of authenticity and of care shows that the style is not ingenuous, the book not a piece of folk art. Twain deliberately creates a linguistic framework and, taking the step which neither Whitman nor Wordsworth attempts, he substitutes for their self-expressive idiom, a new kind of poetic diction. His artifice, in fact, enables Twain to communicate more effectively than he could in his personal idiom. In *The Reign of Wonder*, Tony Tanner compares the stock literary evocation of the dawn in *Tom Sawyer* with the 'vibrant, alive, and luminously rendered verbal re-incarnation of the seen world', when Twain describes the dawn through Huck Finn's eyes (p. 122). The linguistic framework allows Twain to overcome the flaccidity of his own educated speech and, using it, to discover, as T. S. Eliot observed, 'a new way of writing, valid not only for [himself] but for others'.[15]

Despite Mencken's comparison, quoted above (p. 53), this way is not close to Chaucer's. Having decided to use the vernacular, Chaucer replaced one possible language, Latin or French, by the full range of another, English. He wrote the South-East Midland form of English, the *Gawain* poet the North-Western form, because that was what each habitually used. Robinson has noted that a comparison of Chaucer's English with that 'of the contemporary London archives shows the two to correspond in all essentials'.[16] Yank's speech in *The Hairy Ape*, by comparison, represents only a small proportion of the possible forms of American English which might be found in contemporary archives:

> I ain't got no past to tink in, nor nothin' dat's comin' on'y what's now – an dat don't belong. Sure, you're de best off. Yuh can't tink, can yuh? Yuh can't talk neider. But I kin make a bluff at talkin' and tinkin' – a'most git away wit it – a'most! – an dat's where de joker comes in.
>
> (VIII, p. 76)

The writer here is selecting a deliberately limited form of the language and one which is not his own idiom. Of those writers grouped together by Lewis or by Wilson, some, the Romantics of the American

Language Movement, use their own colloquial mode: Dreiser writes as the words come to mind, allowing the reader direct insight into his thought process, unashamed of his careless vocabulary, his elephantine sentences, his clichéd imagery. Others deliberately adopt a dialect or low-colloquial idiom and synthesize a literary style. Amongst such writers we find both Lardner, whose baseball slang has humour and virtuosity as its primary aim, and Stein and Hemingway, who use low-colloquial rhythms to quicken thought and expose the essence of their subject matter.

O'Neill's own position is evident in this extract from *The Emperor Jones*:

(The moon has just risen. Its beams, drifting through the canopy of leaves, make a barely perceptible, suffused, eerie glow. A dense, low wall of underbush and creepers is in the nearer foreground, fencing in a small triangular clearing. Beyond this is the massed blackness of the forest like an encompassing barrier . . .)

JONES. De moon's rizen. Does you heah dat, nigger? You gits more light from dis forrard. No mo' buttin' yo' fool head agin' de trunks an' scratchin' de hide off yo' legs in de bushes. Now you sees whar you'se gwine.

(iii, p. 31)

The Standard English of the stage directions, an equivalent gesture to Twain's 'Author's Note', resembles O'Neill's usual prose style as found in letters and notes, in its Standard syntax, its occasional slang expression, and its uneasy intermixture of 'fine writing' when something particularly striking is being described. 'Drifting through the canopy of leaves', 'a barely perceptible, suffused eerie glow', 'the massed blackness of the forest' – such phrases are literary commonplaces and the eye passes unremarkingly over them. But Jones's utterance demands much closer attention. The rhythm and vocabulary are unusual, the self-attack and self-consolation, joined in this vignette of a man in panic, alert us to what is being said. The speech has a concreteness O'Neill seems unable to attain in his habitual mode. In adopting various forms of the low-colloquial, O'Neill curbs his personal voice and struggles to develop an expressive form of language within a deliberately stunted linguistic framework. Indeed, the extent to which in his early work, he rejects his private idiom, is demonstrated by his avoidance of the regional speech pattern of his own forebears.

O'Neill, a second generation Irish immigrant, many of whose father's acquaintances were Irish, attended two Roman Catholic schools where many of the staff and pupils must have been of Irish extraction and yet there are very few Irish vernacular speakers in the early plays. Paddy in *The Hairy Ape* speaks a long lament, rhythmi-cally similar to those of Maurya in *Riders to the Sea*, and seems to be included largely as a tribute to Synge. Mat Burke in *Anna Christie* and Old Carmody in *The Straw*, are crudely drawn stage Irishmen out of the nineteenth-century theatre. The hairy ape himself, Yank, was modelled on an Irishman O'Neill knew but, developed into a dramatic character, he becomes a New York toughest of the toughs. In creating a linguistic structure to free himself from the embarrassment of using his own idiom, O'Neill also rejects the dialect form that would seem to have been most accessible to him. It is a signal of new confidence when, in the late plays, the majority of the central characters are first or second generation Irish immigrants (see Appendix 2, p: 207).

In the early plays O'Neill, like Twain, uses low-colloquial as a kind of poetic diction. But where Twain found in Huck Finn's dialect a fresher, more intense means of formulating experience, O'Neill finds in the speech of uneducated man a model through which he can show unaccommodated man locked in to himself but unsure, because of the limitations of his communicative faculty, of what that self is. O'Neill prizes the symbolic quality of low-colloquial speech rather than the felicities of individual words and their methods of combination. He uses an individual's inarticulacy to explore the wider inarticulacies of the human condition, as I shall show in my discussion of the plays. It is a method which, after a while, must silence him, and his career after 1924 shows him attempting to rebuild when he has stripped his language down to its bare foundations.

The vernacular and the American stage

Whitman and Twain might be the fathers of the vernacular in poetry and fiction, but there is no comparable figure in the theatre until O'Neill himself. It may seem curious that the form which consists wholly of dialogue should have been the last to imitate speech, unless we realize that a firm convention had developed in which the mode of speech acted as an indication of the moral value of the character. The moral worth of hero and heroine, in nineteenth-century American drama, shone through in the purity of their Standard English (see p. 23, above), and dialect was reserved for scurrilous, comic figures.

The occurrence of the shrewd Yankee on the stage has been traced by historians of the American drama to Royal Tyler's *The Contrast*, of 1783. With David Humphreys' *A Yankee in England* (1815) came the first real attempt to represent Yankee speech and, indeed,

Humphreys included a glossary of dialect terms which seems to have helped determine the stage idiom of subsequent similar figures.[17] During the nineteenth century, it became usual to include a single comic dialect speaker – probably a Yankee, a Westerner speaking the hyperbolic slang of the pioneers, or an immigrant from Ireland or Germany. He is, as well, frequently a drunkard, occasionally money-grabbing and ruthless; often the 'star-turn' of the piece, the humour and local colour of his speech is emphasized. This is Nimrod Wildfire, hero of James K. Paulding's *Lion of the West*:

He was a pretty severe colt, but no part of a priming to such a feller as me. I put it to him mighty droll – in ten minutes he yelled Enough! and swore I was a ripstaver! Says I, 'A'nt I the yaller flower of the forest! . . . my name is Nimrod Wildfire – half horse, half alligator and a touch of the airthquake – that's got the prettiest sister, fastest horse and ugliest dog in the District and can outrun, outjump, throw down, drag out and whip any man in all Kaintuck.'[18]

The farcical nature of the role is sometimes alien to the rest of the play. In Herne's play, *Margaret Fleming*, for example, Joe and Maria Fletcher spar, exchange banter, and chase each other whenever they meet, although on all other occasions Maria is a sober figure, grieving for her dying sister.

Except when given a wife to spar with, as in Herne's play, such characters are quite isolated verbally. Gretchen, Rip's wife in Jefferson's version of *Rip Van Winkle*, speaks a stilted version of Standard, marked by its archaisms, as do all the townsfolk:

Acre by acre you've sucked in his land to swell your store. Yonder miserable cabin is the only shelter we have left; but that is mine. Had it been his, he would have sold it to you, Derrick, long ago, and wasted its price in riot.
                                                              (*American Plays*, p. 405)

whilst Rip speaks quite differently:

Well tham fellers went and tied a tin kettle mit Schneider's tail and how he did run then, mit the kettle banging about. Well, I didn't hi him comin'. He run betwixt me and my legs, an' spilt me an' all them children in the mud; – yah, that's a fact.

                                                              (pp. 407–8)

The idiosyncratic speech pattern must be identifiable immediately. The writer, therefore, isolates and emphasizes a few divergent elements of the dialect – here the word 'mit' and the distorted vowel sounds – and the more frequently a particular dialect is represented on the stage, the more surely will its pattern be fixed, the elements used by one writer being repeated by the next. And, as Norman Page has pointed out in *Speech in the English Novel* (pp. 52–3), until there was widespread broadcasting and easy travel, dialects were usually unknown to the majority of people living outside the region. Conventional representation, therefore, helped to avoid mystification.

The figure is, of course, closely related to the stage Irishman of the London stage and to the long tradition in English drama of comic dialect roles, which reaches back, by way of Sheridan's Sir Lucius O'Trigger, at least as far as Shakespeare's peasants and stage Welshmen. What all the figures have in common is that the dialect speaker is a scallywag or a fantastical character whose speech is remarkably fluent.

The first real departure from the tradition that I have been able to find in the American theatre is Edward Sheldon's *Salvation Nell*. Written in 1908, Sheldon's plot recalls the old melodrama – an uneducated girl, burdened with illegitimate child and drunken lover, searches for a valid way of life, rejects the attentions of a noble young man and finally, by her example, redeems her lover. Nell's speech leans towards Standard, but the New York slum background is unusually convincing because we see a series of domestic episodes and overhear snatches of conversation parallel with and occasionally impinging on the activity of the main plot. Two mid-nineteenth-century plays, Aiken's version of *Uncle Tom's Cabin* (1852) and Boucicault's *The Octoroon* (1859), did contain several dialect speakers but the core of each play was still a group of straight characters who spoke Standard English and, although there were more of them than usual, the dialect speakers remained predictable stage types. Sheldon, by comparison, manages to suggest that we are glimpsing the reality of bustling city life. The dialogue of the prostitutes, drinkers, small time gamblers, children coming and going on errands, who briefly take over the foreground from Nell, has an unaccustomed colloquialism:

SID. Wipe up them pickles. Slow as tar in January!

NELL. Yes, sir. (*She begins wiping the floor near the lunch table.*)

JIM (*to Sid, confidentially*). Say, Sid, does Nelly fit the bill round here? Works pretty hard, I s'pose?

JOE (. . . *roaring to those about the bar*). Tom Blake's scrappin' three rounds wit' the Williams Street featherweight. Got a ten dollar pool. Come on.

CHRIS. Gee! (*He picks up his drink and starts hurriedly for the bar.*)

SID (*loftily*). Nothin' but a chicken fight!

KID. Gimme my drink, Sid! (*He takes it and follows into the poolroom.*)

JIM (*insinuatingly*). Nelly gets two a week? Say that's good o' you, Sid. Now if I was to make her say she'd do it for one-fifty, wouldn't yer pay me what ye owe her?[19]

(I. i)

O'Neill wrote to Sheldon in 1926:

> Your *Salvation Nell*, along with the work of the Irish Players on their first trip
> over here, was what first opened my eyes to the existence of a real theatre as
> opposed to the unreal – and to me, then, hateful – theatre of my father in
> whose atmosphere I had been brought up.[20]

He himself is bold enough to overturn the convention: his characters
in many of the early plays speak only low-colloquial and, speaking it,
suffer loss, know despair and, occasionally, joy. They feel strong
bonds with each other and struggle to find identity. They fear the
future and tremble at the memory of the past. After O'Neill, the
atmosphere was changed beyond recognition. American dramatists,
one after another, have used immigrant or regional dialect or city slang
as the medium for serious drama.[21]

O'Neill's difficulties with language in the first plays

O'Neill did not make a point of selecting working or peasant class
characters at the outset of his career, nor did he give much attention to
developing an appropriate language, except where it affected a particular need of the plot. In each of his first one-act plays, published as
Ten 'Lost' Plays (London, 1965), we find a situation of extreme stress:
a dancer who has loved wealth, a respectable gentleman, and a half-
savage deck-hand are set adrift on a raft without food or water (*Thirst*);
a Belgian peasant, maddened by the slaughter of all his innocent
family, sits in his war-wrecked hovel with a priest who preaches
tolerance, awaiting the advancing German army (*The Sniper*); the
signals to and from a ship in distress are the responsibility of a wireless
operator who has been driven back to sea, despite his secret and
rapidly encroaching deafness, by the needs of his destitute family
(*Warnings*). In pursuing the needs of these strong plots, O'Neill is
often trapped into the formulaic language of the nineteenth-century
stage, against which he was so determinedly pitting his realistic backgrounds and human conflicts. The wireless operator's confession at
the end of *Warnings*, after which he shoots himself, is a pastiche of
confessional phrases from the melodrama:

I should have told you, sir, before we started – *but we're so poor* and I couldn't get
another job. I was just going to make this one more trip. I wanted to give up
the job this time but she wouldn't let me. She said I wanted them to starve –
and Charlie asked me for a suit. (*His sobs stifle him.*) *Oh, God, who would have
dreamt this could have happened* – at such a time. I thought it would be alright –
just this trip. *I'm not a bad man*, Captain. (My italics)

(p. 78)

In *Thirst*, we are not fully engrossed by the dreadful situation because the tired vocabulary and the pedantic syntax deaden the panic and urgency on which the credibility of the subsequent action depends:

GENTLEMAN. I would willingly kill him, as you say, he deserves it. But I cannot even stand. I have no strength left. I have no weapons. He would laugh at me.
DANCER. There must be some way. You would think even the most heartless savage would share at a time like this. We must get that water. It is horrible to be dying of thirst with water so near. Think! Think! Is there no way?

(p. 22)

In these first plays, O'Neill only occasionally uses the vernacular. Several of them have a single minor character, a servant, an old man, a messenger, who speaks low-colloquial, as did countless maids and messengers in the old theatre. There is a more expressive, although erratic, use in *Warnings*. In the scene in which his pathetic domestic poverty is revealed, the wireless operator and all his family, speak low-colloquial Bronx, but in scene two, at sea, O'Neill drops this from his speech and all the characters speak Standard Stage English. Only *The Web*, O'Neill's Zolaesque play, set in downtown New York, is wholly in the vernacular. Occasionally in this play, we have an impression of true dialogue, because the thought of one sentence leads into the next and one character's words pick up and respond to those of the previous speaker. Here, the woman's slang is defiant, the man's harsh and abusive:

STEVE. D'yuh think I'm a simp to be gittin' yuh protection an' keepin' the bulls from runnin' yuh in when all yuh do is stick at home an' play dead? If yuh want any coin git out an' make it, that's all I got to say.
ROSE (*furiously*). So that's all yuh got to say is it? Well, I'll hand yuh a tip right here. I'm gittin' sick of givin' yuh my roll and gittin' nothin' but abuse in retoin. Yuh're half drunk now. An yuh been hittin' the pipe, too; I kin tell by the way your eyes look. D'you think I'm goin' to stand for a guy that's always full of booze an' hop? Not so yuh could notice it! There's too many others I kin get.
STEVE. Can that chatter, d'yuh hear me? If yuh ever t'row me down – look out! I'll get yuh!

(p. 39)

The thought processes and the structure of the sentences are essentially those of Standard English with the addition of grammatical solecisms and a few slang phrases but, whilst the vigour of the exchange quoted is not sustained for more than a few utterances at a time, the dialogue seems altogether less constrained than when Standard is used.

O'Neill's first real achievement comes in the early sea plays,

published as *Moon of the Caribbees and Six Other Plays of the Sea*
(London, 1923). He overcomes the problem of sustaining the idiom
and achieves the fluidity lacking in the earliest dialogue. He still
creates strong situations: smuggling and a drunken brawl; drugs and a
press gang; a man's dying; a suspected spy, but the image that remains
after each of the four *S. S. Glencairn* plays is that of a group of men,
without personal ties, drifting aimlessly through the hard labour of
their lives at the mercy of their desires and rages, finding what bonds
they can in the rough camaraderie of others who share their lot. In
moments of quietness they long for a more meaningful way although
they cannot formulate their longing. By introducing a large number of
characters of different nationality, each speaking his own accented or
dialectal form of English, O'Neill not only improves on private
experience, for the crew of *S.S. Ikalis*, his own ship, had been mainly
from Liverpool, 'with a sprinkling of other nationalities',[22] but makes
the surface of his dialogue newly interesting. Each brief speech
follows and is followed by another in which our attention is caught as
much by the way of saying as by what is said:

COCKY (*mockingly*). A-saivin' of 'is money, 'e is! Goin' back to 'ome an'
mother. Goin' to buy a bloomin' farm an' punch the blarsted dirt, that's wot 'e
is! (*Spitting disgustedly*.) There's a bloody bird of a sailor man for yer, Gawd
blimey.
OLSEN (*wearing the same good-natured grin*). Yust what I like, Cocky. I wus on
farm long time when I wus kid.
DRISCOLL. Lave him alone, ye bloody insect! 'Tis a foine sight to see a man
wid some sense in his head instead av a damn fool the loike av us. I only wisht
I'd a mother alive to call me own. I'd not be dhrunk in this divil's hole this
minute, maybe.

                                        (*The Long Voyage Home*, p. 11)

In suggesting the various dialects, O'Neill relies heavily on typical
national epithets, distorted forms of the verb, divergent pronunciation, all often of the stage dialect kind: 'divil a one', 'ye scut', 'Gawd',
'not 'arf'; 'I disremember', 'gimme', 'here she come'; 'Yust', 'iger-
ence', 'wiv', 'dis woman'. But despite these similarities with the old
theatre, O'Neill is already overturning its usage. As in *The Octoroon*,
there is a group of stage types, but the typification is no longer an end
in itself. It contributes to the several thematic suggestions of the plays:
the mixture of voices, the uneasy coexistence in the isolated meeting
place of the tramp-steamer, the impression the typical phrases give of
former national identities having become petrified, reflect a shadowy
image of the American immigrant experience. The stunted world view
of the men shown in their limited speech and their inability to formu-

late their longing is used by O'Neill to dramatize that longing more effectively. A single example will demonstrate how this can be so.

The dying Yank in *Bound East for Cardiff*, holds death off and prepares himself for it by looking back over his life and trying to make sense of the hardship and privations, the good times and the unfulfilled dreams. The incapacity of the man left lying on the bunk has been stressed by the general exeunt of the other seamen. The hubbub of voices has given way to a single voice; general activity to physical stillness in the two figures who remain on stage so that it is on the words spoken that our attention must focus. As the scene progresses we become aware of a different kind of contrast from that between physical activity and stillness. It is the voice of the dying man that fills the air, as he probes and explores through a succession of extended speeches, whilst the living man, the comforter, can utter only stumbling commonplaces and fearful denials in his occasional, protesting interruptions of Yank's monologue:

YANK. We won't reach Cardiff for a week at least. I'll be buried at sea.
DRISCOLL (*putting his hands over his ears*). Ssshh! I won't listen to you.
YANK (*as if he had not heard him*). It's as good a place as any other I s'pose – only I always wanted to be buried on dry land. But what the hell'll I care then? (*Fretfully*.) Why should it be a rotten night like this with that damned whistle blowing and people snorin' all round? I wish the stars was out, and the moon, too; I c'd lie out on deck and look at them, and it'd make it easier to go – somehow.
DRISCOLL. For the love av God don't be talkin' loike that!

(p. 20)

In Yank's speeches throughout the play, statements, lists of deeds, half-expressed dreams are linked together by his repetition of the word, 'remember' followed by 'that's all' which makes a claim to significance as his mind embraces each part of his life and then shows the dying fall of the claim as each memory fades from his mind. O'Neill also uses several normally neutral words, 'somehow', 'then', 'it must be great to' to make more equivocal the statements which express resignation and, in doing so, characterizes Yank's recognition of his own limitations and his impulse to struggle despite such recognition. And, as I have suggested, the dramatic effect is intensified here because we must take in not only Yank's dying but the response of his comrade who witnesses it. It is less the import of Driscoll's words than the very pattern of his speech which creates the impression of distress before another's spiritual pain and fear and before one's own verbal incapacity to minister to those emotions. The exigencies of dialect usage are leading to greater local control by the dramatist and, at the

same time, O'Neill is developing a sense of the way the interrelation-
ship between the utterances as they follow one on another, can be used
expressively. Throughout the early plays, O'Neill will explore ways of
characterizing man's struggle to be something more than he is and in
doing so, will develop the expressive use of the low-colloquial first
discovered in these sea plays.

T. S. Eliot has claimed that 'a speech by a character of Congreve or
Shaw has – however clearly the characters may be differentiated – that
unmistakable personal rhythm which is the mark of a prose style'.[23]
O'Neill's personal rhythm, as we find it in letters, interviews and stage
directions is exclamatory and often repetitious. It consists of simple or
co-ordinating sentences and is sometimes verbally awkward. In his
early plays, O'Neill avoids the problems of his own style by carefully
patterned representation of American slang or one or other of the
low-colloquial forms of American English and utilizes the difficulties
themselves by making them part of the problems of articulacy of the
characters.

The early plays

As I pointed out earlier, 'the American vernacular' is a generic term.
What emerges most clearly from studies of it is its plurality. Mencken,
with one chapter entitled 'The Common Speech', needed others to
discuss slang and divergent class, regional and immigrant speech
modes. Although commentators make linguistic maps of America,
commonly divided into three major speech areas, 'the Southern', 'the
New York City with the Eastern States', and the rest, called 'North-
ern' or 'Western', they agree that there has been neither sufficient
time, nor sufficient isolation for real dialects to develop.[24] The language of any single group has undergone constant modification. The
press, reinforced more recently by the cinema and broadcasting, has
been present virtually from the beginning[25] to act as a speech unifier.
The speech and cultural patterns of the waves of American immigrants from different areas of the British Isles, from Europe, from
Asia,[26] have impinged successively on the native population whilst the
immigrants, in their turn, have adapted themselves to the norm
through interaction with earlier settlers, through the model of the
media and through the influence of self-help primers and public
education.[27] The internal mobility of America, first Westwards and
then from rural to urban areas, from city to city in search of work and
then, with social advance, from city to suburb[28] has increased the
mixture within any area or within an individual's idiolect. When he

selects a particular idiom, the writer takes ready made into novel, poem or play the associations which that idiom carries and each individual's speech can be used to indicate his environment, his occupation, his antecedents.

O'Neill's vernacular forms are all found in the New England–New York strip of America, a tiny speech area, and yet, because it is the point of influx of European immigrants and because industrialization has drawn black and white labour from the south to New York City for generations, O'Neill finds there an astounding mixture of idioms.[29] What is so striking about O'Neill's work is not that he uses a particular idiom but that he is conscious of the mixture in the American vernacular and is able to project through its means the instability and variety of America. In his drama, we find New York negro speech in *The Dreamy Kid*, *The Emperor Jones* and *All God's Chillun Got Wings*; New England rural in *The Rope*, *Beyond the Horizon*, *Diff'rent* and *Desire Under the Elms*; Bronx in *The Hairy Ape*, *All God's Chillun Got Wings* and *Anna Christie*, where is included, also, the patois of the Scandinavian immigrant, whilst in *The Hairy Ape* we find a melting pot variety, reminiscent of the *S.S. Glencairn* plays.[30]

The forms of the vernacular that O'Neill uses in the early plays contain slang, but not the stimulating slang in which Whitman rejoiced, since O'Neill's characters are barely articulate. Any one speaker's vocabulary is limited; his verb forms are habitually in the present or, occasionally, the past tense, and he rarely uses anything but a simple sentence. This is Chris, the Swedish immigrant in *Anna Christie*:

It's funny. It's queer, yes – you and me shipping on same boat dat vay. It ain't right. Ay don't know – it's dat funny vay old devil sea do her vorst dirty tricks, yes. It's so.

(IV)

This the New York negro of *The Emperor Jones*:

Dis night come to an end like everything else. And when you gits dar safe and has dat bank roll in yo' hands you laughs at all dis. What yo' whistlin' for, you po' fool! Want all de worl' to heah you? Heah dat ole drum? Sho' gits nearer from de sound.

(iii)

And this, Ephraim Cabot, the New England farmer in *Desire Under the Elms*:

Even the music can't drive it out – somethin' – ye kin feel it droppin' off the elums, climbin' up the roof, sneakin' down the chimney, pokin' in the corners

... They's no peace in houses, they's no rest livin' with folks. Somethin's always livin' with ye.

(III.i)

In each case, the construction is similar. The low-colloquial element is marked by confusion of singular and plural, by double negatives, and by the use of the first or second person pronoun with a third person form of the verb. Also common are 'done' [did], 'ain't' [isn't], 'them' [those] and the notation of *th* [ð] as *d* ['den', 'dat', 'dese'] and [θ] as *t'* ['t'ink', 't'ing']. The impression of distinct dialects is achieved by the blending into this common base of select dialect words and characteristic vowel shifts and, also, by the creation of a characteristic rhythm, given to the principal dialect speaker and echoed by others in the community.

The bulk of the dialect words O'Neill uses are monosyllabic not flamboyant. In *Desire Under the Elms*, we find, 'his'n', 'her'n', 'atop', 'afore', 'allus', 'despairful'; in *The Hairy Ape*, 'nuts', 'dat's bunk', 'nix', 'tub' [boat], and in *The Emperor Jones*, 'seem like', 'nohow', 'right heah', 'dem ha'nts' [ghosts], 'crazy mad'. When O'Neill does allow himself an occasional flourish, we register its colour or its pungency but, because of the firm grounding given by these simple words, the dialect representation never seems extravagant as did that in the nineteenth-century drama. 'He skinned 'em too slick', says Sim of his wily father in *Desire Under the Elms* (p. 11). A prisoner, in *The Hairy Ape*, hears the ringing phrases of a senator about the menace threatening the 'very lifeblood of the American eagle' and comments, 'Aw, hell! Tell him to salt de tail of dat eagle!' (p. 59).

In pronunciation notation O'Neill tends to follow literary tradition, as is evident in his use of *oi* to represent the vowel sound in 'church', 'skirt', 'first' in New York City speech, although the sound is actually [3-1]: 'ch3-1rch', 'f3-1rst'.[31] In usage, he is more original. One character's divergent form is sometimes shared by another. Anna Christie, for example, has the American *j* in her normal speech but on the three occasions when she is agitated – immediately before first meeting Chris, during her confession, and when attempting to describe her experience in the fog – her vulnerability is stressed by her echoing of her father's pronunciation: 'yust', 'yob'.

O'Neill is *using* dialect rather than compiling an exhaustive account of it. Unlike the linguist who attempts to arrive at a detailed description of a dialect by accumulating its numerous variant forms, the writer lets the prominent features represent the whole and, using these as markers, attempts to produce an impression of a speech form that is homogeneous and would be suggestive to people familiar with the dialect from which it is abstracted. The illusion of authenticity is more important than authenticity itself. G. P. Krapp, discussing nineteenth-century story-tellers, showed that whilst none of the elements of Bret Harte's vocabulary and syntax were extraneous to the Mid-West dialect, their combination in Harte's writing was such that Twain, having had to rewrite a piece done in collaboration, complained that 'Harte never did know anything about dialect'. The language of Joel Chandler Harris' Uncle Remus stories, on the other hand, although generally regarded as an accurate representation of negro dialect is:

not different from any other dialect form of American English, that is, is merely general low colloquial English with a light sprinkling of words and phrases, which, by custom, have come to have closer associations with negro speech.[32]

What seems to be essential for the illusion of authenticity, is consistency of representation and the blending of the expected into the unexpected.

O'Neill's accuracy, in fact, varies according to the dialect he represents. Negro and New England seem to be directly derived from literary examples, with Twain, Stephen Crane and the American stage as the most probable forebears, whilst New York slang seems to stem from personal observation. 'Purty', 'lonesome' and 'plumb', all common words in Ephraim's vocabulary, occur in Southern and Western country dialects but not in New England,[33] except in literary representation.[34] The vocabulary of New York urban slang used by O'Neill is accurate to the extent that examples from *The Hairy Ape* are given in *The Dictionary of American Slang* to demonstrate usage.[35] But there was a danger inherent in O'Neill's very facility. In his baseball stories, Lardner exploits a situation in order to allow the full pungency of his slang and its variant forms to be revealed. Verbal display is central to his writing. Once or twice in the early plays, O'Neill falls into the trap of virtuosity. One of the T.B. patients in the weight-checking scene in *The Straw*, bursts into a chatter of baseball slang, obviously lifted by O'Neill from Lardner. The ironic effect of the contrast between verbal gesture and physical reality is dissipated because O'Neill, obviously enjoying the slang, includes too much of it. In *Diff'rent*, the values of the shallow Benny contrasted with those of the Nantucket whaling community are reflected in his language which is littered with inappropriate Broadway slang. The device of indicating moral by verbal dishonesty does not work because, again, the character is allowed too much speaking time and the valid point being made is obscured by the tedium of shallow repetition. In the late plays, and most notably in *Hughie*, the handling is more dexterous. We find O'Neill using the display element of slang quite deliberately to reveal the self-enjoyment present in a speaker's rhetoric and frequently, also, to counterpoint the splendid performance with the miserable reality behind the words.

The structural role of language in three early plays

In one of the plays in which the vernacular is used most coherently, *All God's Chillun Got Wings*, the play is structured around different levels of articulacy. The children of the opening scene all use low-colloquial. Black and white are differentiated by pronunciation, black using 'you' and 'yo'', white 'yuh' and 'yer'. Their expletives, 'Lawdy!'; 'land sakes!' on the one hand, 'Aw, gwan, youse!', on the other, and their slang, 'we gwin git frailed', 'you kin git a lickin'' are faint indications of different backgrounds, but the speech is on the whole remarkably similar. Both use 'de', 'dat', 'den'; ''n'', 'kin' [can], 'git', 'ain't'. In scene two, time has passed and a new polarity has entered their speech, differentiating not only races but those who have graduated from those who have rejected their schooling. The speech of the former veers towards Standard, whilst, amongst the latter, racial divisions have hardened both in speech and attitudes. Linguistic markers, now used more densely in the speech of these unemployed youths, boxers, petty thieves and pimps, suggest their need for adolescent display and for identification with a group. This is the aspiring boxer, Mickey:

Can dat name, see! Want a bunch of fives in yer kisser? Den nix! She's me goil, understan'?

(p. 17)

This the unemployed black boy, Joe:

What's all dis dressin' up an' graduatin' an' sayin' you gwine study be a lawyer? What's all dis fakin' an' pretendin' an' swellin' out grand an' talkin' soft an' perlite? What's all dis denyin' you's a nigger – an' wid de white boys listenin' to you say it? Is you aimin' to buy white wid yo' ol' man's dough like Mickey say? What is you? ... Tell me before I wrecks yo' face in! Is you a nigger or isn't you? (*Shaking him.*) Is you a nigger, Nigger?

(p. 24)

The changes, besides marking the passage of time, contribute to our impression of the society against which Jim pits himself. And that society is mirrored further in the speech of Jim's family, which reveals the distance between generations. The speech of Jim's mother, who accepts her lot and is perturbed by change, contains a high proportion of negro markers. The religious overtones of the children's expletives in scene one, have living meaning in her utterance:

I does de duty God set for me in dis worl'. Dey leaves me alone . . . The worl' done change. Dey ain't no satisfaction wid nuffin' no more.

(pp. 42–3)

At the other extreme, her daughter Hattie, whose speech is the most grammatically accurate in the play, has a range of reference that spreads beyond her immediate environment. The contrast between her black consciousness and her full command of the white idiom which includes references to Western culture, indicates, without further comment by O'Neill, the ambiguous position of the emancipated negro in America, who searches for a heritage. This is particularly apparent when she is set in direct contrast with the half-educated white girl, who is unaware of her cultural heritage. Hattie explains to Ella, for example:

It's a mask which used to be worn in religious ceremonies by my people in Africa. But, aside from that, it's beautifully made, a work of art by a real artist – as real in his way as your Michael Angelo. (*Forces Ella to take it.*) Here, just notice the workmanship.

(p. 51)

Through speech, therefore, O'Neill establishes a social context in which there is both stasis and change and is able, without didacticism, to convey his outrage at the truths he reveals about the land of opportunity.

The sequence quoted here is also important in the emotional structure of the play. In it O'Neill draws the audience's attention to the mask that, for most of the action, hangs before them on the stage. Through words, he makes relevant the presence of the seen object, which is in its own right a spectacular part of the décor. The audience's recognition of the gulf between Hattie's words about the mask and Ella's comprehension of her words contributes to their growing recognition of what underlies the inarticulate hatred and fear of the mask which possesses Ella. It alerts them to a substructure of meaning which will make that hatred more convincing and more distressing when it flares up in subsequent scenes. The words in one part of the play are creating a context for action in another and are making a spectacular stage property into an emotionally significant one. Speech mode is an essential element in the characterization of Jim. By giving him speech that is continually developing, O'Neill embodies his aspiration and spiritual search. In act I, scene i, Jim's speech is indistinguishable from that of his fellows:

You know what, Ella? Since I been tuckin' yo' books to school an' back, I been drinkin' lots o' chalk 'n' water three times a day. Dat Tom, de barber, he tole me dat make me white, if I drink enough. (. . .) Does I look whiter?

(p. 12)

We notice him only because his speeches are more extended than those of the other children. As his self-awareness increases, Jim's speech approximates more and more to Standard. He never gains the control his sister has. Her speech mode complements her assured and stable world view whereas, even when he has attained grammatical correctness, Jim continues to use only main clauses and to fall back, in moments of distress, on to the traditional imagery of the Old Testament. We smile sadly at the ingenuous thought and quaint expression of the child, but the image of the small boy drinking chalk is recalled when Jim refutes accusations that he is trying to 'buy white', when Ella declares his love to be the only 'white' thing she knows, when he abnegates himself before her and she seeks to undermine his self-confidence and when, finally, all these are bound together in the symbolic childhood at the end of the play in which despair gives way to joy in the tiny fragment of human inter-dependence that Jim perceives he shares with Ella.

The thematic organization of speech levels and the working and reworking of a single image, such as that of drinking chalk are the kind of devices I had in mind when I suggested earlier that when O'Neill represents the vernacular of inarticulate men he is far more conscious of the role of language in creating meaning than when he uses a more personal idiom. The very limitations which the low-colloquial dialect imposes mean that he must order his words with greater care if he is to make his meaning apparent to his audience who, he must assume, will not themselves customarily speak in low-colloquial dialect. He is, to this extent, using an artificial language and he must so phrase it that he enables his audience to accept its conventions.

The juxtaposing of various idioms in *The Hairy Ape*, allows O'Neill to present the figures of this play in a variety of different relationships.

The central figure, Yank, appears archetypal because each of his attitudes is echoed by the other stokers grouped around him. Ranged against him are Paddy, his spiritual opposite; Long, his political opposite, and Mildred, his social opposite. In the stokehole, Yank is master; on Fifth Avenue, he is insignificant, and amongst the I.W.W. (the anarchist group 'International Workers of the World', otherwise nicknamed 'the Wobblies'), he appears to be a naïve extremist. Mildred, before her aunt, is whining and self-concerned; before the Second Engineer of her father's steamship, is imperious, and before Yank, the brute man, is hysterical.

The figures are distinguished by their speech. Long uses a bastardized form of socialist-revolutionary jargon and the poverty of his speech reinforces our impression of the poverty of his thought and of his personal frustration:

We wasn't born this rotten way. All men is born free and ekal. That's in the bleeding bible, maties. But what do they care for the bible, them lazy, bloated swine what travels first cabin. Them's the ones. They dragged us down till we're on'y wage slaves in the bowels of a bloody ship, sweatin', burnin' up, eatin' coal dust

(p. 11)

Paddy, nostalgic for the old sailing ships and resentful of the industrialization of the sea, has access to a different range of experience and language from Long and the other stokers. O'Neill creates for him a rhythmical speech, which works partly by association. The fluency which his use of co-ordinating and sub-ordinating clauses introduces, the poeticism of his references to colours and to the legendary figure of the flying Dutchman, his use of archaic-sounding words like 'scudding' and, above all, the Irish accent of the actor aided by the interspersed keening 'Oh!', associate the memories of this old sailor with the perceptions and way of life of the characters in Synge's plays:

Then you'd see her driving through the grey night, her sails stretching aloft all silver and white, not a sound on the deck, the lot of us dreaming dreams, till you'd believe 'twas no real ship at all you was on but a ghost ship like the Flying Dutchman they say does be roaming the seas for evermore widout touching a port. And there was the days, too. A warm sun on the clean decks. Sun warming the blood of you, and wind over the miles of shiny green ocean like strong drink in your lungs.

(p. 14)

Mildred, unlike Paddy, has no fluency. 'Bored by her own anaemia', she represents a type of the middle class as the others do types of the working class:

MILDRED (*looking up with affected dreaminess*). How the black smoke swirls
back against the sky! Is it not beautiful?
AUNT (. . .). I dislike smoke of any kind . . .
MILDRED. . . . Do you know what you remind me of? Of a cold pork pudding
against a background of linoleum tablecloth in the kitchen of a – but the
possibilities are wearisome.

(pp. 20–1)

The redundant words, the contrariness indicated by admiration of a
waste product, the contrived imagery of the insult, contribute to our
sense of the artificiality of her utterance, although the image itself is
sufficiently appropriate to be suggestive.

The linguistic world that Yank confronts becomes increasingly
alien. In prison, the senator's words, not spoken directly but quoted
from a newspaper article, are disembodied and their empty rhetoric is
greeted by a chorus of animal barking and yapping from the prisoners
that presents the frustration of those who have neither the power nor
the self-confidence that such language implies. When Yank has
recognized the full extent of his alienation, in the final scene, human
speech is silenced and replaced by the jabbering of monkeys.

In the stage directions, O'Neill specifies a physical presence in the
actor playing Yank which sets him with and yet apart from his
fellow-stokers. Yank is frequently given the dominant position on
stage so that, even whilst watching a group action, our eye readily rests
on him. He is made to adopt and hold one position for most of act four
which attracts the audience's attention both because it is fixed and
because it recalls the well-known posture of Rodin's *The Thinker*. He
is further demonstrated to be a dominant figure, both of and apart
from his fellows by the way they relate to him, even at times becoming
a chorus that echoes his very words. The visual and aural effects create
an impression of Yank as an archetype. But these in themselves would
not be sufficient to hold the audience; for this, verbal depth is also
necessary.

Yank's own speech appears to be as limited in vocabulary and
syntax as that of the other stokers, but O'Neill develops a method of
conveying the restlessness and desperation of the inner man whilst
maintaining the appearance of stunted speech. Yank's speeches are
punctuated by attention-demanding parentheses and interrogatives,
'see?', 'get me?', and sentence after sentence begins with a pronoun,
'Yuh . . . Yuh . . . Yuh . . .', 'I . . . I . . . I . . .' which gives an impression of thrust and attack. The words and meaning of one sentence
are repeated with slight variation in the next until we have several,

circling round and worrying at a single thought and, out of the coalescing of several approximate statements, a precise thought or feeling is conveyed. Yank says to Paddy, for example:

Aw, take it easy. Yuh're awright at dat. Yuh're bugs, dat's all – nutty as a cuckoo. All dat tripe yuh been pullin' – Aw dat's all right. On'y it's dead, get me? Yuh don't belong no more, see. Yuh don't get de stuff. Yuh're too old. But, aw say, come up for air onct in a while, can't yuh? See what's happened since yuh croaked
(p. 16)

To obtain a heightened form of expression, O'Neill intensifies this. In defining who he is, in scene one, Yank begins with a boast in commonplace slang, 'me, I'm young! I'm in de pink!', but as he searches out his meaning, the words become increasingly impassioned:

It's me makes it hot! It's me makes it roar! It's me makes it move! Sure, on'y for me everything stops. It all goes dead, get me? De noise and smoke and all de engines movin' de woild, dey stop. Dere ain't nothin' no more! Dat's what I'm sayin'. Everyting else dat makes de woild move, somep'n makes it move. It can't move witout somep'n else, see? Den yuh get down to me. I'm at de bottom, get me! Dere ain't nothin' foither. I'm de end! I'm de start! I start somep'n and de woild moves! It – dat's me – de new dat's moiderin' de old! I'm de ting in coal dat makes it boin; I'm steam and oil for de engines; I'm de ting in noise dat makes yuh hear it; I'm smoke and express trains and steamers and factory whistles; I'm de ting in gold dat makes it money! And I'm what makes iron into steel! Steel, dat stands for de whole ting! And I'm steel – steel – steel! I'm de muscles in steel, de punch behind it!
(p. 17)

The repeated words now are verbs of action. Loose slang terms are replaced by concrete images of force and power. The new combinations of words show Yank's mind leaping from idea to idea as he declares his faith in himself and his identification with his environment. It is one of the moving ironies of the play that this verbally exciting speech, which offers the audience prose from whose rhythm they can take fire, should be the one which later turns to ashes in the speaker's mouth.

O'Neill also makes Yank's utterance more forceful by linguistic patterning. Certain words and ideas are emphasized by being repeated in a new context. Yank, in the extract quoted, boasts 'I'm at de bottom ... dere ain't nothin' foither, I'm de end', and declares, 'I'm steel, steel, steel'. The words are brought back to mind when, in the next scene, Mildred half echoes him, saying:

Then father keeping those home fires burning, making more millions – and little me at the tail end of it all. I'm a waste product in the Bessemer process –

like the millions. Or, rather, I inherit the acquired trait of the by-product,
wealth, but none of the energy, none of the strength of the steel that made it.
(p. 22)

Without any explicit comment being necessary, the verbal contrast
prepares us for the confrontation between Yank and Mildred in the
third scene. Similarly, we register the words of Yank's dismissal of
Paddy, 'Yuh don't belong no more', because they recall Paddy's own
derisive query made shortly before, 'Is it to belong to that [the
steamship] you're wishing? Is it a flesh and blood wheel of the engine
you'd be?' The word 'belong' is repeated by Yank until it becomes an
emblem of his quest and, because of this first striking usage, we are
alert to the ambiguities inherent in that quest.

Such patterning is even more imperative to the structure of *Desire
Under the Elms*. This is the opening sequence of the play:

(*It is sunset . . . The sky above the roof is suffused with deep colours . . . Eben Cabot
. . . stares up at the sky. He sighs with a puzzled awe and blurts out with halting
appreciation.*)
EBEN. God! Purty!
(*. . . Simeon and Peter come in from their work in the fields . . . Their shoulders
stoop a bit from years of farm work. They clump heavily along in their clumsy
thick-soled boots caked with earth. Their clothes, their faces, hands, bare arms and
throats are earth-stained. They stand together for a moment in front of the house
and, as if with one impulse, stare dumbly up at the sky, leaning on their hoes. Their
faces have a compressed, unresigned expression. As they look upward, this softens.*)
SIMEON (*grudgingly*). Purty.
PETER. Ay-eh.
SIMEON (*suddenly*). Eighteen year ago.
PETER. What?
SIMEON. Jenn. My woman. She died.
PETER. I'd fergot.
SIMEON. I rec'lect – now an' agin. Makes it lonesome. She'd hair long's a hoss's
tail – an' yaller like gold!
PETER. Waal – she's gone. (. . .) They's gold in the West, Sim.
SIMEON (. . .). In the sky?
PETER. Waal – in a manner o' speakin' – thar's the promise. (*Growing excited.*)
Gold in the sky – in the west – Golden Gate – Californi-a! – Golden West! –
fields o' gold!
SIMEON (*excited in his turn*). Fortunes layin' just atop o' the ground waitin' t' be
picked! Solomon's mines, they says! (. . .)
PETER (*with sardonic bitterness*). Here – it's stones atop o' the ground – stones
atop o' stones – makin' stone walls – year atop o' year – him 'n' yew 'n' me 'n'
then Eben – makin' stone walls fur him to fence us in!
SIMEON. We've wuked. Give our strength. Give our years. Ploughed 'em
under in the ground (. . .) – rottin' – makin' soil for his crops! (*A pause.*) Waal
– the farm pays good for hereabouts.
PETER. If we ploughed in Californi-a, they'd be lumps o' gold in the furrow –!

SIMEON. Californi-a's t'other side o' earth, a'most. We got t' calc'late –
PETER (*after a pause*). 'Twould be hard fur me, too, to give up what we've
'arned here by our sweat.

(pp. 9–10)

O'Neill makes use of the stage picture, filling the stage with golden light to suggest sunset and emphasizing, by their earthiness and their clumsy gait, the incongruity of the farm-hands with the stage-pastoral Romantic light. But O'Neill is no Belasco. (A point he makes himself when he uses the same device more explicitly in *A Moon For The Misbegotten*. Here he teases the audience into recognition of the play as play when Jamie gestures towards the sunrise saying 'rise of curtain, Act-Four stuff' (act IV, p, 151).) His interest is not with stage effects but with creating an impression of verbal poverty. Through lighting and gesture, the upturned face and the softened expression, O'Neill reminds his audience of what must be a virtually universal experience – that of wonder before a magnificent sunset. He then has two characters in succession utter the single weak adjective 'purty', as an expression of that wonder. The silent contemplation and the halting statement about personal loss, 'Jenn. My woman. She died.', draw out the moment, emphasizing how tongue-tied the men are. The adjective is used again several times and always in a similar context of significant human experience so that tension between word and feeling is, again, made painfully apparent. The word 'somethin'' is used in much the same way, and three 'stalling words' – words behind which the characters habitually retreat when the world becomes too complex – 'waal', 'mebbe' and 'ayeh', are used repeatedly by all the characters. O'Neill thus epitomizes the extreme inarticulacy of his characters in these few words. As he does also in *Anna Christie*, where the inarticulacy is more directly stated by Chris: 'Anna lilla! Ay – (*He fights for words to express himself, but finds none – miserably – with a sob.*) – Ay can't say it. Good night, Anna' (p. 104). And so he is free to make other parts of his dialogue resonant, without forfeiting the impression that the speech is realistic. It is in fact, as we can already see, highly contrived.

Even in the brief extract quoted here, we find a shift in the expressive quality of the utterance. There is a quickening of rhythm with the introduction of the word 'gold' which creates an effect of excited thought forcing its way into speech, when a series of thought associations is generated. The substitution of a second word, 'stones', cuts the excitement short. The creative thought association is replaced by that method of circling about a single meaning that O'Neill

developed in *The Hairy Ape*. The words 'gold in the West – fields o'
gold' and 'stones atop o' stones – year atop o' year' reverberate
through the play, usually balanced against each other in any given
sequence, and they become identified, increasingly surely, the one
with dream and the other with reality. To those pitted against Nature
in the fight for the New England soil, Californi-a is El Dorado. The
brothers' recurrent song, 'For I'm off to Californi-a', which by virtue
of its rhythm, introduces yet another way of saying into the dialogue of
the play, becomes a ritualistic chant. They use it to convert their
defiance into a spell which will shut out the realities of their harsh life.
As the action of the play proceeds, we gradually realize that they are
re-enacting the dream which Ephraim had found empty when he,
before them, had tried to escape. Already here in the first moments of
the play, through the references to 'gold' and 'stones', O'Neill is
preparing his audience, is setting before them the first elements of the
conundrum of repetition and reduplication between generations of a
family. All the sons will be seen to reiterate their father's greed for the
farm and his lust for Min, whilst Eben who has taken his father's wife
will, when deserted, attempt to escape to the gold fields like father and
brothers before him. The stones come to signify the obstinacy of the
man who has brought fruit to the barren land making it 'pay good',
and to signify the harshness of the servitude his sons have endured and
the grinding life on the farm. They have symbolic meaning for the
characters: 'God's hard, not easy! God's in the stones', says Ephraim,
and, 'I made thin's grow out o' nothin' – like the will o' God, like the
servant o' his hand ... an' he made me hard fur it' (p. 64). Peter's
words, ''Twould be hard fur me, too', interjected into the silence, in
the opening passage, rouse no surprise in Simeon who is supposedly
calculating the journey to Californi-a. Each man is revealed as knowing the other's ways of thought so that no explanation is necessary
between them of the leap in thought from gold to stones. A number of
such moments in the play make it apparent to the audience that reality
will always break through fantasy and that, despite the toll it has
demanded of them, the farm is where the reality of these men is
rooted. We, therefore, have a strong sense of the inevitable when we
witness Ephraim, his world collapsed about him at the end of the play,
turn finally to the stones for solace:

Mebbe they's easy gold in the West, but it hain't God's gold. It hain't fur me. I
kin hear his voice warnin' me agen t' be hard an' stay on my farm ... Waal –
what d'ye want? God's lonesome hain't He? God's hard an' lonesome. (pp.
113–14)

The need to pare down the verbiage which the use of low-colloquial imposes on O'Neill, obliges him to image such deep concerns as the interaction between individual identity and rootedness in family and place, in a few single words. It is this kind of imaging that, as we shall see in the next chapter, is lost in the middle years. It is retrieved in the late plays in a more complex form when questions of identity and rootedness are again O'Neill's urgent concern.

There is more to be said about the language of this play, although it is necessary now to move on to consideration of the plays of the middle years. The possessive pronoun, 'mine', for instance, is another word which recurs and, doing so, draws our attention to the feelings of each character towards the farm and each other; shows how closely possession is bound up with each character's self-respect and self-recognition, and points out for the audience the ambiguity of the word 'desire' in the title of the play. It is another word that helps the audience to make connections between one sequence and another and to which meaning accrues from its repeated use in the ongoing action of the play. And, as with the introduction of the song, O'Neill introduces sequences whose rhythm departs from that of the normal pattern of the play, and in so doing varies the pattern of the audience's response. In the courtship scene, for example, the fervour of the love between Abbie and Eben is presented movingly by the use of a series of antiphonal utterances (pp. 73–4). But before I leave the play, I should like to look in some detail at one specific way in which O'Neill extends the vernacular, because it prefigures one of his major devices in the late plays. It allows him to introduce some of the allusive quality of poetry whilst retaining the impression that the characters are using realistic speech in their interchanges.

Another idiom is intermingled with the rural vernacular. The language of the Old Testament infuses Ephraim's thought and is sometimes echoed by the other characters. Min is 'the Scarlet Woman', Eben's relationship with her is 'sinnin'' and the brothers, mocking him, say he is 'sorrowin' over his lust of the flesh'. They answer his accusations of cowardice with 'An' yew be Samson?' and when they finally abandon work, they do so 'aimin' t'be lilies of the field'. Taunting them, Eben quotes: 'Honour thy father.' In Ephraim's own speech, biblical language is strangely distorted. He woos Abbie with the Song of Solomon; he imitates the prophets, arms raised to Heaven, when he curses his enemies. He does quote directly, 'The days air prolonged and every vision faileth', but, more commonly, New

England vernacular is blended in, 'Lord God o' Hosts, smite the undutiful sons with Thy wust cuss' (p. 47). Ephraim's application of such language to impious acts sharpens our response to the strange mind of the man. The curse is directed against his own sons, and when he kneels down like Hannah to pray for a son in his old age, it is not for a blessing on a barren womb but in order to disinherit his son. O'Neill makes us conscious of the blasphemous nature of Ephraim's language early in the play when Simeon, having learned of his father's new marriage, imitates him:

> 'I'm ridin' out t' learn God's message t' me in the spring like the prophets done,' he says. I'll bet right then and thar he knew plumb well he was goin' whorin', the stinkin' old hypocrit!
>
> (p. 27)

Although such language shocks, we realize it is inaccurate to call it hypocrisy. It is, for Ephraim, a way of expressing intense rage or joy, or great zeal. For O'Neill, at the authorial level, it is a way of retaining the realistic effect of the speech whilst widening its expressive capacity. Moreover, the distortion of biblical language recalls the dream and the distortion of the dream of freedom of the Founding Fathers and, like the accretion of meaning round the two words, 'gold' and 'stones', which are suggestive of the pioneer experience, gives a penumbra of wider significance to the specific dream and reality we see enacted, and associates the action with the nascent mythology of the American continent.

Conclusion

O'Neill's own difficulties with language, the impetus of the American Language Movement, his revolt against the moribund conventions of the nineteenth-century theatre, led him, early in his career, to a form appropriate to his needs at the time. By experimenting with the vernacular he was able to forge a language through which to explore human aspiring, isolation and inarticulacy and to project the puzzlingly heroic stature of certain individuals and the interaction within each man of identity and rootedness. O'Neill eventually found the style he had evolved unsatisfactory. We have seen that, to a certain extent, O'Neill was solving his own problems with language by transferring them to his characters. The danger was that it would cut the writer off from real complexity of thought. For O'Neill's low-colloquial-speaking heroes did not possess the naïve eye of American Romanticism before which all becomes clear. Rather, they struggled to understand, forever trapped by their condition and their inarticulacy. The poetic diction O'Neill had created limited its author in some ways and, by the mid-1920s, O'Neill was ready to break out from the artificial framework he had imposed on his thought. To allow him to develop a more personal voice, he had to develop more sophisticated characters whose vision and verbal capacity would approximate to his own and to that of his audience.

After 1924, O'Neill ceased to use low-colloquial forms. His characters speak Standard American English. With other themes to explore, new things to say, he moved beyond the schematic language he had evolved which had enabled him to absorb his own verbal difficulties. A letter written by O'Neill to Joseph Wood Krutch, in 1929, shows that he was acutely aware of his position. He wrote:

Oh, for a language to write drama in! For a speech that is dramatic and isn't just conversation! I'm so straight-jacketed by writing in terms of talk! I'm so fed up with the dodge-question of dialect! But where to find that language?

(Gelbs, *O'Neill*, p. 698)

4

The failure of language in the middle years

In 1924, O'Neill abandoned the low-colloquial in favour of Standard American English or, as it is more properly called, General American. Low-colloquial dialects are used rarely and then only for minor characters. The General American is used in two ways. In the earlier work of the period, in *The Fountain* and *Lazarus Laughed* and in parts of *Marco Millions* and *The Great God Brown*, it is cast into rhythmical prose or into a quasi-poetic chant. In *Welded, Strange Interlude, Dynamo, Mourning Becomes Electra* and *Days Without End*, as well as in the other parts of *Marco Millions* and *The Great God Brown*, O'Neill uses an idiomatic form of Standard with a light peppering of middle class slang. In the 'poetic' plays, O'Neill is concerned with spiritual experience and with exploration through symbolic means of the mysterious areas of human existence, and he looks to the non-verbal elements of theatre to extend the expressive power of his writing. In those plays whose dialogue is idiomatic, he is primarily concerned to probe and project the individual psyches of the characters he has created. There would seem to be here a deliberate break from the early attempt to synthesize from realistic and expressionistic elements a form through whose means he would be able to present 'Life in terms of lives'.

In this chapter, I shall look first at O'Neill's poetic and then at his more idiomatic style, examining in detail the mechanics of the language of one play in each mode. I shall suggest that the two modes, in intention and effect have a good deal in common and, although at first sight this may not appear to be the case, they demonstrate that O'Neill's approach to dramatic dialogue was consistent throughout the period. I will argue, as the title of the chapter will have already implied, that the middle years were a period of experiment but not of full achievement for O'Neill, and I will show that where there is failure of language it is associated with failure of thought and of dramatic structure.

It may seem to be an oddly negative undertaking that I propose here, and yet it is long overdue. The plays of the middle years have been an embarrassment to many commentators on O'Neill, and they have been the source of sharply conflicting judgements. A. H. Quinn, for example, has written that *Lazarus Laughed* 'is not only lofty poetry; it is also fine drama',[1] whilst Ruby Cohn, on the other side, has declared with equal certainty that the style of the middle plays is 'naïvely explicit and exceedingly flat'.[2] It is only by full discussion of the text that we can decide for one side or the other. These plays were of importance in the history of the American Theatre – for it was for his work in these years that O'Neill won the Nobel Prize, that mark of international respect, and in his experiments with form and subject matter he introduced ideas from Europe that were not at the time current in America. This historical interest has tended to divert critical attention away from the plays themselves, whilst the existence of O'Neill's letters and manuscript notes, his letters of explanation to the press[3] and his habit of commenting in the stage directions on the meaning of the action help to direct critical attention towards the plan behind the play and away from its execution. The more fully we understand the intentions behind a flawed work and the more sympathy we have for the earnestness of the writer's motives, the more necessary it is to keep the text as written clearly before us, if our comments about it are to be valid. If, when we discuss the text closely, we do find it to be flawed in execution and can suggest reasons why this is so then we gain another method of showing what are necessary elements in the ordering of language which *is* fully dramatic.

The poetic style: 'Lazarus Laughed'

The impact of the opening scene derives partly from the careful way O'Neill orders the stage picture and partly from the ability of the audience to pick up echoes behind the text. A sense of awe at the miracle of the risen Lazarus is communicated by O'Neill largely through non-verbal elements of theatre. The lighting plan and the positioning of the figures control the direction of the audience's gaze, drawing the eye inwards from the crowd of anonymous, masked onlookers, placed at the front and sides of the stage, towards the figure of Lazarus, who sits at the rear in a glow of light, the only unmasked figure, the still, silent centre of a tableau, the apex of a triangle formed by his kneeling family. The onlookers gesture towards Lazarus as they speak the first words, in unison:

CHORUS OF OLD MEN (*in a quavering rising and falling chant – their arms
outstretched toward Lazarus*).
Jesus wept!
Behold how he loved him!
He that liveth,
He that believeth,
Shall never die!
CROWD (*on either side of the house, echo the chant*).
He that believeth
Shall never die!
Lazarus, come forth!   (I.i, p. 12)

The chant, composed entirely of phrases from the Gospel account of
the raising of Lazarus in John 11, is likely to stir the auditor's memory
of the wonder and enigma of the ancient story.

The first scene succeeds because it is static. O'Neill seeks only to set
the scene and create a mood of wonder. When Lazarus breaks his
trance-like silence it is to utter a joyfully affirmative 'Yes!' and,
subsequently, a peal of laughter which enthrals those who hear it. The
scene ends with a paean to life, chanted by the chorus and crowd.
What is important is not the precise meaning of the words, but the
suggestive element of voices rising in unison, repeating phrases about
'life' and 'laughter'. O'Neill seems to be writing a deliberately reduced
form of language as if in response to the idea formulated by Craig,
popularized by *The Theatre Arts Magazine* and propounded by
Kenneth Macgowan, that the word in drama is wordiness and should
be subordinated to the sensuous elements of theatre.[4] It is an idea later
preached by Artaud, and developed by him into a theory of drama in
The Theatre and its Double.

It would be difficult to find a stronger denial of the importance of
the word than O'Neill's use of laughter in *Lazarus Laughed*. The
laughter is never described in the dialogue, but O'Neill has recourse to
it at critical moments throughout the play. It is characterized for the
theatre audience primarily by the effect it has on the hearers. Men
capitulate to it: it overcomes rational argument and the blood cry of
warriors with equal ease, Tiberius Caesar and Caligula are momentarily transfigured by it. Lazarus's 'high', 'free', 'exultant' laughter
contrasts with the 'harsh', 'discordant', 'frenzied' or 'drunken' laughter of ordinary men and when O'Neill needs to raise the emotional
pitch of the play, he directs that the one becomes 'higher', 'freer', in
the face of the other's greater harshness. The responsibility for the
pitch and coherence of the action is shifted from the playwright on to
the interpretive faculties of the actor.

The roles of choreographer and director are stressed by O'Neill. Throughout the play, increasingly explicit incidents of physical violence are enacted: mobs slaughter each other, a lion is crucified, there are murders and suicides and amongst all this activity weaves the dancing, chanting chorus. O'Neill approaches most closely to what Artaud will later call 'pure theatre'[5] in a sequence in the final scene of the play. Lazarus is being burnt off-stage and in the flickering firelight Tiberius asks feverishly, what is 'beyond there'. This sequence follows:

LAZARUS (*his voice speaking lovingly, with a surpassing clearness and exaltation*). Life! Eternity! Stars and dust! God's Eternal Laughter!

(*His laughter bursts forth now in its highest pitch of ecstatic summons to the feast and sacrifice of Life, the Eternal.*)

(*The crowds laugh with him in a frenzied rhythmic chorus. Led by the Chorus, they pour down from the banked walls of the amphitheatre and dance in the flaring reflection of the flames, strange wild measures of liberated joy. Tiberius stands on the raised dais laughing great shouts of clear, fearless laughter.*)

CHORUS (*chanting as they dance*). Laugh! Laugh!
    We are stars!
    We are dust!
    We are Gods!
    We are laughter!   (IV. ii, pp. 145–6)

It is tempting to explain the play as an exercise in 'pure theatre' and, in part, this is what it is. Indeed, certain European directors have valued the play highly: Nemirovitch Danchenko and Stanislavski were among the first to claim that the play has greatness, although the censor vetoed plans for production of *Lazarus* at the Moscow Art Theatre,[6] whilst *Lazarus* and *Brown* are advertised in French translation with a quotation from Joseph Losey claiming that they are neglected masterpieces. O'Neill is clearly concerned to utilize the resources of the theatre and there are, among the manuscript notes, pages of set-sketches drawn by O'Neill and various sound and movement plans.[7] But it is evident, in the light of the whole play, that O'Neill has other motives, inconsistent with a drama of 'pure theatre'.

The very wordiness of the play suggests the importance to the author of what is spoken. Lazarus, Tiberius, Caligula, indeed, all have speeches which would last for more than three minutes, a long stretch of performance time. Theatrical elements are frequently used to fix attention on the spoken word: the speaker having been positioned at a focal point, the crowd suddenly falls silent and adopts a still, listening attitude, which it holds throughout the speech. The audience's attention, moreover, is continually distracted from the abstract patterns of movement and sound, to the words. Even in the theatrical sequences which I have discussed, there are gnomic phrases, 'Death is dead' (p. 19); 'my heart reborn to love of life cried "Yes", and I laughed in the laughter of God' (p. 19), which challenge the audience to seek out meaning. Already, by the end of scene i, there have been clues which suggest that Lazarus has a message to preach. The onlookers repeatedly ask what he has witnessed and, although the affirmative cry is momentarily acceptable as indicating stunned joy at the miracle, the queries imply that a moment of revelation, although postponed, is promised.

This latent promise means that the second scene is crucial to our evaluation of the play. When it opens we are no longer amazed at the movement, light and sound on the stage. We have become accustomed to O'Neill's method, and the plot has passed into a new phase, in which memory is no longer quickened by biblical echoes. We look now to the verbal level to reveal the significance of what we have witnessed and, in doing so, are compelled to question the adequacy of O'Neill's method. Two sequences show us the play in miniature: Lazarus speaks his first sermon and, when he is no longer present to inspire them, his followers cry out in terror. The sermon is cast into prose and the followers' cry into a rhythmical chant. The dialogue of the play will alternate between these two modes, and its action will follow the pattern established here when, among different nations and various orders of society, a joyful response to Lazarus's message repeatedly turns to terrified forgetfulness.

At Lazarus's appearance in scene ii the crowd who, until now, have been dancing, chanting and quarrelling, fall silent. The silence is held for a moment, and then music sounds, swelling softly as the background to Lazarus's words. The careful preparation of the moment implies that earlier cryptic phrases will now be explained. Lazarus speaks:

You laugh, but your laughter is guilty! It laughs a hyena laughter, spotted, howling its hungry fear of life! That day I returned did I not tell you your fear was no more, that there is no death? You believed then – for a moment! You laughed – discordantly, hoarsely, but with a groping toward joy. What! Have you so soon forgotten that now your laughter curses life again as of old? . . . That is your tragedy! You forget! You forget the god in you! You wish to forget! Remembrance would imply the high duty to live as a son of God – generously! – with love! – with pride! – with laughter – . . . Why are your eyes always either fixed on the ground in weariness of thought, or watching one another with suspicion? Throw your gaze upward! To Eternal Life! To the fearless and deathless! The everlasting! To the stars! . . . The Master of Peace and Love has departed this earth. Let all stars be for you henceforth symbols of Saviours – Sons of God who appeared on worlds like ours to tell the saving truth to ears like yours, inexorably deaf! (*Then exaltedly*.) But the greatness of Saviours is that they may not save! The greatness of Man is that no god can save him – until he becomes a god.

(pp. 32–3)

The exclamatory structure used, demands a rising tone of voice at the end of every phrase and so imposes a rhythm on the speech which quickly becomes monotonous. The rhythm interferes with our capacity to listen to the words. But the words themselves contribute to the blurring of the thought. Abstract nouns accumulate and we cannot, or we are not tempted to, penetrate their meaning because, apart from the two rather obvious images, we are given no concrete means of relating them to our experience. The curiously neutral speech is the more disappointing because the stage preparation for it and its length have invited us to pay close attention. Such a passage, by default, makes us acutely aware of the functions of dramatic speech. This utterance does little to advance the action and, more seriously, it offers no elaboration or modification of the meanings we have already understood. It repeats what we have learnt from earlier chants and quarrels about human guilt and the need for joy. Equally disturbing, it contains nothing which reveals the character, Lazarus, to us and, whilst it may be inappropriate to look for particularizing human traits in a figure set apart from the rest of mankind, the absence of a stylistic basis for the vaunted spiritual difference of Lazarus from other men means that we have scant belief in that difference. The prose rhythm of Lazarus's speech is identical to that of the carping old men of this scene and to that of Caligula and Tiberius in later scenes.

The dramatic value of the exclamation itself is forfeited. An exclamation in normal speech is unpremeditated and often startles the hearer. It ignores the complexities and formalities of speech. In drama, therefore, it can be used to imply the verbally inexpressible. It can have the appearance of a spontaneous response which reveals a previously concealed or unrecognized aspect of personality, and can suggest the outbreak of an emotion too raw, too deeply felt, to be spoken calmly. Later, in *Long Day's Journey Into Night*, O'Neill uses it to remarkable dramatic effect. In act II (p. 73), Tyrone, pushed to the limit of endurance, cries out his wife's name 'Mary!', and the single cry contrasts with the restraint and studied tolerance that has governed the conversation and shown itself in complex sentences and carefully correct speech. We are therefore able to respond to the outbreak and hear in the cry a note of terrible human despair. But when every phrase is an exclamation, as so often in the middle years, such contrast is impossible and the audience hears only the abbreviated meaning and not the underlying emotion.

The rhythmical chant structure in *Lazarus Laughed* is used always and only for chorus and crowd speeches. The chants do not indicate a change in the pitch of the play, nor does the chorus have a mediating function between play and audience. We do not find the meditative quality of some Greek choric odes, nor the capacity of others for ironic observation.[8] O'Neill's chorus provides a refrain. At the opening of the scene, Lazarus's followers had joyfully cried. 'Laugh! Laugh! There is only life! There is only laughter!' (p. 22). Deserted, at the end of the scene, they voice their horror, saying:

CHORUS.   Forgotten is laughter!
           We remember
           Only death!
           Fear is God!
           Forgotten is laughter!
           Life is death!

FOLLOWERS. Forgotten is laughter!
           Life is death!

ALL (*the Chorus of Old Men and the Crowd joining in*).
           Life is a fearing,
           A long dying,
           From birth to death!
           God is a slayer!
           Life is death!   (p. 43)

'There is only Life!' has now become 'Life is death', but we have been offered no grounds for belief in the reversal. The statement 'God is a slayer, Life is death!' has no verbal power to recreate emotion for the audience. The moral terror the statement attempts to describe, is not actualized.

The structure of the chants is essentially the same as that of the prose passages. A series of exclamatory, simple sentences succeed each other, the verb is usually in the present tense, and virtually every sentence contains an abstract noun. The chants are differentiated from the prose passages by their more concentrated use of repetition and their more regular stress pattern. A few key words, 'life', 'laughter', 'death', recur throughout the play, and are used by O'Neill almost as though they are charms. Each line contains an irregular number of unstressed and two-stressed words, one of which is frequently one of the charm words. Usually the first word, and often the final one, receive the stress, which serves to separate each line from the succeeding one, and the resulting structure is, therefore, extremely inflexible. Since, in addition, each line is commonly end-stopped, O'Neill denies himself the characteristic virtue of *vers libre*, which is its capacity to absorb speech rhythms and to create dramatic tension between line ending and sense ending. It becomes impossible for any idea to be developed with subtlety, when each phrase is an isolated entity. The setting of the play ranges through the lands and degrees of the Ancient World, but the difference between one situation and another, between one mood and another, is lost in the monotony of the rhythm, just as it was in the prose dialogue. Small attempts at variation serve only to emphasize how rigid O'Neill's form is. The enraged shouts of the Orthodox Jews, the joyful song of the Dionysiac Greeks and the triumphant defiance of the legionaries merge into the same sound pattern:

Hear' them laugh'!	Son' of the Light'ning!	Laugh'! Laugh'! Laugh'!
See' them dance'!	Dead'ly thy ven'geance!	Caes'ar no more'!
Shame'less! Wan'ton!	Swift' thy deliv'erance!	War', no more'!
Dir'ty! E'vil!	Behold'ing thy Moth'er,	Wounds', no more'!
In'famous! Best'ial!	Greece' our Moth'er,	Death' is dead'!
Mad'ness! Blood'!	Her beau'ty in bond'age,	Dead'! Dead'! Dead'!
Adul't'ery! Mur'der!	Her pride' in chains'!	(p. 80)
(p. 31)	Hast'en, Redeem'er!	
	(p. 49)	

One can imagine any of these utterances serving its purpose in a different context but, here in the context of the ongoing play, the monotonous rhythmical pattern must numb the receptive capacities of the audience.

T. S. Eliot's play *Murder in the Cathedral*, which in many instances is close to O'Neill's in its subject matter, offers a telling contrast. When Eliot's chorus remember fear and death, there is a suggestive particularity, domestic fears are intermixed with omens from folk-tale and legend:

(*Chorus, Priests and Tempters, alternately*)
c. Is it the owl that calls, or a signal between the trees?
p. Is the windowbar made fast, is the door under lock and bolt?
t. Is it rain that taps at the window, is it wind that pokes at the door?
c. Does the torch flame in the hall, the candle in the room? . . .
p. A man may climb the stair in the day, and slip on a broken step.
t. A man may sit at meat, and feel the cold in his groin.[9]

(1)

When Eliot uses the exclamation, after the slaying of Thomas, to suggest that he is articulating a horror that is scarcely speakable, he combines it with other speech rhythms and so gives pace and shape to the rush of sound, as we see in this extract from the beginning of the speech of the Women of Canterbury:

> Clear the air! clean the sky! wash the wind! take stone from stone and wash them!
> The land is foul, the water is foul, our beasts and ourselves defiled with blood.
> A rain of blood has blinded my eyes. Where is England? where is Kent? where is Canterbury?
> O far far far far in the past; I wander in a land of barren boughs: if I break them, they bleed; I wander in a land of dry stones: if I touch them they bleed.
> How can I ever return, to the soft quiet seasons?
>
> (II, p. 82)

Eliot's massed voices will give an impression of wild clamour, just as O'Neill's do, because of the sheer volume and tone the actors contribute. But the succession of cry, query, lament, offers the audience different ways of perceiving the emotion and concentrates attention on what the words themselves say whereas in O'Neill's chants, as we have seen, it is difficult to hold on to individual words and phrases. Eliot's clamorous sequence, moreover, is carefully placed in the play as a whole. It is immediately followed by the logistics of the knights' self-justification, argued in the prose of modern debate and not, as in O'Neill's play, by another exclamatory sequence which denies the audience any rest or change.

O'Neill clearly is no poet. What are we to make, then, of the very high praise his poetic drama has sometimes received? In an article in *Theatre Magazine* (February 1928), Benjamin de Casseres ranked the play with *Faust*, *Thus Spake Zarathustra* and Flaubert's *The Temptation of St. Anthony*, on account of its 'power, daring and allegorical implications' (p. 12) whilst, in *The Golden Labyrinth*, Professor Wilson Knight wrote that the play is 'as near total drama as any we possess' (p. 392). Whilst Oscar Cargill, in *Intellectual America*, wrote:

The story of Lazarus' victory over death, the stilling character of his presence upon unruly mobs, his reaching affection for the most depraved of mortals, the intoxicating character of his laughter and the great wind of joy from the hilarious crowds sweep this play on to as complete a dramatic triumph as the theatre affords. With utter contempt for the nay sayers we may pronounce *Lazarus Laughed* as much superior to all other dramatic conceptions in its day as were *Faustus*, *Hamlet*, and *Oedipus Rex* to the contemporary drama of their time.

(p. 408)

A similar, if more measured, comment by Lionel Trilling gives a clue to what is drawing such a valuation. In an article on O'Neill in *The New Republic* in 1936, he wrote:

Not only has O'Neill tried to encompass more of life than most American writers of his time, but, almost alone among them he has tried to solve it. When we understand this we understand that his stage devices are not fortuitous technique; his masks and abstractions, his double personalities, his drum-beats and engine rhythms are the integral and necessary expression of his temper of mind and the task it set itself. Realism is uncongenial to that mind and that task, and it is not in realistic plays like *Anna Christie* and *The Straw* but rather in such plays as *The Hairy Ape*, *Lazarus Laughed* and *The Great God Brown*, where he is explaining the world in parable, symbol and myth that O'Neill is most creative.

(vol. LXXXVIII, p. 176)

It is the promise latent in the plays that is valued rather than the plays themselves, the aspiration and enterprise of the writer rather than the writings. O'Neill's drama is rarely mediocre: it is good or it fails badly because the conception has a size and vigour quite different from that of any of his contemporaries. It is for this reason that the plays of O'Neill's middle years can easily seem more significant when they are described than when we read them or see them in performance. The commentator becomes an unconscious mediator who smoothes over the internal conflicts, the inconsistencies of thought and form and makes good the inadequacies of execution, so creating a structure of his own from the diverse and often clumsy elements of the play.

But a more serious problem than the false estimation of the style of the poetic plays by some commentators is what we are to make of the high regard in which O'Neill himself held the writing of these years. In 1926, for example, he wrote of *Lazarus Laughed*:

As for 'Lazarus', what shall I say? It is so near me yet that I feel as if it were pressed against my eyes and I couldn't see it. I wish you were around to 'take a look' before I go over it. Certainly, it contains the highest writing I have done. Certainly it *composes* on the theatre more than anything else I have done, even 'Marco' (to the poetical parts of which it is akin although entirely different). Certainly it is more Elizabethan than anything before and yet entirely non-E. Certainly, it uses masks as they have never been used before and with an intensely dramatic meaning that really should establish them as a sound and true medium in the modern theatre. Certainly I know of no play like Lazarus at all.

(To Macgowan, 14 May 1926)

But, as we have seen, we do not find the linguistic variation, the wit and punning, the assonance and new word formation, the allusiveness, metaphor and verbal propriety, which stimulate the mental capacities of the hearer, and are the signs by which we recognize Elizabethan poetic drama. Nor is *Lazarus Laughed* a single aberrant work. In one after another of the plays of these years, even those in which there is no versification, O'Neill has recourse to the stylistic elements we have identified. When he seeks to charge the dialogue more highly, to convey intense emotion or express sudden spiritual insight, we find the same monotonous exclamatory structure, the same use of abstract nouns to give size to the thought, the same bald repetition, the affirmation unfounded in the action of the play. The result is that, where the meaning should be most sharply defined, it is most blurred. At the climactic moment of *The Fountain*, which O'Neill wrote in 1925, Juan Ponce de Leon is suddenly reconciled to human mortality and cries, when his friend would silence the song of youth and love:

No! I am that song! One must accept, absorb, give back, become oneself a symbol! Juan Ponce de Leon is past! He is resolved into the thousand moods of beauty that make up happiness – colour of the sunset, of tomorrow's dawn breath of the great Trade winds – sunlight on grass, an insect's song, the rustle of leaves, an ant's ambitions. (*In an ecstasy*.) Oh, Luis, I begin to know eternal youth! I have found my Fountain! O Fountain of Eternity, take back this drop, my soul!
(*He dies. Luis bows his head and weeps.*)

(p. 117)

And at the end of *Days Without End*, the final play of the period (1934), John Loving, prostrate before the altar in a church, bathed in a glow of sunlight, resolves the conflict that has tortured him throughout the play, when he echoes Lazarus's words, saying, 'Life laughs with God's love again! Life laughs with love!' (108). The exclamatory structure, the cloying use of visual imagery and the absence of foundation for joy in the body of the play, is likely to recall for the audience the language of melodrama, against which O'Neill had turned so determinedly when he set out to forge his low-colloquial style.

It was his search for a more personally expressive style which led O'Neill to change from low-colloquial to Standard American. But with the low-colloquial medium, he seems to have rejected the organizing skills which he had developed. In his book, *Language as Gesture* (London, 1954), R. P. Blackmur discusses writing whose basic assumption is that if feeling is sufficiently strong it will flow into its own appropriate form without need of, and even deliberately rejecting, traditional poetic craftsmanship (pp. 286ff). He describes this as the idea of 'expressive form' and points out that, unlike work which has been submitted to 'the completing persuasiveness of genuine form', the achievement where the writer looks to expressive form will be bounded by the limits of individual human personality (p. 293). Blackmur's idea is helpful in thinking about O'Neill's writing. Indeed, O'Neill wrote of *The Fountain* that the idea behind the play was 'so fundamental and deep in the root of things that the proper expression ought to flow right out of it' (to Macgowan, 29 March 1921). The writer who relies on expressive form is vulnerable to whatever influences are dominant at a subconscious level. This would be particularly apparent in a writer such as O'Neill who, as we saw in chapter 2, was unusually susceptible to what T. S. Eliot has called 'the invasion of the adolescent self'[10] by cherished writings.

Certain relevant facts about those cherished writings are scarcely to be avoided. Most strikingly, we realize from the account of O'Neill's reading that he was curiously ignorant of contemporary poetry. Although a play by Wallace Stevens was produced by the Provincetown Players in 1919–20, a one-act play called, 'Three Travellers Watch a Sunrise', and William Carlos Williams was also associated with the Players, O'Neill seems to have had little interest in their poetry. There is no evidence that he read either Pound or Eliot before 1932 (see Appendix 1). There is an exception: O'Neill championed the work of Hart Crane, a personal friend, urged Liveright to publish *White Buildings* and even drafted an introduction to the volume in which he wrote of the difficulty of Crane's poetry compared with 'magazine verse', but he did not consider Crane's writing in relation to other innovative American poetry, and although he published work in several little magazines, between 1914 and 1924, he had no connection with either *Poetry* or *The Little Review*. The poets he had enjoyed in adolescence, and whom he reread throughout his life, were the avant garde of an earlier era, whose language had little to offer to a writer struggling with American English in the 1920s. Rhythm rather than linguistic subtlety is dominant in the versification of Whitman, and of Dowson, Swinburne and Symons' Baudelaire. Indeed, for a well-read man, O'Neill was remarkably isolated from current literature in English. With the exception of the Irish dramatists, the contemporary plays O'Neill read were all in translation and, even in the best translation, there is an inevitable separation of the writer's content from his original form. The author's selection of the appropriate word

and the precise verbal construction of his thought are lost. When a
large proportion of what is read is read in translation, there is an
evident danger that approximations of meaning will begin to suffice
and that, in drama, such elements as setting, plot and general construction will come to seem detachable from other aspects of form,
and of more importance. We do not find that speech rhythms are
convincingly transposed into dramatic speech by O'Neill until his late
plays and it is likely that his development was slowed by his isolation
from appropriate literary models for any but low-colloquial forms of
speech.

In my discussion of O'Neill's borrowing from Nietzsche, in chapter
2, I suggested that the references were at once too obtrusive to be
ignored and too cryptic for their significance to be generally available.
This offers at least a partial explanation of the distance between the
audience's response to O'Neill's poetic language and his own faith in
it. His judgement of how rich in meaning the words he uses are, may
have been distorted by the strength of his feeling for their hidden
source. The capacity of these words to stimulate in him a succession of
particular associations is not necessarily felt by his audience. To them,
their recurrence in the dialogue of the play will seem merely repetitious. If we investigate the associations between O'Neill's and
Nietzsche's writing further, we find that the very shape of O'Neill's
poetic prose is derived from the author he so much admired.

Nietzsche's style in *Thus Spake Zarathustra* contains those elements
which we have noted as prominent in O'Neill's: it is aphoristic,
exclamatory and heavily interspersed with abstract nouns. This is
particularly true in the affirmative sequences from which O'Neill's
content is drawn, the hymn to eternity (XL), 'The Drunken Song'
(LXXIX) and the exposition of Eternal Recurrence (LVII, LXXX). But,
even in translation, Nietzsche's writing is more complex and its
internal references more richly patterned. The style embodies the
meaning. The repetition has an inwardly spiralling momentum, the
meaning being tightened with each repetition of a noun, each turn of
the spiral, until it eventually is concentrated in a brief concluding
statement at the central point of the spiral. The final line of section
eleven of 'The Drunken Song', for example, carries echoes of the
previous three stanzas whose meaning it summarizes:

So rich is joy that it thirsteth for woe, for hell, for hate, for shame, for the
lame, for the world, – for this world. Oh, ye know it indeed!

Ye higher men, for you doth it long, this joy, this irrepressible, blessed joy
– for your woe, ye failures! For failures longeth all eternal joy!

For joys all want themselves, therefore do they also want grief! O happiness,
O pain! Oh break, thou heart! Ye higher men, do learn it, that joys want
eternity,

– Joys want the eternity of all things, they want deep, profound eternity.

(LXXIX, p. 389)

This repeats the pattern of each previous section of the song sequence,
each of which develops one of the ideas contained in Zarathustra's
eleven-line roundelay, sung earlier in the book (LIX) as the climax to
the message of Eternal Recurrence and repeated at the conclusion of
the Drunken Song sequence. Nietzsche's expression of joy, for all its
seeming wildness, is thus deliberately ordered and the ordering serves
to emphasize some ideas and make them appear infinitely extensible.

Even such a brief outline of Nietzsche's method as is sketched here,
makes evident the gulf which separates it from O'Neill's, despite the
overt similarities. But O'Neill's poetic style shares its stylistic relationship to Nietzsche with that of George Cram Cook, founder of the
Provincetown Players (p. 26 above) and an ardent admirer of
Nietzsche,[11] to the extent that he eventually retired to Greece in search
of the Dionysiac origins of drama. A brief extract will indicate this.
The hero of Cook's play, *The Spring*, declaring his love, says:

ELIJAH. . . . two such as we might grow to be one person – one person in two
minds – gifted as no one person has been gifted – a new kind of genius – the
end of loneliness!
ESTHER. Can there be such beauty in the world?
ELIJAH. The beauty of the world is infinite. You are a new kind of channel of
inflowing beauty. There'll be fulfilment of hopes more flaming high than the
highest we can form. Maybe the gods were only man's prophetic dream of
what man is to be.[12]

Neither Cook nor O'Neill seems to have realized that he has caught
the echo of *Thus Spake Zarathustra* at the meeting place between
Nietzsche and the despised stage language of the nineteenth-century
melodrama.

O'Neill's experiment in expressive form resulted in a hybrid style
that combined elements of Nietzsche, Cook and Monte Cristo, and
limited what he was able to say more severely than ever the low-
colloquial form did.

But it is not only the style which is hybrid. When O'Neill abandoned the kind of control that had been necessary to develop the
low-colloquial style his own personality was thrust into an exposed
position and we find that, in the middle plays, his inner confusion and

self-doubt occasionally disrupt his more conscious intention. In many of the plays of these years, an undercurrent of feeling pulls against O'Neill's determined protestation of an affirmative philosophy and against the dramatic structures to which his missionary role has led him.

To give an example of this: the characterization of Miriam, one of the half-masked figures in *Lazarus Laughed*, is one of the most disruptive, and most interesting, things in the play. It is a small role and, overtly, supports the trend of the play because O'Neill directs that she laugh triumphantly from beyond the grave in vindication of Lazarus's message. But the scenic image draws disproportionate attention to her, presenting her as Lazarus's opposite. She wears black in contrast to his white and ages as he grows younger. Her speech is the least exclamatory in the play, and the low-toned prose in which she voices her doubt about Lazarus's message suggests, because it seems most like our own, that hers is the voice of sanity. It offers the play's only real conflict. Because the style allows us to concentrate on her words and meaning, her voice seems to frame the questions the audience themselves would ask: after the slaughter of the followers, she questions Lazarus's laughter saying, 'I cannot understand, Lazarus. They are gone from us, and their mothers weep' (II. ii, p. 82); disgusted by the excesses of Rome, she pleads 'This is too far Lazarus. Let us go home' (III. i, p. 88), and in her one long speech, before her death, she attacks the insubstantiality of Lazarus's message, saying, 'Your home on the hills of space is too far away. My heart longs for the warmth of close walls of earth baked in the sun. Our home in Bethany, Lazarus, where you and my children lived and died' (III. ii, p. 112). Her words with their unaccustomed particularity offer us a glimpse of the play that lurks behind the one O'Neill has written. Her final capitulation, less convincing than her protest, leaves us with the impression that O'Neill has side-stepped the real issues Nietzsche's text raised for him. There is, in *The Great God Brown*, too, a much fiercer conflict than the overt one between the world views of the artist and the businessman. The conflict within the man of artistic sensibility whose work draws high praise but who recognizes that he lacks the necessary flare of genius to produce great art is usually latent but, occasionally, erupts in bursts of raw feeling. Dion comments bitterly about his work: 'I got paint on my paws in an endeavour to see God . . . but that Ancient Humorist had given me weak eyes' (I. ii, p. 46), and the audience is briefly gripped by an interest quite different from that roused by the rest of the play.[13]

The uncertainty at the core of *Lazarus Laughed* is reflected in its author's vacillating opinion about what is integral to the play. In one letter O'Neill insisted that masks and chorus 'are in my design of this play',[14] but, subsequently, he suggested cutting the chorus since only the crowd is essential[15] and, still later, he planned to put the crowd off-stage and replace their laughter by music.[16] On completing the play, he declared that it was not philosophy but life,[17] but later stressed the religious ceremonial aspect of it.[18] He said the play contained his 'highest writing',[19] but later suggested that Chaliapin should play the Lazarus part, translated into Russian, since the words were not really essential.[20] And in 1929, although defending *Lazarus Laughed*, as he continued to do throughout his life, O'Neill admitted to having had divided aims in writing the play. He also reasserted the necessity of writing about life first and, importantly, he linked this with the need to gain control over technique. He wrote:

My work will be simpler, more compact and less theatrical ... I certainly admit that my worst plays have all been built around a germ idea that was in its essence theatre first, and life secondarily. In justice to myself, I don't mean this in any meretricious 'theatrical' sense, it simply means that my medium has at times taken the upper hand and become an end in itself and the slumbering director in me (son of Monte Cristo) has swamped the author. 'Dynamo' was a good example of this ... The only fault, in my estimation! with Lazarus is that there is too much direction in the authorship. By straining the collaborative possibilities of the theatre I feel I've at last won to what is my own technique, and it now remains for me to simplify and clarify the technique of its abortive growths and its exhibitionism. Then I can concentrate on saying clearly what I want to say.

(To Clark, 21 June 1929)

It was ten years before he was to achieve this aim.

Realistic dialogue: 'Mourning Becomes Electra'

O'Neill regarded *Mourning Becomes Electra* as his magnum opus from the outset. He let his colleagues know in advance that he would not be hurried into completing it[21] and kept, and subsequently published, a detailed work diary of intentions, new ideas, unsuccessful experiments and revisions. Notes in the diary and letters written at the time make it clear that O'Neill had given much thought to the kind of dialogue he needed in the play and to its function. The notes show that, after experimenting with various stage devices such as masks and interior monologue, he determined to 'get all [these effects] in naturally in straight dialogue – as simple and direct and dynamic as

possible' (21 September 1930). 'Naturalness' and 'simplicity' are
words which recur and they are often opposed to 'fine' writing. In a
letter to Clark, for example, O'Neill wrote:

I do not want you to get the idea that this new work entails any grandiose
poetical flights or any straining after fine writing. It doesn't at all. It is quite
simple.

(27 January 1931)

This reiterated association of lifelikeness with the absence of literary
artifice is found in O'Neill's comments on both his poetic and his
idiomatic style in these years. The theory is derived, as I suggested in
chapter 1, from Shaw but it is only now that it is consciously practised.
Of the poetic style of *The Fountain*, for example, he wrote to Nathan:

I used it to gain a naturalistic effect of the quality of the people and speech of
those times ... with little care for original poetic beauty save in the few
instances where it is called for.

(4 April 1926, quoted Gelbs, *O'Neill*, p. 470)

This helps to explain what is wrong with O'Neill's poetic prose. The
poetic is seen as an embellishment and not, as in Shakespearean
drama, as the linguistic embodiment of meaning itself, tauter and at
once more condensed and more allusive than everyday prose. That the
statement accurately reflects O'Neill's practice is illustrated by his
working notes about his method in *Lazarus Laughed*. In the first draft
of the play, he said, he used 'straight realism in dialogue and construction' and then he completely rewrote the play adding 'the departures
necessary':[22] the play was written in prose and then converted into
poetry. The poetic elements are introduced for a realistic purpose:
they are to convey an impression of distance in time or space. But the
resulting style, as I have indicated, is grandiose, unlike anything
anyone ever spoke.

In writing his idiomatic form O'Neill was anxious to avoid artifice
altogether. He wrote of *Mourning Becomes Electra*:

There was a realistic New England insistence in my mind, too, which would
have barred great language – even in a dramatist capable of writing it – an
insistence on the clotted, clogged and inarticulate.

(*The American Spectator*, December 1932, p. 2)

And, again, in an interview, he said that he wanted 'to get down in
words what people think and feel' and that he wanted 'to make them
say it in the rhythms of this country'.[23] The stage utterance must
strike a chord of recognition in the audience so that the characters'
problems of self-expression will be essential to the emotional structure

of the play. They will draw attention to the private frustrations of each member of the audience, who will derive from the play, therefore, an unusually sharp experience because private truths will seem to be embodied in it.

The complication in this is that O'Neill adopts the realistic fallacy. Although he is selective in other aspects of form, in plot construction, for example, and the manipulation of theatrical devices, in his dialogue he avoids such selectivity. But one does not create emotional recognition of the 'clotted, clogged and inarticulate' simply by putting down on paper the thing itself. It might be said that when O'Neill abandoned his structured version of low-colloquial and embraced expressive form he allied himself to the other section of the American Language Movement and became, for the time being, a Dreiser rather than a Stein. To see what this means in practice we must look in detail at the dialogue of our selected play in the realistic mode.

The climax of the first play of the *Mourning Becomes Electra* trilogy is the murder of Ezra Mannon by his wife, Christine. O'Neill's preparation in the early scenes is so thorough that, by the beginning of act IV, our interest has shifted from the deed itself to the manner in which it will be presented and the relationships it will reveal between the characters involved. The title has indicated a connection with the Oresteia, and the gossip of the minor characters at the opening of the play has made us conscious of the parallels which exist between O'Neill's characters and situation and those of the Greek legend. Aware, therefore, of the course the plot must follow, we know that the Clytemnestra figure will murder the Agamemnon figure. The motive is gradually revealed in the first two acts and threats of betrayal indicate its pressing nature. The method is revealed when the murder is planned on-stage in act II and the discussion of Ezra's weak heart in act III predicts the occasion. The final piece of foreshadowing comes in act IV, when Ezra tells Christine of his premonitions of doom. This sequence follows:

MANNON. And I had hoped my homecoming would mark a new beginning – new love between us! I told you my secret feelings. I tore my insides out for you – thinking you'd understand! By God, I'm an old fool!
CHRISTINE (*her voice grown strident*). Did you think you could make me weak – make me forget all the years? Oh no, Ezra! It's too late! (*Then her voice changes, as if she had suddenly resolved on a course of action, and becomes deliberately taunting.*) You want the truth? You've guessed it! You've used me, you've given me children, but I've never once been yours! I never could be! And whose fault is it! I loved you when I married you! I wanted to give myself! But you made me so I couldn't give! You filled me with disgust!

MANNON (*furiously*). You say that to me! (*Then trying to calm himself – stammers.*) No! Be quiet! We mustn't fight! I mustn't lose my temper! It will bring on – !

CHRISTINE (*goading him with calculating cruelty*). Oh, no! You needn't adopt that pitiful tone! You wanted the truth and you're going to hear it now!

MANNON (*frightened – almost pleading*). Be quiet, Christine!

CHRISTINE. I've lied about everything! I lied about Captain Brant! He is Marie Brantome's son! And it was I he came to see, not Vinnie! I made him come!

MANNON (*seized with fury*). You dared –! You –! The son of that –!

CHRISTINE. Yes, I dared! And all my trips to New York weren't to visit Father but to be with Adam! He's gentle and tender, he's everything you've never been. He's what I've longed for all these years with you – a lover! I love him! So now you know the truth!

MANNON (*in a frenzy – struggling to get out of bed*). You – you whore – I'll kill you! (*Suddenly he falls back, groaning, doubled up on his left side, with intense pain.*)

CHRISTINE (*with savage satisfaction*). Ah!

(*She hurries through the doorway into her room and immediately returns with a small box in her hand. He is facing away from her door, and, even if the intense pain left him any perception, he could not notice her departure and return, she moves so silently.*)

MANNON (*gaspingly*). Quick – medicine!

CHRISTINE (*turned away from him, takes a pellet from the box, asking tensely as she does so*). Where is your medicine?

MANNON. On the stand! Hurry!

CHRISTINE. Wait. I have it now. (*She pretends to take something from the stand by the head of the bed – then holds out the pellet and a glass of water which is on the stand.*) Here. (*He turns to her, groaning, and opens his mouth. She puts the pellet on his tongue and presses the glass of water to his lips.*) Now drink.

MANNON (*takes a mouthful of water – then suddenly a wild look of terror comes over his face. He gasps.*) That's not my medicine!

('The Homecoming', IV, pp. 102–5)

O'Neill does not take advantage of the information we already have to introduce a more complex action here. His characters act out what has been anticipated. The scene is, therefore, a static one despite all its activity. In the late plays, such repetition will be used to establish a sense of timelessness. But, here, O'Neill hardly seems to be aware that the action is repetitious. What elaboration there is is indicated in the stage directions and hardly at all in the structure of the action or the movement of the dialogue. As the stage directions indicate, O'Neill asks the actors to use their skills of voice and gesture to convey Christine's sudden resolution and the extent of her anger and frustration, and to reveal the piteousness of Ezra, the hard man who is vulnerable. The exclamations and simple sentences of the passage quoted and the similarity of the speech of the two speakers recall *Lazarus Laughed*: they have a similar neutralizing effect on the action.

Here, as there, the monotony of style deadens the audience's capacity to ponder motive and deliberate on human relationships although, as the notes to the play make evident, O'Neill had the opposite aim when he wrote the plays. After the first draft of *Mourning Becomes Electra*, he noted that he must prevent the surface melodrama from overwhelming the real drama, but, because the actual doing of the deed is the only new thing offered in the scene, O'Neill fixes his audience's attention on the physical action. We are anxious for the talk to end so that we may witness the deed itself. On this level, O'Neill does not disappoint, but it is the level of traditional melodrama. After the sequence quoted, Ezra falls into a coma, having first cried out his daughter's name; the daughter rushes into the room in time to hear the dying man's accusation, and to see his staring eyes and pointing finger; the murderess swoons, dropping her box of poison; the daughter snatches this up, and the scene, and with it the first play of the trilogy, ends with her oath of vengeance. The audience are passive observers of events. The dramatist fails to create a dialogue and, therefore, an action sufficiently complex to capture the audience's whole attention and to activate their deepest responses. The world of the play lacks reality because it fails to engross us.

We recognize how little O'Neill asks of his audience when we remember the complex patterns of pleading, defiance and rejection in act II, scene iv, of *King Lear* when the daughters, each in her distinct way, taunt their father about his followers and, between them, break him. During the fast and ruthless exchange in which Goneril and Regan reduce Lear's followers from a hundred to none, the auditors must assimilate their appalled admiration of the sisters' method with what they realize the words mean to Lear and with their recognition that it is Lear himself who has given his daughters the power they now wield against him. The one response interacts with the other, until Shakespeare is able to communicate all Lear's loss in the curt query, 'What need one?' Stimulated by what has gone before, the audience are keyed to respond to Lear's extended reply and to grasp the extremity of his rage and grief. Although the action of Strindberg's *The Father* is not so complex and the resulting feeling is not so intense as that of *King Lear*, the audience of the later play also see a man goaded beyond endurance and are themselves compelled to experience something of the sufferings of a human being in extremity. Again, and in contrast with O'Neill's scene, we see that the audience are brought into active relationship with the drama. In the sequence in which Laura goads the Captain, the pace of the scene and the contrast between the speech modes of the two characters contribute, even in translation, to the generation of emotional pressure. The gathering momentum of the scene stems from Laura's short, quick phrases and the agility and seeming logic with which she turns the Captain's slow, brooding speeches to her own cause and inexorably manipulates him into a subordinate position. Even whilst we recognize her cruelty, we are carried along by her argument. When she dominates so completely that her adversary is robbed of speech, the Captain explodes into the violent, irrational and spectacular action of hurling the lighted lamp across the stage. The function of this within the plot, is to provide a triumph for Laura and a deed on which later events will hinge but it also has a direct effect on the audience's way of perceiving the action. Because it is startling, the deed breaks the momentum of the scene, diverts attention from Laura to the Captain, and compels the auditors to reassert their will to think about the whole action. There is no such change and flow of empathy in O'Neill's play and no comparable state of alertness is stimulated because O'Neill, by and large, fails to embody his real concerns in the dialogue and action.

Some passages in the play do work more successfully than the murder scene. This is, perhaps, because the kind of brooding they involve was a habitual personal mode for O'Neill. They are interludes of reverie and description and the language in them is more concrete, their style less exclamatory, than the normal language of the play, so that we listen more attentively to what is said. We glimpse in them something of the O'Neill of the later plays. Indeed, just as O'Neill subsequently will exploit the feeling of time repeating itself which his repetitious action gives, so, also, he will develop a structural device out of his tendency to use more heightened language in passages of reverie. In act II of 'The Hunted', Orin tells of the dreams he has had of warm, peaceful islands and links them with the impression Melville's *Typee* made on him (p. 148). In act III of the same play, Orin recalls his experience of the war (p. 155). Although Orin's literary reference is made clumsily, it is apposite, giving another dimension to the characterization, and a shape to the daydream. The description of the battle is even more successful, both because of the way O'Neill creates an impression of past experience and because he uses this impression in a subsequent episode of the play. O'Neill has linked fog with reverie in other plays, notably *Fog*, *Bound East for Cardiff* and *Anna Christie*, but here the characteristic description of the unearthly effect of the fog drifting over the battlefield, is used as a way of emphasizing the reality of a human death. O'Neill particularizes his description by giving the precise location of the point of the sword as it enters the Rebel's body. We are reminded of Crane's description of Jim Conklin's alertness to visual detail in the battle-charge sequence of *The Red Badge of Courage*. Having responded to the reality of Orin's experience, we listen more attentively to his conclusion. It is a description of a nightmare of the self become an automaton:

Before I'd got back I had to kill another in the same way. It was like murdering the same man twice. I had a queer feeling that war meant murdering the same man over and over, and that in the end I would discover the man was myself! Their faces keep coming back in dreams – and they change to Father's face – or to mine.

(III, p. 156)

The choice of the word 'murder' in the unfamiliar context of a battlefield slaying insists on the reality of the experience for the character and conveys his sense of guilt, without recourse to the elaborate explanations O'Neill usually offers in this play. The stark statement impresses on our minds the image of the over-printing of the hostile by the familiar face, so that, when the image is used again after the murder of Brant, when, seeing his own likeness in the dead man's face, Orin says, 'maybe I've committed suicide' (p. 189), the audience are stirred, as they were not by the murder of Ezra. Although separated from each other by several scenes, the similarities lead us to juxtapose the two sequences and make connections between them.

The difficulty of the play is that O'Neill fails to sustain the impetus of such sequences. After his account of the battle, Orin quickly reverts to the commonplace language characteristic of the play, for example:

Fire away, and let's get this over. But you're wasting your breath – My God, how can you think such things of mother? What the hell's got into you? But I realise you're not yourself.

(p. 157)

Particularly in arguments and when the characters voice deep feelings or state their affection for one another, the speeches consist of strings of clichés. 'My God', 'Good God', 'for God's sake', are used by all the characters as intensifying expletives, with none of the ironic play made by Synge in *The Playboy of The Western World*. The weak adjectives 'horrible' and 'rotten' used by one character after another to voice supposedly specific experience, destroy the illusion of individuality. Affection comes to seem trite when couched in such a trite set of phrases as, for example, 'I'm a damned whining fool! I'm sorry, Hazel. That was rotten of me' (p. 137) and sincere love is no more convincing than feigned, when the same clichés have to bear the load of feeling. The problem is not that O'Neill has reproduced speech: he has not. It is that he has chosen cliché and simple sentence exclamation as his speech markers and has made no strategic use of them.

O'Neill wrote to Arthur Hobson Quinn that he was at once 'very satisfied' and 'deeply dissatisfied' with the play, and added in explanation:

It needed a great language to lift it beyond itself. I haven't got that. And, by way of self-consolation, I don't think from the evidence of all that's being written today, that great language is possible for anyone living in the discordant, broken, faithless rhythm of our time. The best one can do is be pathetically eloquent by one's moving dramatic inarticulations.

(10 February 1932, quoted Quinn, *History of the American Drama*, p. 258)

O'Neill's recognition that the very dysfunctioning of language was part of his material, coupled with the dismal failure of his attempt to write poetic drama, must have strengthened his conviction that dialogue which accurately reflected daily speech was his necessary mode. But in attempting to communicate the 'broken rhythms', he allows himself to become inarticulate.

For drama is not life and its language is not speech but dialogue or monologue spoken in contrived situations by invented characters, which represents speech. The same words spoken in a speech situation and in a dramatic situation can have different meanings. A striking example in illustration of this is the ending of *Dynamo*, another of the middle plays. In the final moment of the play, after Reuben Light has electrocuted himself on the dynamo, Mrs Fife, the only character left on stage, pounds its steel body and says, 'You hateful old thing, you' (III. iii, p. 102). Such words, spoken by an actual woman at a moment of crisis, although banal, could serve to release private emotion, and would therefore be the necessary words for her to utter. Spoken by a character, the communicative function becomes dominant. These words may serve to release but are inadequate to convey frustration and despair. Rather, they briefly superimpose on the image of the character, the image of the author who has lapsed into bathos, and has done so in the final line of the play, which, experience has led us to expect, should be crucial to the play's meaning. We are faced with the obverse of the old question of Miss Bates and boredom. Jane Austen contrives to communicate the tedium of her character's speech without boring her audience because, whilst retaining some of the irritating garrulity, she patterns

Miss Bates' purportedly undirected chatter, so that it offers undercurrents of meaning to the reader. So long as O'Neill is concerned to avoid artifice, his writing may reflect the sterility of American cultivated speech but it is unlikely to draw the audience into a consistently responsive relationship with his meaning or with the sources and effects of the sterility.

O'Neill's identification of the language as the disappointing feature of *Mourning Becomes Electra*, after he had expended so much labour in rewriting and perfecting the play, seems to have been the crucial factor in convincing him that he could only communicate fully by deliberately patterning the speech of his characters. The audience will not reach behind the clichés to discover the characters' real meanings, therefore the writer must so construct his scenes that both meaning and the way words obscure meaning will be made clear to the audience. There is, as we shall see, no transformation of O'Neill's language into poetry in the late plays. The dialogue there is not lyrical, nor euphonious, nor metaphorical, but it is dramatic. And the failures of language in *Mourning Becomes Electra* help us to recognize what dramatic language must do. It must shape our apprehension of individual character, and at the same time convey more to the audience than it communicates between characters. It must present us with a continually developing action as each speech emphasizes, or modifies, or alters our perception of what has gone before. The deeds and the staging must be so related to the dialogue that they become its necessary complement in our experience of the play.

The final sequence of *Mourning Becomes Electra* is peculiarly effective, and is the more interesting because it foreshadows O'Neill's later method. Until now, even in the best of the early plays, endings have been amongst the weakest features of O'Neill's drama. Either his dominating idea has already been expressed and, as in *The Emperor Jones* or *The Hairy Ape*, there is a loss of impetus in the last scene, or he introduces ideas which have little foundation in the body of the play and the ending, as we find in *Anna Christie* is confusing. Occasionally, O'Neill has been divided between two possible kinds of ending. In *Desire Under the Elms*, for example, the stoicism of Ephraim's utterance, 'God's hard and lonesome', is undercut by the spiritual optimism conveyed by Abbie and Eban's walking together into the sunset – already, in 1924, a cinematic commonplace. The stoicism has usually gone completely from the middle plays, leaving only the commonplace image or, in the case of *Marco Millions*, theatrical whimsy. All this is changed with the writing of *Mourning Becomes Electra*. It is

almost as though, in this play, the action has been constructed in order
to present the ending. And, indeed, as early as August 1929, before
beginning the first draft, O'Neill noted in his diary that he had 'given
my Yankee Electra [a] tragic end, worthy of her'. The manuscript
notes and revisions show that, before this, O'Neill had frequently
altered the ending he originally planned for a play, or had had no clear
ending in mind when he began writing. From time to time in my
discussion of the middle plays, I have pointed to elements in the form
and dialogue which will eventually be used purposively by O'Neill but
which are at present disruptive of our sense of the reality of the world
O'Neill is creating. The final sequence of *Mourning Becomes Electra*
has unexpected integrity.

The dominant method of *Mourning Becomes Electra* is repetitious
activity, prepared for and explained in lengthy dialogue whose
thought is limited by the clichés in which it is couched. The form blurs
the force of O'Neill's symbolism and the underlying structure of
doom which he himself saw as the real centre of the play. There are
frequent references to the longing for escape, to the inevitability of
eventual atonement, to the legacy of the past, to premonitions of death
which attach to the Mannon house but, whilst we watch the play, we
find that the significance of these is submerged because they seem so
arbitrary. The references are rarely voiced in such a way that they
relate to our experience of that character's thought and deed. They do
not stimulate us to make vital connections. Orin's reflections after the
murder of Brant were noteworthy because they were exceptional. The
final sequence awakens the audience from the half-aware state into
which the long, slow play has let them lapse because its central idea is
starkly and forcefully expressed. The idea is surprising and yet also
seems inevitable and compels the audience to reach back into the play
for the sources of the ideas and images which culminate here. The
high praise the play has received can probably be attributed to the
effectiveness of the ending. Although the sequence takes only five to
ten minutes of the performance time of a five hour play, it presents the
audience with the image they will take with them from the theatre,
and ameliorates the memory of what has gone before.

Lavinia is left alone on the stage after dismissing her lover in a scene
in which the embarrassment of desperation has made the language
more than usually hackneyed. Seth enters, singing his habitual
melancholy chanty:

SETH. 'Oh, Shenandoah, I can't get near you
Way-ay, I'm bound away – '

LAVINIA. I'm not bound away – not now, Seth. I'm bound here – to the Mannon dead! (*She gives a dry little cackle of laughter and turns as if to enter the house.*)

SETH. Don't go in there, Vinnie!

LAVINIA (*grimly*). Don't be afraid. I'm not going the way mother and Orin went. That's escaping punishment. And there's no one left to punish me. I'm the last Mannon. I've got to punish myself! Living here alone with the dead is a worse act of justice than death or prison! I'll have the shutters nailed close so no sunlight can ever get in. I'll live alone with the dead, and keep their secrets, and let them hound me until the curse is paid out and the last Mannon is let die! (*With a strange cruel smile of gloating over the years of self-torture.*) I know they will see to it that I live for a long time! It takes the Mannons to punish themselves for being born!

SETH (*with grim understanding*). Ayeh. And I ain't heard a word you've been saying, Vinnie. (*Pretending to search the ground again.*) Left my clippers around somewheres.

LAVINIA (*turns to him sharply*). You go now and close the shutters and nail them tight.

SETH. Ayeh.

LAVINIA. And tell Hannah to throw out all the flowers.

SETH. Ay.

(*He goes past her up the steps and into the house. She ascends to the portico – and then turns and stands for a while, stiff and square-shouldered, staring into the sunlight with frozen eyes. Seth leans out of the window at the right of the door and pulls the shutters close with a decisive bang. As if this were a word of command, Lavinia pivots sharply on her heel and marches woodenly into the house, closing the door behind her.*)

('The haunted', IV, p. 287–8)

The play on the word 'bound' in Lavinia's opening words halts our association of the chanty with the dream of escape which has become habitual in the rest of the play. We seem to witness the idea of self-punishment being conceived and developed in the character's mind. Nothing in Lavinia's speech is redundant, nothing laboured, and each sentence elaborates one aspect of the cause, conditions and possible effect of her projected incarceration. The idea with which we are presented is at once shocking, familiar and strangely invigorating. It is shocking because of the associations which have accrued to the house itself. Characters have been loath to enter and have called it 'a mausoleum', 'a sepulchre', whilst the inside of the house has been the setting for murders and suicides, for the laying out of the dead, for the bitterest quarrels and for the private struggles of the characters with their sense of guilt. It is shocking, too, because the detail of having the shutters nailed gives it reality and recalls the joyful Lavinia of an earlier scene, who wanted to throw open the shutters and who found peace away from her home (pp. 244; 238; 250). It is familiar, because it is a cruel distortion of her dream of forgetting the Mannon way of life by closing the house and letting it, with its portraits and its ghosts, crumble and die (p. 276), and also, because Orin has warned her that she has no escape, that 'the darkness of death-in-life' is a 'fitting habitat for guilt' (p. 244), and that 'the damned don't cry' (p. 253). The image O'Neill creates also seems familiar because it recalls a succession of strange American recluses in the literature of New England and the South. It is invigorating, because, despite the horror, Lavinia's spirit flashes out, unbowed. Her self-punishment reveals her as an individual being: it is an act of spirited defiance, an exertion of the human will. Orin has said, 'You'll find Lavinia Mannon harder to break than me! You'll have to haunt and hound her for a lifetime!' (p. 269) and now we can recognize the existence of that fibre. This information brings complexity to the seemingly straightforward words that are spoken, but nothing is laboured. Lavinia's words stir our memories: they do not repeat stridently what we already know and each member of the audience will respond to different suggestions. The finality of Lavinia's decision is communicated by her rejecting the flowers, which were first linked with Christine's need for love and beauty (p. 34) and then with Lavinia's celebration of her new life (p. 274). It is communicated at the surface level, too, by the terseness of the last two exchanges and by the two emphatic actions of closing the shutters and closing the door.

Almost for the first time, we find that the scene as written by O'Neill is the necessary one, and that something is lost when the words and actions are paraphrased.

5

The late plays and the development of 'significant form': *The Iceman Cometh*

In 1933 O'Neill withdrew completely from public life and from active participation in the theatre in order to concentrate on his writing. Between 1933 and 1939, he was involved in an increasingly frustrating struggle with his projected cycle of plays, which were to deal with the private and public lives of an American family from the Revolution to the 1930s.[1] By the end of 1943, his physical health was breaking down, and his slowly worsening palsy was to prevent him from writing during the remaining ten years of his life. But in 1939 he set aside the cycle and within four years had written the five plays which I have called 'the late plays'. Although he held these plays back from production[2] there is a note of confidence and excitement when he mentions them in letters. This is particularly true of *The Iceman Cometh* and *Long Day's Journey Into Night* which he said he had 'wanted to write for a long time'.[3] He wrote to Barrett Clark in 1943:

Although I have done no writing lately, my record since Pearl Harbor is not as poor as it might be. I have finished, except for a final cutting, another non-Cycle play – 'A Moon For the Misbegotten' – and rewritten the 1828 Cycle play 'A Touch of the Poet', done some work off and on on another non-Cycle 'The Last Conquest' – anti-totalitarian state, anti-Instrumentalist philosophy, but useless as present war propaganda because it is a symbolic fantasy of the future, and of the last campaign for the final destruction of the spirit – which (happy ending!) does not succeed.
When, in addition, I consider 'The Iceman Cometh', most of which was written after war started in '39 and 'Long Day's Journey Into Night', written the following year – (these two plays give me greater satisfaction than any other two I've ever done) – and a one act play 'Hughie', one of a series of eight I want to do under the general title, 'By way of Obit', I feel I've done pretty well in the four war years.[4]

The Last Conquest never was written and the scenario and notes which survive are not at present available to scholars.[5] The other five plays,

as O'Neill suspected, and as I have already suggested in references to
them in earlier chapters, represent a different kind of achievement
from his previous work.

Early in his career, as I showed in chapter 1, O'Neill had realized
that the 'ruthless selection and deletion and concentration on the
emotional – the forcing of significant form on experience' were 'the
task' of the writer.[6] Given such early recognition of the necessity of
ordered form, why should O'Neill's writing have achieved 'crisis and
consistency'[7] only between 1939 and 1943? Did his new certainty of
dramatic form allow him to focus his experience more sharply, or did
the pressure of subject matter create the necessary formal rigour?
These two questions can probably not be answered adequately even in
the most probing biography. All we can do is note factors which may
be relevant. We know that O'Neill's isolation allowed him to concentrate on his writing and set it apart from the twenty years of
experimentation, to which he could, therefore, look back as to an
apprenticeship during which he had stretched and tried his medium
until he knew it thoroughly. We can guess that his isolation must also
have given him time and space in which to confront his own past and
measure his present against his adolescent self. And certainly, his
letters show that events in Nazi Germany and the outbreak of war in
Europe had shaken him deeply, and that he sensed there was not
much writing time left to him.[8] But these cannot be more than
suggestions. A study such as I have undertaken cannot explain a
sudden burst of creative imagination. It *can* explore what resulted
from it.

What has emerged most forcibly for me from reading and seeing
performances of the late plays is exactly this, that in each of them we
feel the presence of a creative imagination, shaping and controlling the
elements of the play. Nothing is arbitrary or unfinished as it so often
was in the past. The material, drawn from the period of O'Neill's late
adolescence, is openly autobiographical, but it is treated with an
objectivity which was lacking when similar material was only latent in
plot and characterization in the earlier work. The emphasis in my
discussion will be different from that in the earlier chapters. There, I
suggested that whilst the plays written before 1934 did have intrinsic
interest, their significance lay in what their inventiveness and seriousness contributed to the American theatre and in how their themes and
methods prefigured those of the late plays. I made general points and
illustrated them from particular plays. Now the commentary on
individual plays will be central: the language of *The Iceman Cometh*,

first, and then *Long Day's Journey Into Night*, will be examined in detail.

The variety of language in the late plays and the appropriateness of speech to speaker is striking, particularly in contrast to the monotony of the middle plays. O'Neill now draws on a wide range of dialects and idiolects and juxtaposes standard English with low-colloquial. 'Talk' is no longer a 'straitjacket' and dialect no longer a 'dodge' (see p. 83), because both are used and neither is an end in itself.

In my consideration of *The Iceman Cometh*, I shall be more concerned with broad discussion of how elements are patterned and, in that of *Long Day's Journey Into Night*, there will be more close analysis. It is rewarding to vary the method in this way, because the language of the two plays is organized somewhat differently. Both plays stir wonder and despair about the human condition, both portray the peculiar persistence with which men patch up their lives and go on living against all odds, but these important similarities have blurred recognition of the formal differences between the two plays and of the differing areas of human experience which they explore. The two plays are not alike: they are complementary.

The dramatic effect of *The Iceman Cometh* derives, firstly, from the success with which O'Neill differentiates all seventeen characters who people Hope's bar and makes us interested in them, so that the stage seems to teem with life and, secondly, from the way in which he varies and interweaves their words so that the activity of each at any given point, besides characterizing that figure, contributes to the ongoing action of the play. The effect derives, also, from the fact that one character is treated more fully than the rest and so stands in a different relation to the audience from the other figures and helps to shape their response to the action. I shall, therefore, examine the verbal basis for the differentiation of the seventeen and of their interweaving and will look at the characterization of the differently focused figure, Larry Slade. In *Long Day's Journey Into Night*, there are four central characters, all of whom are at least as fully developed as Larry Slade is. The language does differentiate them from each other, but it also reveals each as being many-faceted and divided against himself. As the play progresses and we seem to know each more fully, the differences between the characters come to seem less significant than the human existence they share. When I discuss this play, I shall investigate the way in which a number of carefully organized linguistic devices help to shape our sense of the living reality of these imagined figures.

The Iceman Cometh

At the opening of *The Iceman Cometh*, all except two of the characters on stage are asleep and most will remain so for three-quarters of the very long first act, only occasionally surfacing from their slumber. There will be very little movement about the stage. Indeed, during the rest of the play, most of the characters will be seated. This physical stillness establishes the mood of inertia which characterizes the 'last harbour' where no-one worries 'where they're going next, because there is no further they can go' (*The Iceman Cometh*, p. 28). It is a daring device, particularly for a writer who has produced plays as monotonous as *Lazarus Laughed* and *Mourning Becomes Electra*. An account of why it succeeds would amount to a description of the changes that have taken place in O'Neill's control over form since he wrote the middle plays. Movement and gesture, for instance, are far more effectively, if less histrionically, used than then. What physical action there is in this generally static play comes at vital moments and makes these more striking precisely because of the contrast with the usual physical stillness. Every character on stage, for example, rouses himself, loses his slouching posture and listens alertly in response to the news that Hickey has been sighted. The concerted movement reinforces the impression we have already gained from the dialogue of the eager anticipation of Hickey's arrival by all the roomers. The greater subtlety now in the handling of movement is matched by the dynamism of the dialogue. The dialogue here entertains the audience, offers them information which augments what they already know or makes them reassess what they thought they knew, and continually stimulates them to make connections. O'Neill's carefully balanced distribution of the dialogue amongst the characters ensures that the audience's attention is continually shifted from one to another of them.

In the opening exchange of the play, O'Neill is already offering visual and oral information, posing questions, raising doubts. When the play begins, a large number of obviously down-at-heel men are asleep around the tables of a dingy bar. Two characters are awake. One is sitting at the extreme left front of the stage. The other passes him a bottle:

ROCKY (*in a low voice out of the side of his mouth*). Make it fast.
(*Larry pours a drink and gulps it down. Rocky takes the bottle and puts it on the table where Willie Oban is.*) Don't want de boss to get wise when he's got one of his tightwad buns on. (*He chuckles with an amused glance at Hope.*) Jees, ain't

de old bastard a riot when he starts dat bull about turnin' over a new leaf? 'Not a damned drink on de house', he tells me, 'and all dese bums got to pay up deir room rent. Beginnin' tomorrow', he says. Jees, yuh'd tink he meant it. (*He sits down on the chair at Larry's left.*)

LARRY (*grinning*). I'll be glad to pay up – tomorrow. And I know my fellow inmates will promise the same. They've all a touching credulity concerning tomorrows. (*A half-drunken mockery in his eyes.*) It'll be a great day for them, tomorrow – the Feast of All Fools with brass bands playing! Their ships will come in loaded to the gunwales with cancelled regrets and promises fulfilled and clean slates and new leases!

ROCKY (*cynically*). Yeah, and a ton of hop!

LARRY (*leans toward him, a comical intensity in his low voice*). Don't mock the faith! Have you no respect for religion, you unregenerate Wop? What's it matter if the truth is that their favouring breeze has the stink of nickel whiskey on its breath and their sea is a growler of lager and ale, and their ships are long since looted and scuttled and sunk on the bottom? To hell with the truth! As the history of the world proves, the truth has no bearing on anything. It's irrelevant and immaterial as the lawyers say. The lie of a pipe dream is what gives life to the whole misbegotten mad lot of us, drunk or sober. And that's enough philosophic wisdom to give you for one drink of rot-gut.

ROCKY (*grins kiddingly*). De old Foolosopher, like Hickey calls yuh, ain't yuh? I s'pose you don't fall for no pipe dream.

(I, pp. 15–16)

The first speaker's words are supported by gesture until we are accustomed to his vernacular. What he says and how he says it indicate his occupation, his social class, and his regional base, tell us where the action takes place, and prepare us, by gesture and through an imitation, to hear the voice of one of the sleeping figures whilst, at the same time, warning us not to believe all we hear. When the second man speaks, we recognize that there is understanding between them. There are some phrases in Larry's speech which echo Rocky's New York City slang, and Larry actually takes over the word 'tomorrow' and uses it with reference to himself and then repeats it twice more, echoing Rocky's warning and extending it to include everyone on the stage. There is continuity between the words of the two speakers, therefore, but there is also a startling linguistic contrast. Apart from the slang phrases, Larry speaks Standard English and uses vocabulary which marks him (despite the obvious poverty of his dress) as of a different social class and educational background from his interlocutor. The pace of his speech is different: unlike Rocky's, all his verbs have subjects, which slows his speech slightly, as does the length and archaic flavour of some of his words, such as 'touching credulity', 'gunwales', 'favouring breeze'. But the contrast goes further than this, and the structure of the speech governs the kind of delivery each actor must adopt. Rocky's speech is crude and terse, Larry's reveals him to be a man who enjoys words, who plays with them, creating pictures, whose way of thinking is reflected in his fluency. His thought is elaborated by verbal devices, by hyperbole, alliteration (most frequently on the 'ls'), and symmetry of phrasing (in the phrase 'cancelled regrets and promises fulfilled', with its past participle + plural noun, plural noun + past participle and its assonance in the repeated '-lled' ending, for example). One image, the 'Feast of All Fools' seems, by a reference to the traditional motif of the ship of fools, to suggest the succeeding one, as Larry spins out his description of the roomers' dreams. The growing length of the sentences also suggests that an idea is being elaborated. But when his subject seems to change in the next utterance and he describes the reality, his tone does not: he uses an even longer sentence (46 words) and an anticlimactic reflection of the same image, in which the feast is cheap alcohol and the ships, with an alliterative flourish, are 'long since looted and scuttled and sunk'.

If the verbal display does not yet, in this first exchange, raise uncertainties about how seriously Larry's philosophy is to be taken, it does indicate that there is some showmanship in him, particularly when it is punctuated by Rocky's cynical interjections, 'de old Foolosopher, ain't yuh?', and, soon 'de old anarchist wise guy dat knows all de answers!' (p. 16). The differences between the speech of the two men help us to perceive each more clearly, and yet the evidence that they converse easily despite those differences is the first signal of how integrated the community in Hope's bar is. Virtually none of this information is stated in so many words by the characters. It is absorbed by the audience from the very shape and organization of the dialogue. Clearly, any one auditor will not register all these points and he will probably register others which I have not mentioned, but he will be aware that the dialogue has a dense texture and that the more fully he concentrates on it, the more he will glean, which creates a state of receptivity in the audience from the outset of the play. O'Neill is ensuring, therefore, in the opening words a degree of engagement by the audience which he achieved only in the final scene of *Mourning Becomes Electra*.

In his one-act sea plays, O'Neill used a variety of regional dialects to differentiate his characters and to create an interesting surface texture (see p. 66 above). As the contrast between the speech modes of Rocky and Larry has indicated, O'Neill returns to this method in *The Iceman Cometh*, although now the variation is more complex and the information it provides more extensive. O'Neill's success in the sea plays depended on each accent being immediately recognizable and being quickly succeeded by a quite different one. The differentiation was bold, if not crude, and each character was derived from the stereotype traditionally associated with the national dialect he used. The variation amongst those sunk to the bottom in Hope's bar is wider than it was on the *S.S. Glencairn*. If those plays offered a shadowy image of America, as I suggested, the image presented here is much more clearly focused.

The speech of thirteen of the characters in *The Iceman Cometh* is individualized, lexically and syntactically. The speech of four more, the tarts and second bartender, is similar to that of Rocky, with whom they form a subgroup among the characters. They have a particular role in the action which will be discussed later. The land, the law, the army, local and national politics, journalism and entertainment are represented here. There are men of various ages and men who are aware of having been sons, husbands, lovers. Not only nationality but class, education and, therefore, degrees of articulacy are communicated through speech. Four characters, Larry (Irish), Jimmy (Scottish), Lewis (English) and Oban (American, upper class), speak Standard English with a slight colouring of national accent, and are able to use a variety of syntactic transformations. The speech of Hickey and Parritt is American Standard with occasional colloquial solecisms. Their sentences are usually simple, sometimes compound. That English is the second language of two, Hugo (Central European) and Piet (Afrikaans), is indicated by pronunciation through vowel and consonant shifts (Hugo: 'leetle', 'vill', 'trink'; Piet: 'plind', 'chentleman', 'dot' [that]); by occasional confusion between singular and plural forms, and by irregular word order ('Always there is blood . . .'; 'Vit mine rifle I shoot damn fool Limey officers py the dozen, but him I miss'). The remaining characters speak New York low-colloquial, but amongst them, too, social degrees are apparent. Harry, Mosher and Macgloin use a great deal of slang vocabulary, and Macgloin has occasional Irish markers, but low-colloquial syntax and phonology is only present in the speech of Rocky's group and of Joe, who also has some specific markers of low-colloquial negro speech. These are much the same as O'Neill developed in presenting New York low-colloquial in the early plays ('boin' [burn], 't'ink' [think], 'dese' [these], 'yuh' [you]. 'Was' generally replaces 'were' and terminal 'gs' are dropped. 'Git' [get], and 'does you?', 'is you?' and 'you better' are used by Joe (cf. p. 72 above)).

O'Neill composes an idiolect for each man by combining regional dialect with occupational dialect. The argot of each man's abandoned occupation intrudes into his speech. It reveals his past but also shows that each man's past still possesses him: his very thought is shaped by the language he retains. We can identify in Hope's bar a one-time confidence trickster ('rube', 'short-change'), a policeman ('fine pickings', 'sugar galore'), a gambler ('play craps', 'my stake') and, amongst the middle class characters, an anarchist ('Bakunin's ghost', 'Hickey the Nihilist'), a journalist ('bitter sorrows', 'losing the woman one loves by the hand of death'), a college student (Willie retains both student slang, 'the rah, rah boys', and student humour, as when he ascribes his bawdy song to Emerson or Jonathan Edwards) and, with Hickey's arrival, a salesman ('honesty is the best policy', 'Now listen, boys and girls, don't look at me as if I was trying to sell you a gold brick. Nothing up my sleeve.').

Dion Boucicault introduced a 'melting pot' cast into his melodrama, *The Octoroon* (1859). The outline given here of the range achieved by O'Neill, shows it to be much subtler than Boucicault's but does not reveal how much more functional it is; for that, the organization of the speech of a few of the characters must be examined in greater detail. I cannot deal with all of them, but my discussion of the way O'Neill handles the speech of these few will serve as a model of what he does with the rest. The individual strands which will be separated here are closely interwoven in the play. The speech of Rocky's group will be examined first and then that of Harry Hope, of Captain Lewis and of Hugo.

Rocky and his group use a large number of slang words. Many of them are variant forms of address. The 'tarts' are also 'pigs', 'hookers', 'hustlers', 'tramps', and 'your stable'; a man is a 'dope', a 'poor sap', a 'louse', a 'sucker', a 'bastard', a 'boob from de sticks'. Cora's face is 'a clock'; the party, 'dis boithday racket'; the bar, 'dis dump'. What is most noticeable is the undertone of abuse, even when none is intended by the speaker. It is exaggerated by the rhetorical way they phrase their questions with a terse 'ain't yuh?', 'dat's you, huh?' and by the violence of their threats: 'I'd like an excuse to give you a good punch in the snoot', 'If yuh opened your yap, I'd knock the stuffin' outa yuh', 'I'd ... mop up de street wid him'.

In an attack on Mencken's praise of American slang, Marius Bewley described such elements and said of them: 'Their intention is nothing less than degradation, for they have their origin in an ancient sense of inferiority (and perhaps guilt) seeking to escape from itself through brutality' (*The Complex Fate*, London, 1952, p. 207). The slang of Rocky's group is, in the first place, suggestive of the limited opportunity of their lives. The roomers have finally fallen to Hope's bar; Rocky and his group begin there. There is social comment as well as comic irony in the fact that their status-illusion is based on semantics and that they recognize fine degrees in their abusiveness: they are 'tarts', not 'whores'; 'bartenders', not 'pimps'. O'Neill emphasized the difference by cutting out phrases like 'a lot of crap' (MS, p. 25), 'shut your trap' (MS, p. 24) from the speech of the roomers in the final draft of the play. There is no real crudity or physical unpleasantness in the play. O'Neill made no use of the choking 'lungers' and freely used spittoons that biographers describe as being commonplace in the bars on which Hope's is modelled,[9] nor does he use obscene language. The language of Rocky's group provides the feeling without any of the distracting horror. Similarly, in the preface to *Oliver Twist*, Dickens comments on his having modified the language of Sykes to give the true flavour whilst avoiding particularly offensive elements.

It has other functions, too. Rocky's group exists partly in Hope's bar and partly in the outside world. Rocky rushes between the public bar and the inner room, the girls burst in from the street, laughing and banging doors. They set the play in relation to external time and society. Because O'Neill shows the outside world through their eyes, a world of 'saps' in which men prey on each other, the harmony and mutual support of the life in Hope's bar is made more valuable and the collapse of that society, when its members confront the world, more grievous. The roomers, too, become abusive and even physically violent towards each other, under pressure of their meeting with the world. At the end of the play, O'Neill keeps Pearl and Margie off stage until after the departure of Hickey. Their harsh voices, as they crash drunkenly on to the stage describing themselves at last as 'whores', come as a reminder to the audience of the outside world which has finally been rejected by the roomers. The lateness of their entrance allows O'Neill to use the visual image of the door being closed on that world.

I mentioned, in my discussion of the opening exchange, the contrast between the speed of Larry's and of Rocky's utterance. Much of the plot is relayed in the exchanges between members of Rocky's group which begin each act. It is relayed economically because they talk faster and more tersely than the other characters. In the final draft of the play, O'Neill cut short some of their speeches to obtain a better dovetailing effect. In the first typescript, for example, Pearl says 'nobody can't call me a whore' (act II, p. 6). In the final text, this becomes:

PEARL. Nobody can't call me a –
ROCKY. Aw, bury it! What are you, a voigin?   (p. 91)

Even sentimentality hardly drags when it is as much to the point as:

ROCKY. You're aces wid me, see?
PEARL. You're aces wid us too. Ain't he, Margie?
MARGIE. Sure, he's aces.   (p. 64)

The cynical name-calling of this group, helps to remind the audience of the self-deceptions the roomers are practising, and their questioning keeps the audience alert. Rocky establishes doubt about Parritt, for example, before this character appears because of his insistent questions: 'Who's de new guy? . . . Why ain't he out dere sticking by her? . . . But what kind of a sap is he to hang onto his right name?' (p. 22).

But if O'Neill saw what Bewley saw in American slang, he knew as Mencken claimed, that at its best it contained 'pungent humour and boldness of conceit' (p. 425), and uses this element, too. In the early plays, O'Neill deliberately limited his use of slang and other forms of low-colloquial in order to project, through their very groping for language, the emotional inarticulacy of his characters. Their vernacular had to be remote from the robust, inventive American speech praised by Whitman and Twain. Now O'Neill can allow his characters to 'spread themselves'.[10] There is a good deal of colourful slang: champagne is that 'old bubbly water' (p. 101) and we hear of 'a case of almost fatal teetotalism' (p. 82). But Harry Hope, the man 'whom every one likes on sight' (stage directions, p. 13), whom we see acting as the benefactor of all the roomers, appropriately has the fullest command of Mencken's kind of slang.

Harry's language draws the audience's affection to him because it is so entertaining. We enjoy listening to him talk. He uses fantastic inventions and farfetched images, in telling of how the bums give him the 'graveyard fantods' (p. 58) or recalling a time when his wife was so annoyed 'she coulda bit a piece out of the stove lid' (p. 56). His use of hyperbole takes the edge off his threats and complaints and gives credence to Rocky's opening comment on him, 'Jees, you'd t'ink he meant it'. It also helps to convey the bar-room mood to the audience as do the yarns the roomers spin and the jokes they tell. This is Harry:

You and Chuck laughing behind my back, telling people you throw the money up in the air and whatever sticks to the ceiling is my share.

(p. 21)

There ain't going to be no more drinks on the house till hell freezes over.

(p. 42)

If there was a war and you was in it, they'd have to padlock the pockets of the dead.

(p. 57)

The kind of inventiveness involved here is often compared by the commentators on American slang with poetic metaphor (see p. 56). I think that these examples show that the two are different largely because their function is so different. The slang phrase is delightful in itself. It draws attention away from whatever is being discussed to its own ingenuity or comic hyperbole. It decorates speech rather than illuminates it, while poetic metaphor takes the reader or auditor inwards into the meaning of the utterance, and is most fully alive in the context for which it was coined. The value of the slang phrase lies in its capacity to be absorbed into the communal vocabulary. Its effective life is limited because repeated usage will gradually dull the pleasure it gives. O'Neill avoids this problem of dulling by using, quite appropriately since the play is set in 1912, slang which is no longer in common usage and so will not be blunted by being well-known to the audience. I have cross-checked O'Neill's slang against several collections of American slang and, interestingly enough, found that virtually all the lexical items he uses were authentic and are recorded in one or another of the dictionaries.[11] This includes some of the particularly appropriate epithets, which one might have imagined were coined by O'Neill: 'foolosopher' (Weseen, *Dictionary of American Slang*, p. 336), an expression that Professor M. C. Bradbrook tells me was current in Elizabethan English, 'Harp' [Irishman] (Weseen, p. 347), 'rah, rah boys' (Weseen, p. 384). But whether it is invented or remembered, O'Neill's slang *seems* authentic because of the use of hyperbole and of ingenious elaboration.

O'Neill utilizes the affection Harry's speech rouses in the audience, to bind them emotionally later in the play. When Harry returns, the first to have failed Hickey's challenge, he is badly shaken so that even Hickey admits 'I didn't think he'd be hit so hard. He's always been a happy-go-lucky slob' (p. 175). Harry's language reinforces this testimony. O'Neill makes his words harsh and crude, 'Bejees, you're a worse gabber than that nagging bitch, Bessie was' (p. 174) and then lets his language shrink into terse sentences of monosyllabic words, 'I

want to get drunk and pass out. Let's all pass out. Who the hell cares?'
(p. 175). It is the degraded aspect of American slang which is now
apparent in his speech, reflecting his mental state. The audience
listens as eagerly as the roomers when, after Hickey's departure,
Harry reverts to his earlier robust way of expressing himself. The
spiritual resurgence is clearly displayed in the linguistic resurgence.
The speech which initiates the change is a remarkable one. It is
rhythmically patterned: a personal cry, beginning with his habitual
oath, 'Bejees', and the first person pronoun, alternates with a general
statement about Hickey's mission which begins with the third person
pronoun, 'it':

> *Bejees*, fellers, *I'm* feeling the old kick, or *I'm* a liar! *It's* putting life back in
> me! *Bejees*, if all *I've* lapped up begins to hit me, *I'll* be paralysed before I
> know it! *It* was Hickey kept me from –. *Bejees, I* know that sounds crazy, but
> he was crazy, and he'd got all of us as bughouse as he was. *Bejees, it* does queer
> things to you having to listen day and night to a lunatic's pipe dreams . . . (my
> italics).

He is almost singing when he reaches the climax,

> Bejees, it's good to hear someone laugh again! All the time that bas– poor old
> Hickey was here, I didn't have the heart – Bejees, I'm getting drunk and glad
> of it! (*He cackles and reaches for the bottle*.) Come on fellers. It's on the house.
>
> (pp. 215–16)

Harry seems to lead the others back to life with this joyful paean. The
emotional response of the audience derives less from the paraphrase-
able meaning of the utterance than from its rhythmic and syntactic
structure and from its relationship to all Harry's preceding utterances.

But the roles of Rocky and Harry Hope are central in the play and it
might be expected that the dramatist would pay particular attention to
their speech. We will see, when we turn to the two minor roles, that
each character is fully integrated into the action. We have the impression that Hope's bar is peopled with all sorts and conditions of men
because each is etched sharply, and, in every case, the speech is the
man. Among the notes for the play there are detailed descriptions of all
the characters. How clearly O'Neill heard each from the outset, is
evident in the scenario, which consists of snatches of what will become
characteristic dialogue, joined by a running commentary;[12] how clearly
he saw each character is evident in the detailed descriptions in the
introductory stage directions. At every turn of the action, we hear every
man's voice, even if, in the interests of economy, the voice is sometimes
limited to a single utterance. This brings a feeling of multiplicity to the

play such as O'Neill intended in *Lazarus Laughed* but failed to achieve despite the complicated mask scheme. The difference between the two plays reveals how necessary that early dictum of O'Neill's, 'Life in terms of lives', was to his particular kind of dramatic imagination. The way in which O'Neill makes time for every voice to be heard in this play, makes a claim for the individual value of every man, and is one of the major positive statements of the play. In *Death of a Salesman*, Miller tells us that 'attention must be paid' to Willy Loman. O'Neill has no need for such didactic commentary. The very presence of each character is a demand for attention.

O'Neill's portrayal of Captain Lewis comes closest to using a national stereotype. Lewis's command of syntax tells us that he is educated, and his articulacy is emphasized because we usually hear him in conversation with Wetjoen, whose English is halting and heavily accented. That he is English is established by his use of characteristic epithets, 'my dear fellow', 'old chum', 'the only bloody sensible medico', and by a certain pomposity of phrasing, 'my *profound* apologies', and of attitude: this destitute man will save for a *first* class passage home and will accept any job however humble, but 'not *manual* labour, *naturally*'. The jauntiness of the ex-army officer is marked by the occasional use of 'what?' as a rhetorical coda at the end of sentences and by the liberal use of 'bloody'. But O'Neill also plays with the stereotype, to make the character more complex. Lewis gives his word 'as an officer and a gentleman' when he clearly has no intention of keeping it. The stiffness associated with the British in America is reflected in the pedantry of Lewis's speech, but the pedantry is, in its turn, often a source of deliberate humour on Lewis's part, as when he avoids discussion of an outstanding debt with the words, 'Sorry. Adding has always baffled me. Subtraction is my forte.' Our appreciation of the humbug underlying this kind of humour is reinforced by the information that Lewis came to America to work in the Boer War spectacle at the St Louis Fair, so that it is with a delighted recognition of the inevitable that we discover that, just as the boasts of great strength of his sparring partner, Wetjoen, are belied by what we see of his physical weakness, so Lewis, too, has betrayed his stereotype by having embezzled regimental money.

The presence of Lewis, like that of every character, contributes to the central action. Specifically, it does so through his seemingly inconsequential description of his friend as 'my balmy Boer who walks like a man' which is followed by a joke in which he compares Wetjoen to a baboon. The response of the other characters implies that this is a habitual joke, and this impression is reinforced when the joke is repeated in act III and the pun laboured by being explained. When the joke is told a third time, after Harry's paean, the repetition of the familiar acts as a signal to the audience that the roomers are following Harry's lead and are beginning to reconstruct their former life style.

We are constantly aware of Lewis, although his is one of the smallest roles in the play. His physical presence sketched in some detail by O'Neill in the stage directions is as striking as his words – he is tall and erect, is bewhiskered and frequently strips off his shirt to reveal a ragged scar. Every other character is intended to be equally distinct visually. The description given here of Lewis together with what we have seen of the pattern of his speech indicates O'Neill's method in the play. The figures are not fully rounded as we shall see those in *Long Day's Journey Into Night* are, but nor are they simply types or humours. In each case, O'Neill sketches the outline of a whole man, and adds to this a few telling details. By developing and rearranging these details, he projects the character. This is the art of the caricaturist. O'Neill is adopting the method used by Dickens when he depicts figures like Micawber or Betsy Trotwood and the figures in Hope's bar have comparable clarity. They are memorable in a way that more fully drawn characters could not be and, because we can therefore hold them in our minds simultaneously, O'Neill is able to interweave them to form the patterned action. The discovery by O'Neill's biographers of prototypes for each of the roomers in Hope's bar, reinforces rather than contradicts this point. O'Neill himself wrote:

The dump in the play is no one place, but a combination of three in which I once hung out. The characters all derive from actual people I have known – more or less closely or remotely – but none of them is an exact portrait of anyone.

(To Macgowan, 29 November 1940)

Doris Alexander's detailed description of Hyppolyte Havel, for example, demonstrates convincingly that Hugo is derived from him.[13] But to show that O'Neill worked from life is not to prove that he recreated that particular life on the stage, and to suggest that he did is to miss what he is actually doing.[14] The caricaturist, too, works from life.

Hugo is described by O'Neill as having the appearance of 'the type anarchist as portrayed bomb-in-hand in newspaper cartoons' (p. 10). His speech and action are more restricted than those of any other figure on the stage. His appearance is bizarre and so is his manner of suddenly waking from sleep to cry the revolution before sleeping again. He speaks almost entirely in two- to six-word exclamations, made more elliptical by his foreign syntax and pronunciation and by his frequent use of revolutionary jargon: 'Capitalist svine! Bourgeois stool pigeon! Have the slaves no right to sleep even?' (p. 17). This first utterance of his is typical, and conveys the extent to which he has atrophied in Hope's bar. It is reminiscent of the speech of the revolutionary socialist, Long, in *The Hairy Ape* (see p. 75) but, as the play progresses we see how differently it is handled. We find that, whilst the shape of the utterances continues to suggest Hugo's sterility, O'Neill rearranges the content making it surprisingly expressive both of the Hugo that once was and of the Hugo who, for all his atrophy, still has the remnants of human emotions, still feels panic and fear and still needs to maintain some kind of belief in himself. After Hickey has quietly pointed out that Hugo's anger when the champagne is not properly iced is incongruous with the revolutionary ideals he boasts, O'Neill endorses Hickey's point and, suggesting Hugo's panic, gives an impression of unconscious thought welling into speech, because he includes in Hugo's outburst a succession of self-condemning oppositions and incongruities, 'I love only the proletariat! I vill lead them! I vill be like a Gott to them! They vill be my slaves!' (p. 146). Any comparable signs of bad faith in *The Hairy Ape* served to distance Long from the audience and make him appear ridiculous but here, because we are allowed to perceive Hugo's self-recognition, and his attempts to hide from it, they have the reverse effect and make him seem more pitiable. His insistence on his need for sleep is a case in point. O'Neill makes this appear like some panacea clutched from childhood. Similarly, the protestation that he is drunk is repeated too often to carry conviction: 'I am very trunk, no, Larry?', he says, 'I talk foolishness. I am so trunk Larry, old friend, am I not, I don't know what I say? ... Yes I should sleep. I am too crazy trunk' (p. 147). The very turning to another for support, is expressive of his own doubt.

Because Hugo's speech is so attenuated, his words are more explicit than those of the other characters, his thoughts more immediately exposed, and so his speech acts as a kind of indicator of the general mood. This happens, for example, at the end of act III when Harry staggers back, having failed the challenge. Harry, as we have seen, has lost his capacity to describe his fury and fear, or to voice his subsequent despair but, because of the juxtaposition of his entrance with one of Hugo's outbursts, Hugo, who appears so oblivious of the world, is able to speak for him:

I vill trink champagne beneath the villow – But the slaves must ice it properly!
Gottamned Hickey! Peddler pimp for the nouveau riche capitalism! Vhen I
lead the jackass mob to the sack of Babylon I vill make them hang him to the
nearest lamp-post the first one! . . . I hear myself say crazy things. Do not
listen, please . . . What's matter, Harry? You look funny. You look dead.
Vhat's happened? I don't know you. Listen, I feel I am dying, too. Because I
am so crazy trunk. It is very necessary I sleep. But I can't sleep here vith you.
You look dead.

(III, pp. 173–4)

We perceive in speeches like this that O'Neill, whilst giving an
impression merely of creating speech appropriate to the speaker, is at
the same time using language to intensify the whole drama.

Hugo has one cry, 'The days grow hot, O Babylon. 'Tis cool
beneath thy villow trees!' which is curiously corrupted in the speech
addressed to Harry which I have just quoted – 'I vill trink champagne
beneath the villow' – and which is varied by O'Neill on other occasions
to give a succession of striking images in which the changing mood of
the play is epitomized. As it stands, the cry implies the remains of a
revolutionary faith of a different order from that suggested by the
jargon. Whether or not the audience recognize the source, the quotation is made available to them in a way that the references to Nietzsche
in the middle plays were not.[15] The phrase will be evocative for them
because of its suggestion of relief from the heat in the cool shade, and
because of its echo of Psalm 137, 'By the waters of Babylon we sat
down . . . we hanged our harps upon the willows'. In the convivial
atmosphere of Harry's party, Hugo cries, 'Ve vill eat birthday cake
and trink champagne beneath the villow trees' (p. 127). When the
society in Hope's bar begins to disintegrate, O'Neill demonstrates
Hugo's snobbery and the real divisions that exist between the roomers, in Hugo's substitution of 'hot-dogs' and 'free vine' for 'cake' and
'champagne' in his derisive promise of the happiness which the
revolution will bring to Rocky's group (p. 146). When the general
collapse is apparent, Hugo's cry, in response to Hickey's announcement that his wife has been murdered, 'Always there is blood beneath
the villow trees! I hate it and I am afraid' (p. 178) is fitting, but it also
expands out of the world of the play with something of the power of
poetic metaphor. At the end of the play, the audience's relief at the
return to life, is qualified by their recognition that the new optimism
of the roomers is founded on Hickey's lie, and that the festivity is a
means of pushing out of mind the blood beneath the willow trees and
the dark knowledge of their own futility to which Hickey had led the
roomers. The significance which has accrued to Hugo's cry makes its

emotional effect as the final line of the play terrifyingly complex. The characters can deafen themselves by pounding their glasses and chanting together, ' 'Tis cool beneath thy willow trees!', but the echo, 'If I forget thee, O Jerusalem . . .', persists in the ears of the audience.

The speech of each character, then, establishes his identity. It also contributes to the central action of the play. They interweave: figures in the same dance. And it is to their interweaving that we must now look.

The outline of the action can be given simply. In act I, everyone waits, dreams, exists. Hickey arrives. In act II, there is general uneasiness and the roomers veer between mutual affection and hostility. In the third act, real discord is apparent with each man concerned only for himself. The fourth act begins with each isolated from the rest, withdrawn into his own despair but, with Hickey's departure, they are able to revive their former existence. In the first act, each character's habitual mode of speech is established for the audience. Changes in that speech, in the second and third acts, convey the spiritual collapse and, at the end of the play, the revival is signalled by a return to the habitual modes. This is reductive, the dance has a liveliness we do not perceive in the notation for it, but it does demonstrate the pattern which underlies the action of *The Iceman Cometh*. The outline is filled out because of the interest O'Neill makes us feel in the lot of each of the seventeen characters. Even more important than any one individual, is how credible and how valuable he makes the community appear.

The roomers in Hope's bar have their idiosyncratic speech but they also have speech in common. We saw that Larry, in the opening exchange of the play, had some American slang mixed with his Standard English. Certain slang words and phrases are shared by all the roomers. This is most noticeable amongst the words they use for alcohol and the epithets with which they address each other. Larry is the 'old foolosopher', the 'old wise guy' and, when Hickey christens him 'old Cemetery', this name, too, is taken over by the others. Whiskey is 'the booze' or 'rot-gut'; they are 'the bums', 'the gang'. They also share the language of deception. All 'smoke' the same 'hop', all have 'pipedreams' and, although not slang, the word 'tomorrow' has special significance amongst the roomers. We saw that Larry took the word over from Rocky in the opening sequence, and thereafter it is uttered with affection by one after another character. This one will pay tomorrow, that one will go out, the other will find a job: they are all self-admitted members of the 'tomorrow movement'. The shared language helps us to realize not only that each man is living under a delusion, but that each deliberately reinforces the others' dreams in order to make his own dream more convincing. This collusion is the basis on which the society in Hope's bar is founded, and the shared language is, therefore, functional in communicating one of the central ideas of the play. Joe will invite everyone to the opening of his gambling house and stake them all, 'If you wins, dat's velvet for you. If you loses it don't count' (p. 52). The sympathetic hearing of which each is confident, gives him stature in his own eyes. Mosher and Macgloin flatter Harry, who glows and willingly supports them in return. Wetjoen and Lewis dream and squabble together about their native lands. Willie suggests Macgloin engage him as legal counsel and Macgloin joins in the fiction, replying, 'Sure I will, and it will make your reputation' (p. 55). The shared language shows how mutually supportive and also how artificial a construct the society is. The collapse, when it comes, seems more complete because O'Neill uses the same examples. The close friends are the first to insult each other: Joe boasts that he will return to the bar, a rich man, able to jeer at the roomers (p. 148), and Macgloin scoffs at the idea of retaining Willie's notoriously dishonest father's son as his lawyer (p. 159).

Lloyd and Warfel describe people who share particular items of language as a 'speech community' and make this point:

> People share speech habits in regard to matters about which they communicate with each other. Each one is thus a member of all the groups he customarily moves in, and an outsider in all the groups in which he does not. His language is a coherent system; it is all of a piece. He may not find it easy to tell which of his familiar expressions is generally known and used and which is current only in one place or among a few people.
>
> (*American English in its Cultural Setting*, p. 54)

But the audience is able to tell, because the community in Hope's bar is isolated and because O'Neill introduces an outsider who shares neither their language nor their mores. Parritt calls the roomers 'tanks' which is legitimate slang for drunkards but not a word used among Hope's roomers who, we have seen, are 'bums'. Parritt's presence helps us to realize that the deep structure of what the roomers would say is identical although transformed at the surface in response to the idiosyncrasies of each. Addressing Parritt early in the play, Larry says, 'The rules of the house are that drinks may be served at all hours' (p. 25). Hugo makes the same point, 'Don't be a fool! Loan me a dollar! Buy me a trink!' (p. 35), and Willie says, 'Yes,

Generous Stranger – I trust you're generous . . .' (p. 38). Lewis tries to
catch Harry unawares by saying suddenly, 'I will have a drink, now
you mention it, seeing it's so near your birthday' (p. 47); when Cora
appears with her day's takings she immediately treats everyone to
whiskey (p. 69), and Hickey, finally arriving, having greeted the
roomers with 'Hello, gang', firmly establishes himself as one of them,
whatever the subsequent action might bring, when he throws a roll of
dollars on the bar and cries, 'Do your duty, Brother Rocky. Bring on
the rat poison' (p. 72). Parritt, in contrast with Hickey, is a real outsider, who hides his roll. Joe dismisses him as a 'one-drink guy' (p. 27)
and Rocky calls him 'tightwad' which soon becomes the accepted
name for him amongst the roomers, ostracizing him more completely.
Parritt responds to the literal meaning of statements which are neutral
amongst the roomers: Hugo's denunciation, 'Got-tamned stool
pigeon!' and Willie's confidential whisper, 'No-one will ask you where
you got it', are rebuffed angrily by Parritt. This draws our attention to
what the roomers have actually said, indicates the nature of Parritt's
guilt, and also shows the emotional distance between Parritt, the
isolate, and the other characters. The text leads the audience to make
connections which allow the subtextual meanings to grow. When the
roomers listen tolerantly to each other's pipedreams, the clear-sighted
outsider cries, 'What a bunch of cuckoos!' But when, later, that
outsider can find no-one to listen to his self-justifying explanations of
his own behaviour, we are made aware of how necessary such self-
deceptions are. Parritt commits suicide partly because he exists in
isolation from other men and has no social context to give him belief in
himself. His is a minor role, but his presence in the play makes us
more conscious of its allegorical implications.

As I have half-suggested here, Parritt is also used as a distorting
mirror in which Hickey is reflected, and I will refer to this use again
later, and also to his function as a catalyst who stimulates the reaction
within Larry. In *Long Day's Journey Into Night*, as we will see in the
next chapter, the device of revealing a man's spiritual alienation by
giving him the slang of a community different from the one we see on
the stage, is of central importance in the characterization of Jamie
Tyrone.

The shared slang and the intrusive presence of Parritt convince us
that the roomers form a mutually supportive community but the
language is also functional in binding the audience to that community,
and making it matter. Just as we enjoyed listening to Harry Hope talk,
so we enjoy the atmosphere of Hope's bar. O'Neill deliberately took

time to achieve this end, as a note he wrote to Macgowan reveals. He wrote, explaining why he would not cut the play:

After all, what I've tried to write is a play where at the end you feel you know the souls of seventeen men and women who appear – and the women who don't appear – as well as if you'd read a play about each of them. I couldn't condense much without taking a lot of life from some of these people and reducing them to lay figures. You would find if I did not build up the complete picture of the group as it is in the first part – the atmosphere of the place, the humour and friendship and human warmth, the *deep inner contentment* of the bottom – you would not be so interested in these people and you would find the impact of what follows a lot less profoundly disturbing.

(13 December 1940)

We have seen that in the play, O'Neill explores the dramatic potential of American slang and of the variety of dialects found within America. In keeping with this, we find that, in creating the atmosphere of Hope's bar, he also draws on the traditional resources of American folk humour: jokes based on incongruities, outrageous anecdotes and tall stories.

Stamm has claimed that *Ah, Wilderness!* is the 'only one of [O'Neill's] plays in which we find humour'.[16] It *is* the only play which might be regarded as wholly optimistic, but that is not quite the same thing. As the audience's reaction to any stage production bears witness, *The Iceman Cometh* is at times extremely funny, as are all the late plays. The black depths it touches in its presentation of human life are blacker because of the contrast with our laughter at other moments of the play. Some of the most emotionally harrowing moments are those which come when jokes and tall stories no longer have power to lighten the mood.

In the first act, Joe retells Mose Porter's joke about distinguishing anarchists from socialists (p. 24), he tells the tale of Joe and de Chief (p. 46), Jimmy tells the tale of Jimmy and Dick Trumbull (p. 51), Mosher tells of The Swindling of Bessie (p. 56) and the tarts describe their Victories Over the Saps Outside (pp. 62, 68). Each is a dramatic narrative complete with dialogue and gesture in the tradition of Twain's 'Celebrated Jumping Frog'.[17] These tales, which become more elaborate as they make their way towards the punch-line, demand a particular kind of attention from the audience and so help to vary the pace of the play. One never follows immediately on another but is followed by a quick, broken action which involves several characters: after one, a new character enters, after another, a round of drinks is served, a friendly quarrel breaks out. Hickey's capacity as tale-teller, contributes to the enthusiasm with which he is awaited. 'What the hell you think happened to Hickey?', says Hope, 'Always got a million funny stories ... Remember that gag he always pulls about his wife and the Iceman? He'd make a cat laugh' (p. 59).

The audience warms to the characters as it laughs with them, although sometimes it is startled into awareness of its own complicity when a character draws an unexpected moral from the tale, to the delight of the others. When, for example, Mosher comments in high self-esteem after demonstrating his swindling technique, 'In those days I could have short-changed the Keeper of the Mint', or when Chuck caps Cora's outrageous tale of robbing a drunken sailor with, 'Ain't Uncle Sam a sap to trust guys like dat wid dough'. O'Neill contrives to demonstrate the unchanging, habitual life style of the community without letting the demonstration become tedious, because of the variation. The same process operates in the shorter jokes. Early in the play Rocky makes a straight comparison, 'Dis dump is like de morgue *wid all dese bums passed out*' (p. 18). When Margie and Pearl enter, the comparison is turned into a quip and the common slang is replaced by a more idiosyncratic phrase, 'Jees, Poil, it's de morgue *wid all de stiffs on deck*' (p. 60), and, when Cora enters soon afterwards, we are treated to a picturesque elaboration, 'Jees, de morgue *on a rainy Sunday night*' (p. 66).

Not unexpectedly, given what we have seen of his method already, O'Neill builds on this firm basis of habitual action. Because the Iceman joke has been relished beforehand, Hickey's failure to tell it as expected disturbs the audience's as well as the roomers' expectations, and marks the beginning of his assault on the community. We recognize that Mosher is pitting the whole society against Hickey when, at the end of act I, he temporarily restores the good humour of the community which Hickey's strange words have shattered, with a tall story about a doctor whose prescription for longevity was alcohol and no work. This draws the last burst of unstrained and unmalicious laughter until after Hickey's departure in act IV. The yarns told at the end of the play help to ensure, along with Harry's return to his robust slang, Lewis's repetition of his joke, and several similar idiosyncratic markers, that relief is one of the conflicting emotions felt by the audience at the end of the play.

But the humour also gives rise to other emotions. The audience is aware of a new harshness in the manner of the roomers towards each other in act II. Even if they do not realize that the tales have stopped, they know that the roomers are no longer as entertaining as they were.

Because of this, they probably share some of the resentment against
Hickey which they see displayed on stage and are more ready to be
partisan. Early in act II, they have heard the secret suspicions Larry
harbours about Hickey and, using a tension-raising device from the
old melodrama, O'Neill does not scotch these suspicions at once but
lets the suggestion grow in the auditors' minds. (O'Neill's relaxed
attitude to melodrama and his ability to make *conscious* use of its
devices is a further indication of how much more confident he is with
his form than in the early years.) When Larry suddenly turns on
Hickey, they are likely to be intrigued about how the question will
affect Hickey's equanimity. This sequence follows:

LARRY. I notice you didn't deny it when I asked you about the iceman. Did
this great revelation of the evil habit of dreaming about tomorrow come to you
after you found your wife was sick of you?
(*While he is speaking the faces of the gang have lighted up vindictively . . .*)
HOPE. Bejees, you've hit it, Larry! I've noticed he hasn't shown her picture
around this time!
MOSHER. He hasn't got it! The iceman took it away from him!
MARGIE. Jees, look at him! Who could blame her?
PEARL. She must be hard up to fall for an iceman!
CORA. Imagine a sap like him advisin' me and Chuck to get married!
CHUCK. Yeah! He done so good wid it!
JIMMY. At least I can say Marjorie chose an officer and a gentleman.
LEWIS. Come to look at you, Hickey, old chap, you've sprouted horns like a
bloody antelope!
WETJOEN. Pigger, py Gott! Like a water buffalo's!
WILLIE (*sings to his 'Sailor Lad' tune*).
  'Come up', she cried, 'my iceman lad,
  And you and I'll agree—'
(*They all join in a jeering chorus, rapping with knuckles or glasses on the table at the
indicated spot in the lyric.*)
  'And I'll show you the prettiest (*Rap, rap, rap.*)
  That ever you did see!'
(*A roar of derisive, dirty laughter . . .*)

                                                    (II, pp. 131–2)

The audience's attention is caught by the quickened pace of the
sequence, and they are likely to be propelled forward with the roomers
as each brief utterance is succeeded by the next. Each familiar voice
contributes its word, and one member of each of the familiar pairs,
Pearl and Margie, Cora and Chuck, Wetjoen and Lewis, elaborates
the remark made by the other. Together they compose a delighted and
malicious substitute for the bawdy tale Hickey failed to tell on arrival.
The sequence affects the audience with something of the excitement
and surprise we know in the real world when several people suddenly

find their minds working in concert, and the ideas accumulate to a climax in Willie's neat adaptation of his habitual song. The pattern of the sequence is broken when O'Neill directs that the whole company join in the chorus of the mocking song, supplementing the sound of their voices with loud rapping. The change gives the audience time to perceive themselves and so separates their response from that on the stage. The vision of a chanting group and a silent individual against whom they are all pitted is in itself frightening. O'Neill used it once before, in rather cruder form, to redirect the flow of empathy, when his stokers in *The Hairy Ape*, were made to chant 'Drink, don't think!' The three loud raps, a traditional call to attention in the theatre, also contribute to the emotional distancing of the audience, since they are likely to recall the striking suggestion made in act I, that Willie was knocking on the door of death. I have said that shared laughter creates an emotional tie between the participants, and O'Neill here utilizes the obverse of this, which is that one-sided laughter creates a barrier. It is unlikely that the audience will laugh with the roomers at the end of Willie's song and this moment, when enjoyment is not shared, establishes a doubt about the nature of the society in Hope's bar which will co-exist for the rest of the play with the positive response to that society which we have already noted. When Hickey replies to the mockery with the announcement that his wife is dead, the roomers are silenced and shamed and the audience are made more acutely aware of their own brief complicity in the persecution, and are, therefore, alerted to future ambiguities in the action.

A problem with this kind of commentary is that, because the play is broken into constituent parts, it appears more schematic than it is in performance when everything is closely interlocked and the audience receives a continuous flow of suggestions, echoes and images. The first distorted version of the iceman joke, for example, created here by the whole community is echoed by a second. Hickey's confession in the fourth act is, in effect, a longer, more chilling and more serious version of it. Part of the reason why we listen with such fascination to the confession, and it lasts for a quarter of an hour of performance time – an extraordinarily long time – is that we have been so well prepared, for the method, by the tales of the first act and, for its emotional impact, by this sequence at the end of act II. We will have already been alerted to the possibility that there is allegorical meaning in the references to 'the iceman' because the word appears in the title of the play and so we will take the association of the iceman with death from the juxtaposition of the roomers' taunting joke with Hickey's announcement. Alerted by sequences such as the one under discussion, the frequent references to death in the play begin to press in upon us. At first, we have been scarcely more conscious of the death imagery in the jokes and slang of the roomers than we are of the latent metaphor in everyday words. 'Kill a pint'; 'It's a dead cinch'; 'When I don't want a drink, you call the morgue'; 'What is this, a funeral?' – we don't count off such expressions as they occur, nor do we anxiously seek out their meanings, but, by their very frequency, they serve to provide a context within which the more directly relevant statements: 'Would that Hickey or Death would come'; 'Death was the Iceman Hickey called to his home', reverberate. As the community in Hope's bar crumbles, we find ourselves convinced by the cold touch Hickey has introduced there and we recognize it as the touch not of physical but of spiritual death.[18]

A comparison between the first and final drafts of this sequence demonstrates how the play took on significance in the writing. The scene was mapped out in the scenario in this way.

Larry (suddenly). How's your wife, Hickey? – Hickey (startled). What makes you ask about her? Larry (with amused carelessness). You always used to talk about her, show photo – H. Never when I was sober. But thank you for enquiring. Evelyn is taking a long, much deserved rest. – Margie, A vacation, you mean, – with the iceman? – H. (with a strange smile). Yes, I think you might say she is in the arms of the iceman. I'm sorry to have to tell you that my dear wife is dead. At once, all except Larry full of contrition.

(p. 11)

As originally conceived, only one character besides Larry contributed. There is no suggestion in the scenario of a change in tempo, nor of the malice of the final text. There is nothing to implicate the audience. Hickey's metaphorical play on the word 'iceman' at this juncture allows a much less subtle subsequent development than the juxtaposition later adopted by O'Neill. Similarly, it was originally intended that the tension at the end of act I should be relaxed not by Mosher's somewhat inconsequential tall story, but by all the roomers joining in with Hugo's cry ('Scenario', p. 7). Had this been retained, the final chant of the play would have been a direct echo of it and would therefore have recalled a moment of relief. This would have given the play something of the mechanical regularity of the early plays. In writing, the pattern lost such easy symmetry. By transferring the first use of voices in chorus to act II and using the device in the menacing way it is used, O'Neill makes the final chant echo an emotionally ambivalent rather than an optimistic moment of the play. The ending of the play is correspondingly more complex as a result.

Before I leave *The Iceman Cometh* I want to comment on the role of language in the characterization of Larry Slade who, as I have suggested, is a more rounded character than the others and, as such, gives a foretaste of the characterization in *Long Day's Journey Into Night*. I may seem, in leaving the discussion of the other characters where I have, to have given some of them, particularly Hickey, short shrift, but I think that once the method is clear, it is readily applicable to each of the characterizations. Although Hickey's role is much the largest in the play, his language parallels that of the other figures. His presence causes their disintegration but, at a later stage of the play, he disintegrates in just the way they have done. What strikes us most forcibly about his speech, and this is consistent throughout the play, is the contrast between its restlessness and the peace he preaches. The language of efficient salesmanship sits as ill with his message as it does when associated with the Christian message in some brands of evangelical religion, as O'Neill himself reminds us in Hickey's references to his preacher father (see act IV, p. 197). The essential point made by his language is that he is one with the roomers.

At one level Larry, too, is one with the roomers and elements in the shared language of the bar which apply directly to him, help to make his presence there credible. I described the principal idiosyncrasies of Larry's speech in my discussion of the opening scene of the play, and will just add to that a note about his Irishness since, although not noticeable there, we do become aware of it in other parts of the play and its use foreshadows that in *Long Day's Journey Into Night*. (See my discussion of Irish dialect, Appendix 2.) The Irish dialect marker, 'sure' used to begin a sentence, is occasionally added to Larry's Standard English. It is used entirely to signal light banter, and we are left in no doubt that it is deliberately assumed by Larry since, when he flatters Pearl and Margie with 'Sure, I love every hair of your heads, my great big beautiful baby dolls', Pearl comments, 'De old Irish bunk, huh?' (p. 94–5). But without making an obvious point of Larry's Irishness, O'Neill flavours his speech and suggests the fluency of Irish English. This effect seems to derive from the choice of one kind of word order rather than another. He forms questions, for example, by means of subject/predicator inversion: 'Isn't a pipe dream of yesterday a touching thing?', 'Didn't I tell you he'd brought death with him?' rather than by the addition of a clause: 'I told you

he'd brought death with him, didn't I?' Either form is equally acceptable in Standard English, but the former is used far more frequently
by Larry. In this sentence pattern, the stressed question word leads us
into the sentence and allows the significant word to come in the rising
cadence at the end of the sentence. It lends itself more readily to being
spoken with an 'Irish lilt'. A similar pattern of stress and cadence
derives from Larry's frequent use of introductory phrases, 'Be God
...', 'By all accounts ...', 'What the hell ...'

Larry stands in a different relation to the audience from the other
figures, because in the early part of the play he acts as a narrator. He is
positioned at the side of the stage, from where he describes the bar and
its inhabitants to the outsider, Parritt. In the original plan for the play,
Larry was not affected by Hickey's mission but was to be an observer
of it. In some notes dated June 1939, we find him described in this
way: 'Terry[19] – who sees and is articulate about real meaning of what is
going on – who regrets they can't leave themselves alone – can't
forgive themselves for not being what they are not.' As we have seen,
the play, born out of O'Neill's nostalgia, was much slighter and more
benign in its original conception, than in its final form. No internal
conflict is stirred in Larry in the scenario by the presence of Potter
[Parritt] and he bears no responsibility for the younger man's suicide,
which comes as a direct response, not to him but to the typical cry
from Hap [Hugo], 'Traitor to the gallows!' Larry merely comments,
'Justice has taken its course', before joining the other roomers in their
festivity, with the words, 'out of great drunkenness, comes great
wisdom'. The character grew in the writing, although the role of
narrator, retained from the original conception, helps to distance
Larry and prevents our concern with his private struggle from becoming the central issue.

The Larry of the play differs from the other roomers in that we seem
to see more fully into his consciousness. This impression derives in
part from the tenor of his speech. So many of his utterances are
warnings to the others, to distinguish poison from 'the real McCoy' (p.
81), to drink themselves oblivious of Hickey, that he seems to take
responsibility for their fate. He wrestles with Hickey on their behalf,
'Leave Hugo be ... Have you no decency or pity?' (p. 102), and they
in their turn admit their distress to him, 'It's been hell in that damned
room, Larry' (p. 107), 'I'm glad you're here, Larry' (p. 108). The
result is that, when we see their individual torment, we are also aware
of Larry, sitting at the side of the stage, sharing their suffering. But
the image of Larry is complicated by the presence of Parritt. Parritt is

increasingly identified with Larry, since he addresses his words almost entirely to the old anarchist. He addresses Larry familiarly from the outset, although Larry never uses his name in return, and the disparity alerts us to Larry's attempt to hide. Parritt is a reflection of some aspects of Hickey and frequently is used to relay Hickey's words to Larry with a taunting, 'What did he mean by that, Larry?', 'What do you say to that, Larry?' (p. 109). His presence on the stage, serves to project Larry's internal conflict. Under pressure from Parritt, Larry becomes terse and avoids direct replies. When he becomes almost completely silent in act IV, Parritt's voice, mocking, challenging, pleading, keeps Larry's struggle in the audience's mind and, at the tensest moment of Hickey's confession, there, too, is Parritt, whispering his confession, for Larry's ear alone.

The state of Larry's consciousness is revealed also through the very structure of his speech. His style becomes plainer when he is disturbed, and his syntax is organized to convey the unconscious processes of his thought. In the example here, I have separated the sentences and italicized certain words in order to demonstrate this point more clearly:

It's nothing to me what happened to him.
But I have a feeling he's dying to tell us, inside him, and yet he's *afraid*.
He's like that damned kid.
It's strange the queer way he seems to recognize him.
If he's *afraid*, it explains why he's off booze.
Like that damned kid again.
Afraid if he got drunk, he'd tell –   (II, p. 98)

As the recurrent adjective moves to the beginning of the sentence, the idea of fear is expressed first as an after-thought, then as a supposition and, finally, as a positive statement. This implies a preoccupation with Hickey on Larry's part which contradicts his first statement, 'It's nothing to me ...' The repetition of the reference to the 'kid', shows in a similar way, how dark a shadow Parritt's presence has cast upon his mind. Larry scarcely participates in the opening exchange of act IV, although he has figured prominently in parallel sequences of earlier acts. What he does say confirms the impression his silence gives, of his extreme anxiety. His replies to the demands of other characters are all denials, 'No, it doesn't look good ...', 'I don't think anything ...', 'Stop shoving your rotten soul in my lap'. After a hopeless attempt to prevent Hickey's confession, he does not speak again until after Hickey has gone. The contrast with his former readiness to comment on any eventuality draws our attention to him and, when his suffering finally spills over into words, we feel it the more fiercely because the words Parritt has begged from him are scarcely coherent, 'Go! Get the hell out of life! God damn you, before I choke it out of you! Go up –!' (p. 213). The two oaths in quick succession show how remote his present speech is from his earlier care and delight in elaboration, and the alliteration here does not decorate but serves to increase the choked staccato effect of the exclamations. The self-contradictory nature of Larry's last speech (p. 222) reveals his final position more fully than does the meaning of the individual words. His speech has become what Blackmur has called 'the language of gesture'.[20]

The verbal gesturing, indeed, interacts with and draws meaning from the physical gesture and the stage picture. The tables and chairs in Hope's bar have been slightly redistributed between acts I and IV, as O'Neill's own sketches for the stage plan (illustration 3) make clear. The redistribution marks the difference between the easy, aimless atmosphere in the bar at the opening of the play, and the roomers' clustering together for support at the end. First Hickey leaves his position at the middle of the stage (see sketch b in illustration 3), then Parritt exits from the table at Left Front, so that there is an imbalance in the distribution of characters on the stage. The imbalance is emphasized when Hugo, in the last minutes of the play, moves across to join the other roomers and, in doing so, leaves Larry isolated in his corner of the stage.

The fact that Larry is revealed so fully does not contradict the logic of the play since his illusion is ontological and, of necessity, when Hickey strikes at it, he strikes at Larry's very mode of thought. But it does place Larry in a special relationship to the audience and makes his role a vital one in their perception of the action. When he continues to sit absolutely still and apart during the sequence in which the roomers reconstitute their lives he, the only one to have accepted the consequences of Hickey's message, seems to absorb into himself all their former despair. He becomes the spectre at the feast, the image of everyone's reality.

José Quintero, who produced the first major revival of the play, in 1956, said of it:

My approach in directing *The Iceman Cometh* was different from that used in any play I had ever done. It had to be for this was not built as an orthodox play. It resembles a complex musical form, with themes repeating themselves with slight variation, as melodies do in a symphony ... My work was somewhat like that of an orchestra conductor, emphasising rhythms, being constantly

a

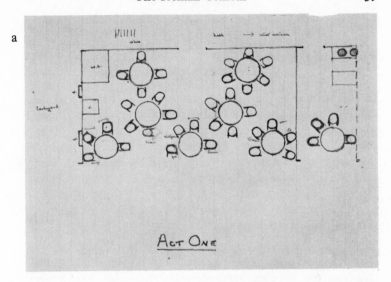

b

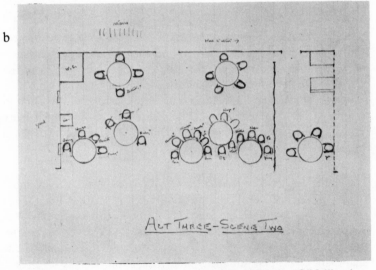

3. *The Iceman Cometh*: stage plans sketched by O'Neill. (O'Neill subsequently relabelled act III. ii, act IV.)

aware of changing tempos; every character advanced a different theme. The paradox was that for the first time as a director, I began to understand the meaning of precision in drama – and it took a play four and one half hours long to teach me, a play often criticized as rambling and overwritten.

('Postscript to a Journey', *Theatre Arts*, XLI, p. 88)

In contrasting the play with 'orthodox plays', I think Quintero is really defining *The Iceman Cometh* as major dramatic writing. The words with which he describes his discovery about the form of the play could be applied equally to any play which convinces the audience of the reality of its world and which draws an emotionally complex response from them. One might compare with his account, Peacock's discussion of 'intertexture' in *The Art of the Drama* (pp. 166–7), Styan's commentary on the organization of the plays of Chekhov,[21] or this description by Clemen, of Shakespeare's mature plays:

Again and again, when we are watching or reading attentively, a later act or scene, we are reminded of a phrase or an image or even of a situation in the earlier parts of the play. There are numerous echoes, correspondences, variations and repetitions in each of the tragedies which help to bind the parts of the play together and make it a living organism of which all the parts are interrelated.   (*Shakespeare's Dramatic Art*, p. 9)

An attempt has been made in this examination of *The Iceman Cometh* to retain the experience we have in performance of its presence as a living organism and to show that this experience derives from the precision and flexibility of the language. It does not exist in spite of it. I hope the discussion has demonstrated the meaning of my claim in chapter 4 that the language of this play, although not much more lyrical, euphonious or metaphorical than that of the middle plays, is dramatic.

The holograph of *The Iceman Cometh* is dated June to November 1939. Although O'Neill did not begin the first draft of *Long Day's Journey Into Night* until the following summer, there is amongst his notes a character list for the play, dated June, and a six-page scenario, dated, July 1939, a page of which is reproduced in illustration 4. The final shape of the play and many of its most telling details are already evident in the scenario, as three brief extracts will demonstrate:

1. 'Sneaking one, eh?' – 'I feel lousy and he won't miss one' – 'See if he's still talking by the hedge' Y.S. goes to window – 'Yes' – E.S. takes one puts water in bottle to line.

(Act II, see text II, i, pp. 46–7)

4. *Long Day's Journey Into Night*: page of O'Neill's scenario

2. Mother enters. E.S. bitter – stares at her – makes meaning remark. Y.S. angry. 'Shut up' E.S. apologises – then bitter again stares at her, then says to his brother you can see what I was afraid of is true – Y.S. mad but frightened, 'It's a lie' Mother guilty and strange – 'I don't know what you mean. I took a nap. I feel so much better' – 'So I see'

(Act II, see text II, i, pp. 52–5)

3. E.S. .... quotes Kipling mockingly, 'If I were hanged on the highest hill I know whose love would follow me still, Mother of mine' – Y.S. 'Stop it, damn you. Leave her alone.' – E.S. Don't worry, she's safe, you can't touch her now' – Mother goes round looking vaguely 'Something I lost a long time ago. What is it?'

(Act V, see text IV, pp. 142; 152)

In the play itself, the first extract is developed into an incident which reveals the closeness of the family relationships: a habit is shared, a trick enjoyed, a reference to a third, unnamed character immediately understood. The second extract makes it evident that, already in the scenario, O'Neill planned to darken the mood by making one character deny the response looked for by another. And the third extract shows that he planned, too, to make the same kind of refusal appear in a crueller and more tangled form in the final act. The bitterness of the elder son, the miserable and clumsy protectiveness of the younger and the terrifying dissociation of the mother from both, which we find projected so painfully in the play, are all indicated here. The use of quotation, which will be a central device in the play, is also beginning to take shape. Such close relationship between scenario and final text, makes it evident that, although the second play was written some time after the first, *Long Day's Journey Into Night* was present in O'Neill's consciousness in something remarkably close to its final form throughout the writing of *The Iceman Cometh*. This would help to explain why the two plays complement each other in quite the way they do.

6

Significant form:
Long Day's Journey Into Night

Both *The Iceman Cometh* and *Long Day's Journey Into Night* are set in 1912, and present a group of people isolated together from the world. But they are antithetical in several ways. One takes place in a New York City bar, the other in a family home in a New England small town. In the one play, a large group of men of widely different backgrounds are met in a society constructed by them to meet their needs and O'Neill explores their relationship to each other and to that society, letting us glimpse more intimate personal relationships through the eyes of only one of the participants. In the other play, the scale of the action is narrowed to just such intimate relationships. The four characters belong to a nuclear family and O'Neill explores the nature of their bondage to it and to each other. For all its breadth, *The Iceman Cometh* is the less complex of the two plays in construction and emotional effect. The images it projects disturb the audience and make them sharply aware of contradictions normally thrust aside in the activity of daily living. Those of *Long Day's Journey Into Night* take the audience into their very selves. In both plays, the audience are made conscious that chaos and isolation lie threateningly behind the action but, whereas in *The Iceman Cometh* the character who perceives this most fully is continually moved to the periphery of the action, all four characters in *Long Day's Journey Into Night* move steadily closer to articulation of such knowledge.

The multiplicity of *The Iceman Cometh*, the impression we have of there being many changes and happenings to take into account, the theatrical zest of the piece, derive from the astonishing range of character projected. In *Long Day's Journey Into Night*, there are four major characters, where in the earlier play there were seventeen. Whatever variety or intensity, sadness or humour the play has must come from the dialogue and gesture of these four. My purpose in this chapter is to consider how it does so.

The language offers an immediate measure of the change in focus between *The Iceman Cometh* and *Long Day's Journey Into Night*. The bold range of national and class dialect of the earlier play is not found in the later, where all four characters speak Standard American English. Their speech is no less clearly differentiated than in the earlier play but the process of recognition here is a slower one. The audience gradually becomes attuned, through shifts in the syntactic and lexical arrangement of the dialogue and through recurrent topics of conversation, to the various registers which exist within the speech of each character.[1] The smaller number of characters and the more gradual method of projecting them, allow O'Neill to probe behind the idiosyncratic surface and explore the varying and even conflicting elements of individual identity. The method is similar to that used in presenting Larry Slade but is developed in a more intensive way. Whereas the old anarchist sat alone at the edge of the stage, the characters here are all fully embroiled in the action and continually interact with each other. When new information causes us to alter our assumptions about a character then our idea of his relationship with each of the other characters is altered, too.

The conventions associated with drama help to shape the audience's acceptance of the illusion of the reality of the stage world. Compared with people in life, the characters of *The Iceman Cometh* are caricatures and yet, as we have seen, they have an extraordinary vitality during the play. In his essay on Tourneur, Eliot pointed out the necessity of characters being 'real in relation to each other' if the conventions are to operate and said:

[Tourneur's characters] may be distortions, grotesques, almost childish caricatures of humanity, but they are all distorted to scale. Hence the whole action, from their appearance to their ending, 'no common action' indeed, has its own self-subsistent reality.

(*Elizabethan Dramatists*, pp. 110–11)

Having noted the importance of internal consistency, we must also acknowledge that there are plays whose action and emotion seem more searingly close to ourselves than is usual, whose characters, as Eliot says elsewhere of Shakespeare's figures, 'represent a more complex tissue of feelings and desires as well as a more supple, a more susceptible temperament' than we normally find in plays.[2] In the common shorthand, such figures are labelled 'fully rounded' or 'three dimensional'.[3] But whilst such characters have been readily enough identified, there have been few attempts to discover how they are created in the dialogue.

Many commentators, attributing the roundedness of the characters of *Long Day's Journey Into Night* to the autobiographical origins of the play, have been concerned to describe O'Neill's private relationships in the period in which the play is set.[4] But this is to slide away from the crucial questions about how the play works, since autobiographical writing is not, *per se*, binding on its audience. Although the personal nature of the material may well quicken the writer's imagination, it can only speak to the audience when it has been shaped by that imagination into an artistic form with its own unity, apart from the life.[5]

If the play is an emotionally harrowing experience, it is so because of the stage characters and the stage action. However lifelike they seem, characters have their existence only in relation to the stage action, and exist in their particular form because of the way the writer has selected and organized words and gestures. The dramatist writes dialogue, not speech, and presents not the O'Neills, who are people, but the Tyrones, who are characters.

In the wake of the various psychological and sociological descriptions of personality of the last hundred years, have come a succession of attacks on the idea of richly delineated, autonomous characters in fiction by writers who claim that these belie reality with their false coherence.[6] In the Preface to *Lady Julie*, in one of the earliest of such statements, Strindberg argued that if the dramatist is to reveal ourselves to ourselves he must do so through figures that are characterless since, far from being the self-consistent wholes generally portrayed on the stage, people are unpredictable, 'vacillating', 'riven asunder'. His own characters he described as being:

conglomerations from past and present stages of civilization; they are excerpts from books and newspapers, scraps of humanity, pieces torn from festive garments which have become rags – just as the soul itself is a piece of patchwork. Besides this, I have provided a little evolutionary history in making the weaker repeat phrases stolen from the stronger, and in making my souls borrow 'ideas' – suggestions, as they are called, from one another.

(trans. C. D. Locock, *International Modern Plays* (Everyman), p. 9)

But such is the force of the convention that we assimilate and order the fragmentary information and create for ourselves a clear idea of the three individuals, Julie, Jean and Kristen, who appear on the stage. The audience draws from the text the kind of characterization that the pattern of set, plot and coherent dialogue leads it to expect. It is only when Strindberg robs us of these expectations by positing the play as a dream and not a mimesis of life, in the Chamber plays and *To*

Damascus, that the audience finds itself unable to naturalize the text in this way.

O'Neill seems to have shared Strindberg's theory of human personality but, in writing the play, takes the audience's ordering impulse as his starting point. He develops an idiosyncratic language pattern for each character, thus differentiating them and giving each an identity. He then proceeds to vary and occasionally break these patterns so that each speaks with several different and even conflicting voices. Each appears many-faceted, an unpredictable amalgam and yet, at any given moment, still himself, distinct from any other figure on the stage.

The method of *Long Day's Journey Into Night*, like that of *The Iceman Cometh* was prefigured in a less complex way in the early plays. As we saw in chapter 3, Jim Harris' low-colloquial speech, in *All God's Chillun Got Wings*, was modified towards Standard by stages throughout the play. At the realistic level, his growing articulacy indicated his educational progress and marked the passing of time whilst, at the symbolic level, it signalled his spiritual growth. In *Desire Under the Elms*, O'Neill attempted something rather more complicated. Ephraim's New England low-colloquial was coloured by an idiosyncratic use of biblical vocabulary and syntax which became more evident when he was roused by anger or lust. Filtered into the speech of other characters, particularly at moments when they sought to defy Ephraim, such religious language revealed the influence of the old man on them. So, James Tyrone's speech mode in *Long Day's Journey Into Night* varies according to his emotional state and, at times, both sons echo his manner. Mary Tyrone's utterance is closer to the model of Jim Harris in that her speech changes under the influence of the drug she takes and is actually different from act to act. Changes in her speech serve to mark the passage of time too although, here, the movement is not from present to future, but from present to remembered past. Jamie uses two distinct and conflicting registers, one of which is usually consciously adopted but sometimes seems to take demonic possession, whilst Edmund, still a young man with several paths open to him, has a range of voices some directly imitative of Jamie or of the writers he admires, but none so distinct as those of the other members of the family. To see how these patterns evolve on the stage, creating as they do the feeling and meaning of the play, I shall first investigate the consistencies, shifts and surprises of the dialogue through which each of the four characters is projected.

The dramatic effectiveness of supposedly neutral dialogue: the four
characters

When he creates a stage presence for his characters, O'Neill is conscious of the effect of their speech and of their physical being. In the
stage directions, he notes not only costume and appearance, but
bearing and quality of voice. Tyrone

> is sixty-five but looks ten years younger ... his bearing ... has a soldierly
> quality of head up, chest out, stomach in, shoulders squared ... a big, finely
> shaped head ... His voice is remarkably fine, resonant and flexible ... There
> is a lot of solid earthy peasant in him.
>
> (p. 11)

and the description is complemented by a speech mode that is equally
robust and straightforward.

The majority of Tyrone's sentences fall into the subject–verb–
complement pattern of the normal English sentence. The subject is
usually a personal pronoun and only rarely a nominal phrase or clause.
The sentences are usually simple or co-ordinating and there are few
adjuncts. When O'Neill wants to intensify Tyrone's speech he does so
by adding one or two new elements or by concentrating the habitual
syntax and making it strikingly regular. In act IV, for example, when
Tyrone in one of the crucial speeches of the play confesses to Edmund
that he has betrayed his dreams for financial security, his self-
searching is conveyed by just such grammatical intensification:

> I've never admitted this to anyone before ... *That God-damned play* I bought
> for a song and made such a great success in – a great money success – *it* ruined
> me with its promise of an easy fortune. I didn't want to do anything else, and
> by the time I woke up to the fact I'd become a slave to the damned thing and
> did try other plays it was too late. They had identified me with that one part,
> and didn't want me in anything else. They were right, too. I'd lost the great
> talent I once had through years of easy repetition, never learning a new part,
> never really working hard. Thirty-five to forty thousand dollars net profit a
> season like snapping your fingers! It was too great a temptation. Yet before I
> bought the damned thing I was considered one of the three or four young
> actors with the greatest artistic promise in America. I'd worked like hell. I'd
> left a good job as a machinist to take supers' parts because I loved the theatre. I
> was wild with ambition. I read all the plays ever written. I studied Shakes-
> peare as you'd study the Bible. I educated myself. I got rid of an Irish Brogue
> you could cut with a knife. I loved Shakespeare. I would have acted in any of
> his plays for nothing, for the joy of being alive in his great poetry. And I acted
> well in him. I felt inspired by him. I could have been a great Shakespearian
> actor if I'd kept on. I know that!
>
> (pp. 130–1, my italics)

The confession begins with a more complicated construction than is usual in Tyrone's speech. The subject is not a simple noun ('The play') but is a nominal group ('That God-damned play ...') which contains besides adjectives and nouns, two post modifying clauses ('[which'] I bought ...' and '[which I] made such a ...'. It is disjoined from its verb and placed in apposition to the pronoun, 'it'. Randolph Quirk has noted that this type of construction is common in spoken English where it is used for emphasis and clarity[7] and, certainly, the unusually complicated syntax here, does suggest Tyrone's anxiety to communicate a difficult insight into himself as accurately as possible. The impression is reinforced by Tyrone's use of parenthetical intensifiers, 'They were right, too'; 'I know that', and, later in the speech, 'And it was true'; 'Ask her what I was like in those days'. Tyrone's speech seems to become more animated when he recalls the crucial period in his past. His normally preferred construction becomes completely dominant, 'I read ... I studied ... I educated ... I got rid of ... I loved ...', and the succession of short parallel sentences makes the distant experience seem close, until the simple past tense gives way to the hypothetical past tense in two conditional clauses, 'I *would* have acted ... for nothing ... I *could* have been ... a great Shakespearean actor', reminding us that all the effort and devotion was forfeit and pushing the events back into the distant past.

Syntax is similarly important in structuring our response to the words of the other characters. O'Neill seems to take us into Jamie's mind in the course of his confession in act IV. After a sequence of boisterous camaraderie, Jamie introduces a more serious note into the conversation:

Nix, Kid! You listen! Did it on purpose to make a bum of you. Or part of me did. A big part. That part that's been dead so long. That hates life. My putting you wise so you'd learn from my mistakes. Believed that myself at times, but it's a fake. *Made* my mistakes look good. *Made* getting drunk romantic. *Made* whores fascinating vampires instead of poor, stupid, diseased slobs they really are. *Made* fun of work as a sucker's game. Never wanted you succeed and make me look even worse by comparison. Wanted you to fail. Always jealous of you. Mama's baby, Papa's pet! (*He stares at Edmund with increasing enmity.*) And it was your being born that started Mama on dope. I know that's not your fault, but all the same, God damn you, I can't help hating your guts–!

(p. 146, my italics)

The parataxis at the beginning has much the same function as the complicated syntax at the opening of Tyrone's speech. Jamie is reaching around for his meaning. Then, in a succession of parallel sentences beginning 'Made ...', we are presented with a catalogue of Jamie's self-blame until, at the end of the passage, the self-blame is suddenly replaced by accusation. The shift in thought is marked by the significantly childish insult, 'Mama's baby, Papa's pet!', after which we have the impression of a deeper, darker impulse overcoming the original goodwill of the confession. A syntactical shift underlines the change, signalling that we have moved to a different level of Jamie's consciousness. He himself says later that he had not meant to tell 'that last stuff', adding 'Don't know what made me'. Obviously, we do not respond to the grammar at a conscious level noting, 'Ah, parataxis! Ah, a syntactical shift!', but we can see how instrumental the syntactical shift is if we try to rewrite the passage substituting a continuation of the elliptical pattern of the earlier part of the speech for the complete sentences with which the passage concludes in O'Neill's text. If we read, for example, 'Wanted you to fail. Always jealous of you. Resented your being born. Said started Mama on dope. Know not your fault, but can't help hating you', we find that the change from self-blame to self-justification is lost and, with it, the impression the last part of the passage gives of suppressed thoughts spilling over into speech. In both confessions, O'Neill communicates the secret emotion of his characters through his structuring of their speech. The audience is made to feel something about the characters without being conscious of the machinery that shapes their feeling.

Tyrone is given an alternative register of speech, which is used when he is hurt, embarrassed or angry, and acts as a kind of subliminal preparation for his confession. Although he is given particularly resonant quotations from Shakespeare to roll around the theatre with his fine and flexible voice, his alternative register is not the prose of Shakespearean drama but that of the melodramatic stage. In this mode, colourful nominal phrases replace the pronouns – Shaughnessey, for example, is 'that blackguard' – and a string of synonymous verbs or a succession of imperatives replace his normal verb pattern. In act II, for example, Tyrone berates Jamie:

You ought to be kicked out in the gutter! But if I did it, you know damn well who'd weep and plead for you, and excuse you and complain till I let you come back.

(p. 65)

On such occasions, he adopts not only the speech structure but the attitudes of melodrama. The register is made to appear more flamboyant because it is used most frequently in argument with Jamie, whose speech on such occasions is terse.

O'Neill uses the histrionic side of Tyrone to bring vigour and variety to the play's surface. We enjoy Tyrone's delight in recitation and fine words and relish his flourishing gestures when we see them or hear them described, as for instance by Mary who describes the stage bow she sees him direct towards haughty neighbours passing in their smart car. In act IV, O'Neill produces a brilliant *coup de théâtre*. A squabble between Tyrone and Edmund, developed from a petty clash of wills over whether the lights should be turned off or not, becomes bitter when Edmund taunts his father with his meanness and bigotry. The angry tirade with which Tyrone replies is stilled on his recollecting his son's illness and, in one of those moments of sudden quiet which O'Neill creates from time to time between the members of this family, Edmund, ashamed, gets up to turn out the lights. He is forestalled by his father whose anger is replaced by an equally overstated self-pity, accompanied by a magnificent gesture:

Let it burn! (*He stands up abruptly – and a bit drunkenly – and begins turning on the three bulbs in the chandelier, with a childish, bitterly dramatic self-pity.*) We'll have them all on! Let them burn! To hell with them! The poorhouse is the end of the road, and it might as well be sooner as later! (*He finishes turning on the lights.*)

(p. 111)

The whole quarrel has collapsed into broad comedy.

But O'Neill does not create such a dramatic moment without integrating it into the structure of the play. Drinking and brooding over Mary, occasionally returning to their card game, the two men again become hostile when Edmund accuses his father of planning to send him to a cheap sanatorium in order not to waste money on attempting to cure a fatal disease. The vicious aspect of Tyrone's meanness is felt more sharply because the audience has enjoyed its comic aspect. This cruel exchange exposes a rawer level of emotion and, in order to make the return from this extreme position, O'Neill must present us with something as intense in a positive instead of a negative way. It is here that he introduces Tyrone's confession. When Tyrone concludes with the wry inquiry, 'What the hell was it I wanted to buy, I wonder?' (p. 132), his claim on our sympathy has been re-established. But, suddenly, the initial obstinacy and the splendid gesture are recalled and the audience are shifted back to the humour of the beginning of the sequence, when Tyrone says:

The glare from those extra lights hurts my eyes. You don't mind if I turn them out do you? We don't need them, and there's no use making the Electric Company rich.

(p. 132)

The conflict between our recognition of Tyrone's uncertainty and broken dream and our sense of the ridiculous ensures that our response to James Tyrone will remain ambivalent. If we recall the melodramatic stage clichés which swamped O'Neill's writing at the beginning of his career when he attempted to convey strong emotion (see the discussion of *Warnings* p. 64, above) and compare the strategic use to which they are put here, we have some measure of the kind of control O'Neill is exerting.

O'Neill uses contrast between the melodramatic and the plain-speaking register, to create an impression of heartfelt sincerity in Tyrone in sentences which, out of context, would seem neutral enough. He sometimes does this by a direct juxtaposition as in this utterance, for example, when the register of Tyrone's attempt to comfort Edmund in the first part contrasts with that in his apos-trophizing of Jamie in the second part:

don't take it too much to heart, lad. He loves to exaggerate the worst of himself when he's drunk. He's devoted to you. It's the one good thing left in him. (*He looks down on Jamie with a bitter sadness.*) A sweet spectacle for me! My first born, who I hoped would bear my name in honour and dignity, who showed such brilliant promise!

(p. 148)

At other times, our recognition of what Mary's surrender to the drug means to the family is sharpened because words fail the usually fluent Tyrone. In act II i, when it is apparent that Mary has yielded to the drug, Tyrone remains slumped and silent (pp. 58-9). One of the most moving moments of the play comes later when Tyrone simply cries out his wife's name, and then adds a brief appeal, 'For the love of God, for my sake and the boys' sake and your own, won't you stop now?' (p. 73). The actor in the theatre uttering the cry, can hardly fail to make use of the long gliding dipthong in the final word, drawing on the very sound of the word to express the pain. Under pressure of strong emotion we may, as Yeats has suggested, be capable only of looking 'silently into the fireplace'[8] but, if the appropriate context has been created, those will be speaking silences.

At the beginning of the play, O'Neill emphasizes how normal the manner and matter of Mary Tyrone's speech is. She has the preoccu-pations and the slang of polite middle class America ('I've gotten too fat, you mean. I really ought to reduce'; 'As soon as your head touches the pillow'; 'I do feel out of sorts'; 'You must have gotten out of the wrong side of the bed this morning'). She is self-possessed, rarely speaking except to pacify. In the first draft of the play, O'Neill made Mary's speech tense and erratic at the outset, but he later cut the explicit signals of her anxiety so that now the implication that she is not as calm as she might appear filters in only slowly and does so primarily through gesture – a hand patting hair, fingers drumming on the table top, and through two quickly curtailed outbursts. A hardly stated impression of resentment is conveyed through a series of comments which, individually, would appear as light teasing of Tyrone but, taken together, form a complaint. The audience are alerted to her unease by the conversation between Jamie and Tyrone (p. 25–34) during Mary's first absence and, from this point onwards, have a new sensitivity to the implications of her utterance. At her return, Mary replies to Jamie's comment that Hardy is not a good doctor:

Oh. No, I wouldn't say he was either. (*Changing the subject – forcing a smile.*) That Bridget! I thought I'd never get away. She told me all about her second cousin on the police force in St Louis. (*Then with nervous irritation.*) Well, if you're going to work on the hedge why don't you go? (*Hastily.*) I mean, take advantage of the sunshine before the fog comes back. (*Strangely, as if talking aloud to herself.*) Because I know it will. (*Suddenly she is self-consciously aware that they are both staring fixedly at her – flurriedly, raising her hands.*) Or I should say, the rheumatism in my hands knows. It's a better weather prophet than you are, James. (*She stares at her hands with fascinated repulsion.*) Ugh! How ugly they are! Who'd ever believe they were once beautiful.   (p. 35)

In such a speech, O'Neill rewards the expectations he has created and stimulates further concentration. We miss Mary's earlier coherence. The individual sentences are neutral enough, what makes them striking is their erratic combination. She seems to respond to some private significance in her seemingly commonplace remarks which she hastens to qualify. Each sentence begins with a conjunction or a parenthetical phrase, as though she were beginning mid-sentence. The distracted movement of her speech is ominous, following the men's discussion, and so is the harshness with which she rebuffs Jamie's attempt to reassure her at the end of the scene (p. 36).

Towards the end of the first act, therefore, Mary's probable return to the drug is signalled by the shape of her speech. In the subsequent acts, the fragmentation of her personality under the drug is also imaged in the structure of her speech. In acts II and III, O'Neill presents us with an extraordinary study of the human mind under the influence of morphine. Freed from the normal restraints of intercourse, Mary speaks her fears and harboured resentments, her impulsive warmth and her perceptions about the personality of others. She moves in panic between the present and the past in search of the explanation of her suffering until, in act IV, she comes to rest, cut off from reality, at a point of security in the distant past.

Four main patterns alternate in Mary's speech in acts II and III, and one slowly comes to dominate. One pattern recurs when Mary is obliged to deal with present anxieties. Her speech then becomes frenetic, a combination of excited protests and nagging questions, with which she torments both herself and the men:

Why is that glass there?   Did you take a drink?   Oh, how can you be such a fool?   Don't you know it's the worst thing?   You're to blame, James.   How could you let him? ...

(p. 58)

I won't have it!   Do you hear, Edmund?   Such morbid nonsense! ... Your father shouldn't allow you ...

(p. 78)

I won't have it!   How dare ...!   How dare ...!   What right ...?

(p. 103)

The busy persistence of such speeches and the uniformity of their tone make them hard to listen to and present a distressing contrast with the peacemaking Mary of act I. O'Neill establishes a guilty allegiance between the audience and the listening characters by following such outbursts with an abrupt and unsympathetic demand for peace from one of the men: 'Mama, stop talking!' (pp. 58; 94); 'Stop talking crazy' (p. 104), and, more harshly, in protection of a third person, 'Mary! Hold your tongue' (p. 78). When Mary finally arrives at her resting place, isolated from the present, the audience's response is qualified by a feeling of relief at being able to listen easily to her words.

There is also a vein of quiet sharpness in Mary's speech. She utters words lightly which are not light for the character who hears them. Nothing is explicitly stated – the onus of making the connection between the two figures present before them on the stage being put on to the audience, who thus become acutely conscious of the emotion of the silent listener. This is not a new device for O'Neill, although it is used more consistently here than elsewhere. In the first part of *Mourning Becomes Electra*, for example, the inert dialogue briefly comes alive in a speech in which Christine says of the Mannon house:

Each time I come back after being away it appears more like a sepulchre! The 'whited' one of the Bible – pagan temple front stuck like a mask on Puritan grey ugliness! It was just like old Abe Mannon to build such a monstrosity – as a temple for his hatred. (*Then with a little mocking laugh.*) Forgive me, Vinnie. I forgot you liked it.

(p. 34)

Her mocking apology, alerting us to the significance of the words for her listening daughter, are more telling than all Lavinia's lengthy reminiscences of her mother's failure to love her as a child.[9] Mary's words can seem as cutting, as they do, for example, in the sequence which comes after Mary has recalled her first meeting with Tyrone. He replies to her query, 'Do you remember?':

TYRONE (*deeply moved – his voice husky*). Can you think I'd ever forget, Mary? (*Edmund looks away from them sad and embarrassed.*)
MARY (*tenderly*). No. I know you still love me, James, in spite of everything.
TYRONE (*His face works and he blinks back tears – with quiet intensity.*) Yes! As God is my judge! Always and forever, Mary!
MARY. And I love you, dear, in spite of everything.
(*There is a pause in which Edmund moves embarrassedly. The strange detachment comes over her manner again as if she were speaking impersonally of people seen from a distance.*)
But I must confess, James, although I couldn't help loving you, I would never have married you if I'd known you drank so much.   (pp. 97–8)

The calmness of the repudiation after the moment of intimacy makes it seem particularly cruel. Later in the same act, O'Neill uses the device over an extended sequence of the action, rousing and then undercutting the audience's feelings of hostility to Mary. Edmund exposes his misery to his mother in a desperate attempt to draw sympathy from her. She rebuffs him with a light denial:

You're so like your father, dear. You love to make a scene out of nothing so you can be dramatic and tragic. If I gave you the slightest encouragement you'd tell me next you were going to die –   (p. 104)

and then, when her son has left in despair, replies with shocking indifference to Tyrone's query about him, 'Perhaps he's going uptown again to find Jamie. He still had some money left, I suppose' (p. 106). The contrast between this and her sudden bare cry, 'Oh, James, I'm so frightened. I know he's going to die' (p. 106), which is accompanied by her reaching out for physical contact and then sobbing, is distressing, and confuses our certainty of who is strong and who weak, who caring and who cruel. The emotional force of the device depends on the audience's consciousness of the listener and, therefore, belongs peculiarly to the drama where we can watch one character whilst listening to the other. As we shall see, the auditor's consciousness of the tangled emotions of the silent listeners, is used to remarkable effect in the final line of the play.

The audience is made aware of the inconsistencies in Mary's self-portrayal. Her regret at not having become a nun, for example, must be accommodated with Cathleen's astonishment at the notion (p. 87), with her delight in describing her wedding dress (p. 100), and with her account of her first meeting with Tyrone, in which the details confront us not with a nun but with a coquettish schoolgirl concerned about the redness of her eyes and nose (p. 91). Sometimes O'Neill shows us a Mary who veers within a single speech from one line of thought to another, from one emotion to another, contradicting in one sentence the idea of the previous one. This third pattern in her speech gives us the impression of her incoherence without ever being allowed to become itself incoherent because O'Neill limits its use to a few strategic points in the action. It occurs in the utterance which tells Tyrone she has returned to the drug (p. 57–8); again, immediately after the three men have left (II. ii, p. 82); immediately before they re-enter (III, p. 92); at the end of her long recollection of the past (p. 95), when her excursion to buy the drug is discussed (p. 101), and, finally, when she briefly faces the truth about Edmund's illness (p. 106). These are all occasions on which the present intrudes on her reverie about the past or she is forced to acknowledge her close ties with one of the three men.

My example is the monologue spoken before the men's entrance in act III:

You're a sentimental fool. What is so wonderful about that first meeting between a silly romantic schoolgirl and a matinee idol? You were much happier before you knew he existed, in the Convent when you used to pray to the Blessed Virgin. (*Longingly.*) If I could only find the faith I lost, so I could pray again! (*She pauses – then begins to recite the Hail Mary in a flat, empty tone.*) 'Hail, Mary, full of grace! the Lord is with Thee; blessed art Thou among women.' (*Sneeringly.*) You expect the Blessed Virgin to be fooled by a lying dope fiend reciting words! You can't hide from Her! (*She springs to her feet. Her hands fly up to pat her hair distractedly.*) I must go upstairs. I haven't taken enough. When you start again you never know exactly how much you need. (*She goes toward the front parlour – then stops in the doorway as she hears the sound of voices from the front path. She starts guiltily.*) That must be them – (*She hurries back to sit down. Her face sets in stubborn defensiveness – resentfully.*) Why are they coming back? They don't want to. And I'd much rather be alone. (*Suddenly her whole manner changes. She becomes pathetically relieved and eager.*) Oh, I'm so glad they've come! I've been so horribly lonely!

(pp. 92–3)

Clearly, the interpretation and voice control of the actress are extremely important in creating the effect of such speeches but the dramatist guides her with his structuring of the passage as well as with his stage directions about tone and bearing. Mary uses the second person pronoun to address herself in her expressions of self-contempt at the opening of her speech. This somewhat impersonal form gives way to the first person pronoun when she speaks longingly and the thrusting questions and accusations are replaced by the conditional form of the verb. The epithets she applies to herself, 'sentimental fool', 'silly romantic schoolgirl', are bitter enough when contrasted with the joyfulness we heard in her account of that meeting a few speeches earlier but they are, nevertheless, the same kind of language. When, soon afterwards, she calls herself a 'lying dope fiend' we have the impression that there has been a real mental shift, because Mary is now using a different and cruder kind of slang. In the last section of the monologue, her contradictory response to the men's return is expressed by the juxtaposition of a snatch of Mary's nagging, questioning, with a snatch of the register which we have heard frequently in the central acts and which will dominate her speech at the end of the play.

We are prepared for the state of withdrawal which Mary will have achieved at the end of the play by her own testimony and by that of the men. 'She'll listen but she won't listen. She'll be here but she won't be here', says Jamie, and Tyrone endorses this, 'Yes ... there'll be the same drifting away from us until by the end of each night –' (p. 67). And equally suggestive, if less explicit, are the other comments: 'If you're that far gone in the past already, when it's only the afternoon, what will you be tonight?' (p. 74); 'You're not so far gone yet ...' (p. 102), and, finally, when it is already late evening, Edmund predicts, 'She'll be nothing but a ghost haunting the past by this time ... Back before I was born –', and Tyrone replies, 'Doesn't she do the same with me? Back before she ever knew me' (p. 118). And the words 'far', 'back', 'beyond', 'far away' recur in that part of Mary's speech, the fourth strand that we find in acts II and III which I will call 'reverie'. As we listen to the various passages of reverie, we realize that it is not one particular event Mary is trying to retrieve, but a state of mind: of faith, perhaps, but faith in herself as well as in the Deity, and faith that there is meaning and purpose in existence. She searches back into her past until she finds a time when life was forward looking, and there were still choices to be made.

O'Neill underlines this by using as the language of reverie, the eager, effusive elements of girlish speech. 'Lovely', 'beautiful', 'dreadful' are recurrent adjectives. The same word is repeated with a different function or meaning within a brief section of her utterance: 'All' is used like this in act III, 'I forgot *all* about ... *All* I wanted was

... And in *all* those thirty-six years ...' (p. 91), and 'sure' in the final speech of the play, 'how *sure* ... to make me *sure* ... as *surely* as ... I must be more *sure* ... If I was so *sure* ... If I still felt *sure* ...' (p. 155). The impression of trusting naïveté, so moving when heard from the mouth of the white-haired woman, cruelly worn by her experience of the world, is conveyed by the use of 'and' to pile up adjectives in descriptions of people and events: of Tyrone, for instance, who was 'simple, and kind, and unassuming, not a bit stuck up or vain' (p. 99), or of Mother Elizabeth, who is lovingly described in the final speech. It is conveyed, too, by the use of school-girl slang, 'stuck-up', 'my good points', 'all mixed up', and girlish intensifiers, 'I was *really* shocked', 'her eyes look *right* into your heart', 'it was *simply* a waste of time' (p. 155), 'I was so mad at myself' (p. 90). We begin to see here how effectively O'Neill uses the seemingly insignificant words in presenting a verbal image of personality. Indeed, the use of the intensifier 'so' recurs at crucial moments of the play and becomes remarkably expressive as a result. 'I worked *so* hard', 'I was *so* bashful', 'I was *so* excited and happy': such remarks occur frequently in the reverie and show us Mary at her most girlish, untouched by disappointment. To express Mary's present desolation, O'Neill uses the same construction, but combines 'so' with 'alone', 'lonesome', or 'lonely'. The assonance here on the 'o' sound is even more striking in Standard American than in Standard English because the vowel sound can be held on to longer when uttered with an American intonation. The echoing cry 'so lonely' is fixed more securely in the auditor's mind because not only are these the last words Mary speaks before the men enter in act III, but they have also been uttered as the final words of act II, scene ii, the mid-point of the play, and the most probable place for the interval in a stage production. That this effect was consciously produced by O'Neill is evident from alterations he made to the first draft of the play, in which he cut away the original ending until these words were prominent. The parallelism of the phrases 'so happy' / 'so lonely' means that each calls the other to mind. It is no mistake that the final line of the play should be, 'I fell in love with James Tyrone and was so happy for a time.'

Mary's affliction, which makes a ghost or a fog person out of a flesh and blood human being, is the result of chance and circumstance and, as such, is a peculiarly powerful image through which O'Neill can project the tension between received ideas of order and experience of disorder, between faith and unwilled scepticism. On paper, Jamie Tyrone would seem to be one of the weaker elements of the play, his condition a paler version of his mother's, since alcohol is less strange to us than morphine, its effects less immediately drastic and its influence less clearly the result of accident or of a single blow of Fate. The characterization is more vulnerable to distortion in the event of any looseness on the part of the author because the audience are likely to have preconceptions about alcoholism which may sway them towards sympathy, sentimentality or hostility, making this figure seem less real than the other three. The characterization is similarly threatened by the traditional stage stereotypes of the charming wastrel and of the drunken buffoon. In the event, O'Neill demonstrates how complex Jamie is in contrast to the stage stereotypes and so draws the character as to leave no room for any private gloss by the audience. Jamie is as credible and as mysterious as the other three characters, and his presence is as essential in creating the fine balance which exists between them.

Jamie is presented as living a death-in-life but the 'dead part' of him is responsible for his sharp tongue, from which much of the humour and vigour of the play derives. The audience, therefore, responding to his recitation, his jokes, his startling but frequently apt remarks about the other characters, finds itself drawn into partial collusion with him. Moreover, since a large part of the information about Jamie derives from the testimony of other characters which must be modified subsequently in the light of actual words and deeds, we are continually forced to recognize that he is more complex than the testimony allows. We are constantly confronted with the positive elements of a largely negative figure.

In the opening scene of the play, Jamie compliments his mother, laughs at his brother's joke, shrugs off his father's attacks, but actually says very little. What he does say is commonplace enough] The audience is thus alerted to the disparity between what they observe and the hyper-sensitivity of the other characters towards Jamie. Edmund is quick to notice and parry attacks on him; Mary becomes defensive when she catches him looking at her, Tyrone attacks him without noticeable provocation Prompted by the testimony, we are led to see that Jamie's neutrality is a deliberate withdrawal from any demanding situation: Let's forget it' (p. 19), 'Oh, all right, I'm a fool to argue' (p. 27), 'All right, Papa, I'm a bum. Anything you like so long as it stops the argument' (p. 28). If this seems to support Tyrone's opinion of his son's shiftlessness (p. 19), the few times when Jamie does initiate the conversation present a different picture. In the atmosphere of mystification, we find that his impulse is towards the truth: 'The Kid's damned sick' (p. 25), 'I think it's the wrong idea to let Mama go on kidding herself' (p. 25), 'He thinks it's consumption, doesn't he, Papa?' (p. 26), 'God, this ought to be the one thing we can talk over frankly without a battle' (p. 32). When the promised sneers do come, therefore, late in act I, the audience is prepared to find accuracy as well as malice in them. Their vigour is probably more surprising.

O'Neill couches Jamie's sneers in New York City slang drawing particularly on its habit of hyperbole and extravagant abuse: 'If Edmund was a lousy acre of land you wanted, the sky would be the limit' (p. 26); 'I know it's an Irish peasant idea consumption is fatal. It probably is when you live in a hovel on a bog, but over here with modern treatment ...' (p. 29). His words are, therefore, projected forcefully, drawing our attention to the accuracy beneath the sneer. We begin to recognize that the other characters fear the sneers themselves less than the possibility that they represent the truth, and suspicion and appreciation conflict in our response to him. It is Rocky's rather than Harry Hope's kind of slang that Jamie usually speaks. We are conscious of the note of abuse even when no deliberate insult is intended. A man is 'a louse', 'a sap', 'a boob', 'a sucker', 'a dumbell', living in a world of 'hick burgs', 'hooker shops', 'cheap dumps' and talking 'the bunk' or 'drunken bull'. At its lightest, the humour is uncomplimentary, achieving its effects through bathos, 'I was half-way up the walk when Cathleen burst into song. Our wild Irish lark! She ought to be a train announcer' (p. 46), or derisive incongruity, 'I shall attain the pinnacle of success! I'll be the lover of the fat woman in Barnum and Bailey's circus' (p. 141). But the slang usage is developed differently here from in the earlier play.

In *The Iceman Cometh*, the shared slang helped to reveal the communal feeling of Hope's roomers. This effect is now reversed. Jamie's slang indicates his alienation from his own home where no-one shares his language. His 'foul tongue', his 'rotten Broadway loafer's lingo' is specifically rejected by the other characters and the gulf is the wider because of the half-echo we find in Edmund's speech. The younger man occasionally adopts the lexis but never the spirit of the slang and it is from him that the sharpest repudiation of it comes in his scornful parody:

They never come back! Everything is in the bag! It's all a frame-up! We're all fall guys and suckers and we can't beat the game! (...) Christ, if I felt the way you do –!

(pp. 65–6)

The other difference is that Jamie is not limited to a single variety of English. In the first act, slang words and attitudes are loosely interspersed with Standard and do not become persistent until after Mary's return to the drug. It is only rarely used with full force, but when it is then it is the kind of slang Bewley proscribed:

> ... no fresh language, but a tired, thin-blooded language, dead sophisticated in a popular way, and afraid to stop moving lest it should not easily get into motion again.
>
> (*The Complex Fate*, p. 209)

The shock of his sudden brutal coarseness, 'Another shot in the arm!' (p. 65), 'Where's the hop-head?' (p. 142), is reinforced by the response of the stage listeners, by Tyrone's anger and by Edmund's swift physical reflex action, as well as by Jamie's own subsequent collapse into silent sobs. When O'Neill wishes Jamie's words to carry conviction he uses no slang. To Tyrone's accusation that his son sneers at everyone except himself, Jamie replies, 'You can't hear me talking to myself, that's all' (p. 28) and, in explanation of his bitterness towards his mother, 'She thinks I always believe the worst, but this time I believed the best. I suppose I can't forgive her – yet. It meant so much' (p. 143). The simplicity of the language here gives the actor the cue to the tone in which they must be spoken. As so often in this play, it is the contrast with what occurs elsewhere which makes the particular words moving.

Jamie's absence during act III has a realistic explanation, but it is also strategic. He is removed at the point in time when his tongue, were he to remain on stage, must become most callous. His harshness is communicated by means of reported rather than direct speech and so is tempered. The references to Jamie are frequent but usually brief, 'You say such mean bitter things when you've drunk too much. You're as bad as Jamie or Edmund' (p. 103); 'That loafer! I hope to God he misses the last car and has to stay up-town' (p. 115). Two are rather more extended: Mary in her reverie projects a picture of Jamie's childhood. There is no didacticism here because the information about Jamie is given almost by the way – our recognition of his early emotional deprivation is gleaned between the lines of Mary's telling of her own tragic experience of life (p. 75). Edmund's discussion of Jamie in act IV (p. 115–17) is more direct. He presents a hypothetical image of Jamie's actions off-stage at the moment of speaking. The presentation is ambivalent because Jamie's thought is satirized through the quotation of two poems with whose writers Edmund, only a short time before, has identified himself. Edmund's own position is again in question, as it was when he parodied Jamie's 'lingo'. We gather that the relationship between the brothers is less straightforward than either claims, and that the intimacy between the two can be betrayed by the younger as well as by the older. When Jamie enters, the reality of his action is superimposed on the image. Since image and reality almost coincide, our attention is fixed on the few differences. Jamie has indeed been reciting poetry to a fat whore in a brothel but his wry recognition of the humour in the situation shows us a self-knowledge greater than had been allowed. Where Edmund's account was narrated and generalized, Jamie's is particularized and delivered as a series of performances: Mamie beefing, Fat Vi giving a 'grand bawling out', Jamie crying and sentimentalizing whilst conscious of the reactions of the onlooker. We find a vitality in the speech of the man, who is able to produce nothing, that is lacking in the words of the incipient writer. We find, too, that Jamie's deliberate selection of Fat Vi has been an act of impulsive sympathy towards another human being so that in this, as well, he has proved larger than the portrait.

If we are repeatedly made to feel that there is more to Jamie than meets the eye, we find that his younger brother continually eludes our grasp. Edmund's identity seems to be unformed rather than shifting like those of the other members of the family. He is ten years younger than Jamie, but seems a lifetime away from brother and parents because he is the only one for whom possibilities remain. He is the one link the Tyrones have with the future. He stands at that point in time to which Tyrone and Mary both look back and which Jamie can never experience. O'Neill casts a particularly dark shadow on this seemingly doomed family by making him the character whom tuberculosis will possibly kill.

O'Neill achieves this effect of Edmund's being not quite formed, not yet an adult, by emphasizing his clumsiness and enthusiasm. His eagerness to reassure Mary, at the end of act I, is for her the signal of mistrust which finally pushes her back to the drug, whilst his inexperience and optimism make him slow to realize that she has returned to it, in act II, scene i. He is stoutly optimistic, but when he attempts to act on his hope, we see at once that there is no substance to it. He cannot begin to talk on equal ground with his mother. She manipulates him verbally in act I, and avoids his appeal in act III. The awkwardness of his revolt against his father invites comparison with Jamie's verbal dexterity. In reply to Tyrone's quotation of Prospero, for example, Edmund rephrases Shakespeare's words:

Fine! That's beautiful. But I wasn't trying to say that. We are such stuff as
manure is made on, so let's drink up and forget it. That's more my idea.

(p. 114)

We are aware that Jamie would never have been so rash as to rewrite
Shakespeare but would have parried Tyrone's optimism by silent
scorn or by the witty selection of another accurate quotation whose
meaning would be distorted by the context to reflect his cynicism. The
contrast is telling and warns us against too easily discussing the
character's clumsiness as if it were the dramatist's. Edmund's inexperience is revealed, too, when his sensitivity to the response of the
outside world breaks through incongruously at moments when
private grief would be expected to be uppermost. It is the character
who in the bright morning had declared in support of Tyrone's
independent attitude, 'He's right not to give a damn what anyone
thinks. Jamie's a fool to care about the Chatfields ... whoever heard
about them outside this hick burg?' (p. 38), who later cries to his
mother, 'For God's sake, Mama! You can't trust her! Do you want
everyone on earth to know?' (p. 101) and says to his father:

to think when it's a question of your son having consumption, you can show
yourself up before the whole town as such a stinking old tightwad! Don't you
know Hardy will talk and the whole damned town will know?

(p. 126)

When he is not talking a great deal, as in his narration of the joke in act
I or during the vigil he shares with Tyrone in act IV, he talks noticeably
little. Indeed, of his eighty-five separate utterances in acts II and III,
sixty-three consist of only one or two terse sentences or half sentences,
and only nine of five or more sentences. Since it is in these acts that the
family afflictions become apparent, this brevity helps to indicate the
difficulty he finds in coping with the situation. Many of his utterances
are appeals to the others for silence, 'Cut it out, Papa' (p. 67); 'Don't,
mother' (p. 78); 'Stop talking, Mama' (p. 94). And, of all the characters, it is he who resorts most often to gesture because words have
failed him. He twice attacks Jamie physically (p. 142, 151) and once
recollects having done so (p. 103) and in his misery at the end of act III,
he runs out to hide himself in the fog.

We catch echoes of all the other characters in Edmund's speech: of
Jamie's slang, Mary's vocabulary, Tyrone's delight in the sound of
words. He adopts Jamie's slang, for instance, particularly in conversation with or about his brother, but his usage is woolly. Expressions
like, 'Nix on the loud noise' (p. 136); 'Don't look at me as though I'd

gone nutty' (p. 113), lack the callousness but also the pungency of Jamie's idiom. They are sufficient to indicate both the influence of brother on brother and the limits of that influence.

The characterization is not as negative as my discussion so far suggests. What at one moment we call 'unformed', at the next we might describe as 'not fixed'. His retreat from the word might equally be seen as self-assertion through physical action. His sensitivity to the situation implies a degree of feeling not hardened by habit. Although the other characters fear Jamie's tongue, the most cutting comments on the situation come from the lips of the naïve son. His mockery of Jamie's melancholy self-analysis stops his brother short (p. 141); his appeal at the end of the play, almost impinges on Mary (p. 154) and it is he who shows Tyrone that his symbol of the past is to be equated with Mary's when, in what is in its implications one of the cruellest lines of the play, he suggests that Booth's praise for Tyrone's Othello 'might be in an old trunk in the attic, along with Mama's wedding dress'.

One sequence in Edmund's utterance demands detailed attention for it is one that has been praised as poetic and denounced as embarrassing. It seems to me to be a scene in which the difference in the dramatist's control between the first and second parts of his career is clearly evinced.

We have seen that in the first part of his career, O'Neill adopted a heightened form of language, notable for its flowing rhythm, in passages of reverie, of confession or of recollection of the past. It was sometimes effective, as when Anna Christie dreamed in the fog or Orin Mannon brooded about the battlefield but, almost always, it was out of key with the rest of the play – an interlude in the action, not an integral part of it. There is no equivalent passage in *The Iceman Cometh*. Larry Slade's speech breaks down when he begins to probe his own consciousness and, in Hickey's confession, O'Neill emphasizes speech rhythms, making use of the parentheses, redundancies and syntactical irregularities of talk. The confessions of Tyrone and Jamie, in act IV of *Long Day's Journey Into Night*, follow this pattern. They are idiomatic rather that lyrical. And Mary's reverie is cast into an idiosyncratic form which is an extension of one of her habitual speech rhythms. But what are we to make of Edmund's confession? The character based on the young O'Neill uses the register we have identified with O'Neill's personal voice to recount an experience of ecstasy. Not surprisingly, Edmund's comment on the passage has been taken as O'Neill's assessment of his own work and discussion has usually centred on the statement 'it will be faithful realism, at least. Stammering is the native eloquence of us fog people'. This has led to the divorce of the passage from its context and the subsequent discussion of its merits as literary prose in isolation from its dramatic function.

The passage does read awkwardly but to label it an unfortunate patch in an otherwise well-written play and then pass on, will not do. It occupies a long stretch of performance time at a crucial moment of the play and if it did not contribute positively to the ongoing action, it would damage it badly. Since experience of performance suggests that there is no such damage here, it is necessary to consider whether it could succeed as dramatic dialogue whilst failing as literary prose.

It is necessary to quote a rather longer sequence than usually suffices and, even then, it is important to remember that the scene modifies and is modified by previous and subsequent scenes. Edmund speaks to his father:

Yes, she moves above and beyond us, a ghost haunting the past, and here we sit pretending to forget, but straining our ears listening for the slightest sound, hearing the fog drip from the eaves like the uneven tick of a rundown, crazy clock – or like the dreary tears of a trollop spattering in a puddle of stale beer on a honky-tonk table top! (*He laughs with maudlin appreciation.*) Not so bad, that last, eh? Original, not Baudelaire. Give me credit! (*Then with alcoholic talkativeness.*) You've just told me some high spots in your memories. Want to hear mine? They're all connected with the sea. Here's one. When I was on the squarehead square-rigger, bound for Buenos Aires. Full moon in the Trades. The old hooker driving fourteen knots. I lay on the bowsprit, facing astern, with the water foaming into spume under me, the masts with every sail white in the moonlight, towering high above me. I became drunk with the beauty and singing rhythm of it, and for a moment I lost myself – actually lost my life. I was set free! I dissolved in the sea, became white sails and flying spray, became beauty and rhythm, became moonlight and the ship and the high dim-starred sky! I belonged, without past or future, within peace and unity and a wild joy, within something greater than my own life, or the life of Man, to Life itself! To God, if you want to put it that way. Then another time, on the American Line, when I was lookout on the crow's nest in the dawn watch. A calm sea, that time. Only a lazy ground swell and a slow drowsy roll of the ship. The passengers asleep and none of the crew in sight. No sound of man. Black smoke pouring from the funnels behind and beneath me. Dreaming, not keeping lookout, feeling alone, and above, and apart, watching the dawn creep like a painted dream over the sky and sea which slept together. Then the moment of ecstatic freedom came. The peace, the end of the quest, the last harbour, the joy of belonging to a fulfilment beyond men's lousy, pitiful, greedy fears and hopes and dreams! And several other times in my life, when I was swimming far out, or lying alone on a beach, I have had the same experience. Became the sun, the hot sand, green seaweed anchored to a rock, swaying in the tide. Like a saint's vision of beatitude. Like the veil of things as they seem drawn back by an unseen hand. For a second you see – and seeing the secret, are the secret. For a second there is meaning! Then the hand lets the veil fall and you are alone, lost in the fog again, and you stumble on toward nowhere, for no good reason! (*He grins wryly*.) It was a great mistake my being born a man, I would have been much more successful as a sea-gull or a fish. As it is, I will always be a stranger who never feels at home, who does not really want and is not really wanted, who can never belong, who must always be a little in love with death!

TYRONE (*stares at him – impressed*). Yes, there's the makings of a poet in you all right. (*Then protesting uneasily*.) But that's morbid craziness about not being wanted and loving death.

EDMUND (*sardonically*). The *makings* of a poet. No, I'm afraid I'm like the guy who is always panhandling for a smoke. He hasn't even got the makings. He's got only the habit. I couldn't touch what I tried to tell you just now. I just stammered. That's the best I'll ever do. I mean if I live. Well it will be faithful realism, at least. Stammering is the native eloquence of us fog people.

(*A pause. Then they both jump startledly as there is a noise from outside the house, as if someone had stumbled and fallen on the front steps. Edmund grins*.)

Well, that sounds like the absent brother. He must have a peach of a bun on.

(pp. 133–5)

Unlike such passages in the earlier plays, the reverie here is set within a frame. The speaker introduces and afterwards comments on it, so that attention is directed towards the efforts of the nascent poet to express his experience as well as towards the experience itself. The somewhat bizarre sentence with which the passage begins, and with sixty-five words it is the longest in the play, takes us, at the outset, past the meaning to the mode of expression. The vague, literary description of Mary in the opening clause gives way to an accurate observation of the present ('here we sit, pretending to forget, but straining our ears listening for the slightest sound'). This, in its turn, is diffused by the comparison between the fog and the 'rundown, crazy clock' which, somewhat awkward, distracts the audience's attention to itself. What establishes the difference between the effect of this and of similar stylistic mixtures in the middle plays is that the dramatist, conscious now of the impression created, is able to use it. The elaborate description of the clock appears to distract the speaker, too, from his meaning to his style so that he ends the sentence with the exuberant anticlimax of 'or like the dreary tears of a trollop spattering in a puddle of stale beer on a honky-tonk table top!', and then adds the self-conscious comment, 'Not bad that last, eh? Original, not Baudelaire.'[10] The experience of ecstasy is introduced equally self-consciously ('Want to hear mine? Here's one'), and is punctuated by prosaic reminders that a speaker is communicating with a listener ('Then another time ... And several other times ...'). The description of the scene ('Full moon in the Trades', 'the high dim-starred sky', 'watching the dawn creep ...'), and the thought ('I belonged to Life itself', 'belonging to a fulfilment', 'you see and seeing the secret, are the secret') tell us little about the experience, as do the literary echoes we catch (of Dana in the sequence about the bowsprit,[11] Wordsworth in the references to 'wild joy' and 'unity', and Shelley in the image of the veil). The descriptive passages are clichés and unfocused abstractions, whilst the literary echoes, reminding us of the greater coherence of the source, are disturbing rather than illuminating. But, because of the frame which encloses them – the speaker's self-consciousness – both descriptions and echoes lead us to the character and not, as they did in the middle plays, to the struggling dramatist.

O'Neill uses the literary effusiveness of his own late adolescence for purposes of characterization. A play could not bear many such passages, but it can bear this one because of the support given by the surrounding dialogue and its consistency with what we have learnt of the character. We find in it, Edmund's clumsiness, his enthusiasm, and his delight in the words of poets. The word-play of the 'dreary tears of the trollop' sequence, with its pattern of plosive consonants, has a disarming excess, of a kind we meet again. Images are taken too far ('became the sun, the hot sand, the green seaweed anchored to a rock swaying in the tide') and nouns, adjectives or adverbs tumble over each other in the eagerness of expression ('feeling alone, above, and apart', 'Men's lousy, pitiful, greedy fears and hopes and dreams'). Although verbally imprecise, the passage has a rhythmic coherence. The medley of ideas in that opening sentence, for example, are bound together by the repeated use of the continuous present form of the verb ('haunting ... pretending ... straining ... listening ... hearing ... spattering'). And in the reverie itself, which moves from the past tense ('When I was ...') through the present ('for a second you see ...') to the continuous form of the future ('I will always ...'), the separate sentences are bound into larger periods by patterning. In Edmund's first sea memory, for instance, each of four consecutive long sentences is introduced by a first person pronoun and a simple past tense ('I lay ... I became ... I dissolved ... I belonged ...'). Within the first two sentences, ideas are grouped in pairs, within the second, they are arranged in sets of three, associated by the reiteration of the verb in one set ('I dissolved ... *became* white sails and flying spray, *became* beauty and rhythm, *became* moonlight and ...'), of the preposition in the other ('I belonged, *without* past or future, *within* peace and unity and a wild joy, *within* something greater ...'). Attention is focused on the climax of this first vision because the rolling sentences are replaced by a sudden brief one, 'To God, if you want to put it that way.' The audience, swept along by the rhythm and by the boyish voice speaking into the silence in an urgent tone, is likely to concur with Tyrone's comment, 'Yes there's the makings of a poet in you all right.' But as soon as the utterance ceases qualifications will begin to flood in. Our recognition that we have been led by the rhythm and the enthusiasm to a spurious response is immediately absorbed by O'Neill into the action of the play when, in the coda to Edmund's utterance, the qualifications are put into the character's own mouth in language that breaks the pattern. A precise image and a wry pun phrased in earthy slang replace the abstractions, and short, disjointed sentences replace the rhythmic flow. The recognition of failure is spoken in a direct, unfurbished statement, 'I couldn't touch what I tried to tell you just now.' O'Neill makes us aware of the gulf between longing and capacity and confronts us at a more complex level with that area of human experience he explored in *Desire Under the Elms*. Like the early patterned use of the word 'purty', Edmund's reverie with its plain-speaking coda makes us conscious not only of his inarticulacy but of his pain at being unable to articulate his deeply felt experience. It is this pain which activates the private emotions of the audience.

If we also catch a reference to the dramatist's private experience in the 'stammering' comment, the frisson we feel helps to intensify the response much as happens if we seem to hear Shakespeare's voice speaking with Prospero's in the 'Our revels now are ended' speech in *The Tempest*. If we return to the speech after the play to seek out the writer, we find a nice irony in the fact that one of O'Neill's most memorable lines in a play in which he is so fully master of his form should have been written about his verbal infelicity. But, in the play, such consciousness could only be fleeting because Jamie is heard entering and seriousness gives way to the farce of the drunken man stumbling in the fog of his inebriation. Our viewpoint is already being shifted and new impressions are modifying those just made. Edmund's clumsy slang, 'He must have a peach of a bun on', reminds us that he is also a novice in Jamie's world where, if metaphors are inappropriate, they are deliberately and grotesquely so. The audience themselves feel the edge of Jamie's cynicism because it is directed against the moment of intimacy just witnessed between Edmund and Tyrone, which has seemed one of the few wholly positive exchanges in the play: 'He's been putting on the old sob act for you, eh? He can always kid you. But not me. Never again' (p. 138). And, before long, the mood has darkened again with the third and cruellest of the self-exposures in which Jamie, in his turn, achieves his own kind of stammering eloquence.

Empathy and alienation: O'Neill's structuring of the play

One of the more firmly fixed dramatic conventions is that there should be a hero, a central figure. Much of the emotional intensity of this play derives from O'Neill's deliberate breaking of the convention. The audience's impulse to identify with one character is continually satisfied and then frustrated. At any given moment, one of the four dominates the action revealing his thought in such a way that our sympathy is engaged but, immediately, his words and gestures alienate that sympathy and his place is taken by another. The resulting tension binds the audience to the action by insisting that they hold the claims of all four characters in mind and delay judgement on what they see. Even as one figure expresses his spiritual isolation, we find ourselves relating his words to each of the other three and, by extension, to all human experience. The relationship between the four characters, from which none can wholly separate himself, is as much O'Neill's subject as is the quest of each for individual meaning. As the play proceeds, we recognize that each character is both supported and crippled by the relationship and that these elements are tightly enmeshed. O'Neill uses particular linguistic devices to create what might be called a 'family rhythm'. These are responsible for much of the surface variety of the play and also for its underlying coherence, since they permeate the action, seeming to root the characters together in their shared past.

Most obviously, but nevertheless importantly for the tone of the play, the characters address each other familiarly. They tease each other about little personal matters, snoring, reducing, digesting. They laugh at the same jokes. The Shaughnessey joke, for example, told by Edmund in act I (pp. 19–22), is humorous in itself, but is used by O'Neill as a surface event behind whose cover he can demonstrate the patterns of grievance and affection which coexist between the characters. The family comes together to share the joke but breaks

apart immediately when father turns the laughter into an attack on
son, and the story itself is repeatedly interrupted by the tangential
comments of the listeners which reveal their private attitudes and
indicate their habitual positions. Quarrels, too, flair out of nothing
and are quickly deflated, allegiances shift and each character puts in
his word in a manner possible only amongst people with a history of
such interactions. O'Neill is confronting the audience with the pattern
of its own familiar conversations and asking them to leap its gaps and
understand its shared assumptions. Something of this can be seen in a
fairly lighthearted exchange early in act I: Edmund breaks into a
conversation about other matters with a reference back to Mary's
earlier complaint about Tyrone's snoring:

EDMUND. I'll back you up about Papa's snoring. Gosh, what a racket!
JAMIE. I heard him, too. (*He quotes, putting on a ham actor manner*.) 'The Moor,
I know his trumpet.'
(*His mother and brother laugh.*)
TYRONE (*scathingly*). If it takes my snoring to make you remember Shakes-
peare instead of the dope sheet on the ponies, I hope I'll keep on with it.
MARY. Now, James! You mustn't be so touchy.
(*Jamie shrugs his shoulders and sits down in the chair on her right.*)
EDMUND (*irritably*). Yes, for Pete's sake, Papa! First thing after breakfast!
Give it a rest, can't you?
(*He slumps down in the chair at left of table next to his brother. His father ignores
him.*)
MARY (*reprovingly*). Your father wasn't finding fault with you. You don't
have to always take Jamie's part. You'd think you were the one ten years
older.

(pp. 18–19)

Jamie caps Edmund's words, Edmund Mary's and the dialogue flows
quickly from statement to reaction, the alternation of second and first
person pronouns helping the movement of the sequence. Each utterance endorses, contradicts or extends the preceding one. The startling
personal attack by father on son and the speed with which the other
two characters intervene, suggest that there is knowledge involved
which predates the play and alert us to meanings beyond the common
core of the words spoken. Using the predisposition of the audience to
seek out significance, O'Neill embeds his exposition of situation and
character into the flow of the dialogue. There is no narration in this
play of the kind spoken by Larry to Parritt at the opening of *The
Iceman Cometh*. There are only fragments which the audience must
piece together. The use, here, of the continuous form of the verb, and
of adverbs of time, such as Mary's 'always', suggest that we are

witnessing a habitual response, and this impression will be reinforced when these two features recur, as they frequently do, in expressions of irritation between the characters ('Papa, if you're starting that stuff again!' p. 18; 'You always imagine things' p. 23; 'I could see that line coming! God, how many thousand times' p. 28). We gather specific information, too, about Jamie's wastrel life, the relative ages of the two brothers, Tyrone's respect for Shakespeare, and we can deduce that both brothers must have been awake during the night although the significance of this will only become apparent with the accumulation of several such hints. Similarly, we hear a comic distortion of a quotation and an irritable response to it – the first piece of a pattern which will be elaborated during the play.

The open method of exposition is particularly appropriate to this play. What the audience learns about the past might be detailed, but it can never be fixed because it is refracted through the consciousness of one or other of the characters and, far from endorsing any one account, O'Neill lets each contradict the others. Whilst some details are allowed to seem fairly stable, other topics – homes, doctors, the electric light, the fog, alcohol – are raised, dropped and taken up again by each character, each new reference modifying the audience's viewpoint until, by the end of the play, each topic is fraught with suggestion. To take one small example: we have seen that there are numerous references to the electric light which gradually becomes a symbol of Tyrone's financial anxiety, the cause of much of the family suffering and bitterness. When Jamie enters drunk in act IV we seem to be being presented with the traditional stage comedy of the drunken man. All the elements are here, the slurred speech and lurching movement; the recourse to tired, moralistic proverbs and the attribution of human intentions to the objects with which he collides, but there is also a succession of references in word and gesture to fog and clarity, darkness and light ('Ought to be a lighthouse out there'; 'What the hell is this, the morgue?'; 'Lesh have some light on sibject'; 'Ford o' Kabul river in the dark! ...'; 'Can't expect us to live in the Black Hole of Calcutta') which not only communicates Jamie's hostility to his absent father but recalls the long scene between Edmund and Tyrone and contributes to the symbolic undercurrent of the play.

We catch echoes of one character's speech in that of another. The speech of both Tyrone and Mary has an Irish shape much like that of Larry Slade (see p. 135) which appears most noticeably when they tease each other affectionately or dream of the past. This helps to suggest the warmth of their feeling at such moments and also marks the experiential gap between parent and child. The brogue itself is not used but a cluster of references makes the idea of Ireland into a signal of the insecurity of the uprooted man. The American-born sons can cut deep with scornful references to the ancient homeland. Tyrone's tale of self-help follows the classical American immigrant pattern of rejection of origins coupled with staunch loyalty to them. He has rid himself of his brogue but has surrounded himself with his own tribe in the shape of tenant, housemaid, drinking companions. Elsewhere, shared language can mark the deep, unacknowledged bond between parent and child. Edmund's speech in act IV which begins, 'The fog was where I wanted to be' (p. 113), is a moving example of this. Although he, as much as the others, has resented his mother's retreat into herself, Edmund, here, not only echoes her longing to withdraw but, in doing so, takes over the words which recur in her speech and in descriptions of her: 'fog', 'alone', 'lost', 'hide' and 'ghost'. Soon after this, Jamie comments drunkenly on his own quotation of Wilde's 'The Harlot's House', saying, 'Not strictly accurate. If my love was with me I didn't notice it. She must have been a ghost' (p. 139). The uncanny impression of Mary's presence, created by the collocation in Edmund's speech of words normally associated with her, is likely to make the audience sensitive to the word 'ghost' when it occurs again in Jamie's speech. Without making anything explicit, O'Neill allows the audience to perceive the unconscious irony of Jamie's words and to recognize the part his relationship with his mother has played in warping his life. We might contrast, here, the explicitness of the Freudian statements O'Neill used in the middle plays, particularly *Strange Interlude* and *Mourning Becomes Electra*, about the relationships between parents and children. By using associations established in the earlier scenes of the play as the material for the dramatic metaphors of the later scenes, the dramatist binds the play into a whole.

Denials and barriers of silence occur frequently. They are as telling as the shared language in revealing what the characters have in common and, as they accumulate, we become aware of their thematic significance. Certain truths are avoided by the Tyrones as firmly as others were in Hope's bar. Things are implied but not stated, a topic is suddenly changed, a speaker falls silent in mid-sentence and the listener forbears to comment. During the first act, for example, we observe the men's concern for Mary, we hear her demands that they trust her and their eager reassurances and we also piece together a

grimly comic picture of all three men simulating sleep on the night
before the action of the play whilst listening intently to Mary's restless
moving about. When any of the men attempts to discuss this the
others deny having been conscious of anything extraordinary. The
audience's curiosity is aroused. In the second act, the anxiety and
shirked confidences of the men are recalled, just before Mary's
entrance, in the pause which occurs during this brief exchange:

EDMUND. She didn't get much sleep last night.
JAMIE. I know she didn't.
(*A pause. The brothers avoid looking at each other.*)
EDMUND. That damned foghorn kept me awake, too.   (p. 48)

The admissions which flood into such silences are more marked
because they are spoken only in the minds of the audience. They are
ominous because they draw attention to but do not solve the mystery
already sensed. Euphemisms are used in the play, with similar effect.
Tyrone refers to the drug as 'the poison', 'her curse', and the other
characters avoid naming it. All use the euphemism 'summer cold' to
disguise their fear of Edmund's illness from themselves and each
other. If, in his anxiety, one character forgets the tacit agreement, the
others quickly remind him and the pattern of reticence and uneasy
collusion is reinforced. For example:

MARY. You mustn't mind Edmund, James. Remember he isn't well.
(*Edmund can be heard coughing as he goes upstairs.*)
(*She adds nervously.*) A *summer cold* makes anyone *irritable*.
JAMIE (*genuinely concerned*). It's not just a cold he's got. The Kid is damned
sick.
(*His father gives him a sharp warning look but he doesn't see it.*)
MARY (*turns on him resentfully*). Why do you say that? It is *just a cold!* Anyone
can tell that! You always imagine things!
TYRONE (*with another warning glance at Jamie – easily*). All Jamie meant was
Edmund might have *a touch of something else*, too, which makes his cold worse.
JAMIE. Sure, Mama, *that's all* I meant.
TYRONE. Doctor Hardy thinks it might be *a bit of* malarial fever he caught
when he was in the tropics. If it is, quinine will soon cure it.
                                                                  (p. 23)

Such passages help to show the guilt and panic underlying the relationship. The soothing words, which infiltrate the speech of all the
characters, as my italicizing in the extract demonstrates, represent a
shrinking from the deeper reassurances and admissions for which all
long. The euphemisms make us sensitive to the family's private
taboos, and it is the effect of a taboo being broken as much as the

sudden coarse slang which makes Jamie's bitter attacks on Mary so shocking (pp. 65; 142), or Edmund's cry, 'Mama, it isn't a summer cold! I've got consumption' (p. 154), so piercing and Mary's refusal to respond so final.

Throughout the play such denials occur, shifting attention from facts and events to their emotional effect, and infiltrating our consciousness with the looming despair of the Tyrones. We are made painfully aware that the time will never be ripe, that opportunities will always be missed, because O'Neill juxtaposes some of the cruellest denials with moments of brief sympathy, frustrating the expectations of change which are beginning to be shaped. So, in act I, Jamie and Tyrone break apart with mutual recriminations after their brief understanding (pp. 26–9). And, when one character tries to break through to another by crying out an appeal, the other retreats in confusion or resentment, as Tyrone does from Mary in act II (p. 60) and she from him in the following act (p. 73). Such withdrawal, as we have seen, becomes a dominant pattern in Mary's speech.

A similar pattern of accretion underlies our impression that the relationship also has its positive aspect. This is most immediately apparent in the confessions of act IV, in which, one after another, each character reveals his trust by attempting to expose his deepest thought. But it is apparent too in much slighter devices. Tyrone, for example, usually avoids Jamie's Christian name. This emphasizes his resentment much as did Larry Slade's avoidance of Parritt's name in The Iceman Cometh. But here the pattern is occasionally and significantly broken. In the early part of the play, Tyrone uses the name when there is brief but unambiguous sympathy between the two men, when they discuss Mary (pp. 23; 32; 33; 35) or worry about Edmund's sickness (pp. 30; 56; 69). Each expression of affection, although minimal in itself, is strengthened by being linked with others through the recurrent use of the name. The current of feeling so created is a small but persistent one, so that when we hear the name being used by Tyrone in his final utterance, 'Pass me that bottle Jamie. And stop reciting that damned morbid poetry. I won't have it in my house' (p. 154), ambiguity creeps in and the audience are reminded of the underlying affection as well as of the habitual irritation. O'Neill's originality, indeed, derives from his capacity to make both the closeness and the resentment within a whole web of relationships[12] – between parent and child, husband and wife, brother and brother – apparent, by intertwining the negative and positive elements. In this, his material differs from Strindberg's in The Father and *The Dance of Death*, with which his plays have often been compared, and from Edward Albee's, in *Who's Afraid of Virginia Woolf?*, which was probably influenced by O'Neill.[13] Perhaps of all the forerunners, only Ibsen creates quite the same kind of tension: in the relationship of the two sisters in *John Gabriel Borkman*, for example.

Our sense of the necessity of the family unit to each member, despite all the horrors it holds for them, is established in part by the image we are given of the Tyrones keeping face before the outside world and revealing their fragmented, uncertain selves only to each other. When Tyrone, in act III, quiets Mary with the words, 'Hush now! Here comes Cathleen. You don't want her to see you crying' (p. 106), he bears witness to the existence of an intimacy which does allow her to cry before him. O'Neill presents the difference dramatically by introducing the fifth character, Cathleen. She represents on stage the world beyond the walls of the house. When she is present, and it is only in the central acts, not in the concentrated final section of the play, nor in any of the tauter sequences, the audience briefly see the characters as they would present themselves to the outside world, the world of the pub and the club and the theatre, the whorehouse and the small town. Cathleen is not developed in the way the other characters are, nor is she given the Dickensian individuality of Hope's roomers. Her speech is marked by complacent generalization ('Everybody healthy snores', p. 85; 'It's a good man's failing', p. 86; 'He's a fine gentleman and you're a lucky woman', p. 91) and stage-Irish dialect ('Sure, didn't it kill an uncle of mine in the old country', p. 45; 'I'd think you'd a drop taken', p. 90). Her words rarely offer more than their surface meaning and her utterances are short, except when O'Neill needs a contrast with Mary's words when the other three Tyrones are off-stage. Then, he is able to emphasize the seriousness and strangely distant innocence of the mistress's words by means of a painfully humorous contrast with Cathleen's vacuous chatter.[14] A brief extract will demonstrate the effect:

CATHLEEN. . . . . Give him half a chance and he's pinching me on the leg or you know where – asking your pardon, Ma'am, but it's true.
MARY (*dreamily*). It wasn't the fog I minded, Cathleen. I really love fog.
CATHLEEN. They say it's good for the complexion.
MARY. It hides you from the world and the world from you. You feel that everything has changed, and nothing is what it seemed to be. No one can find or touch you any more.
CATHLEEN. I wouldn't care so much if Smythe was a fine, handsome man like

some chauffeurs I've seen – I mean, if it was all in fun, for I'm a decent girl. But for a shrivelled runt like Smythe – ! I've told him . . .

(pp. 84–5)

Cathleen is, in essence, the conventional comic servant of the nineteenth-century theatre. Because conventional, she is neutral and, so, acceptable as a minor character. She has not sufficient intrinsic interest to intrude on our impression of the family's isolation and, by the same token, can serve as the mirror in which the public face of each is reflected. In her eye, the sons are carefree men about town, Tyrone a good husband and generous gentleman, Mary a considerate mistress and loving mother. The audience is made conscious of the contrast between ordered image and confused reality, without any of the clumsy paraphernalia of masks and scenic devices which were so distracting in the middle plays.

Quotation is a major structural element in *Long Day's Journey Into Night, A Touch of the Poet* and *A Moon for the Misbegotten*. In the early plays, there were echoes and half-quotations from other writers, the implications of which were often inappropriate to O'Neill's meaning. I suggested in chapter 2 that these were often unconscious intrusions but that when O'Neill wrote *Ah, Wilderness!* he had become sufficiently self-aware to use his feeling for particular literary works as a key element in characterizing the hero of the play. As with O'Neill's other experiments, when the use of quotation appears in the later plays, it is developed with greater complexity.

Three of the characters quote frequently in *Long Day's Journey Into Night*. Their choice of writer and the way in which his words are used show the individual minds engaging with life. All three Tyrone men quote from Shakespeare. Tyrone's quotations seem spontaneous because he interrupts himself to utter them:

There's nothing wrong with life. It's we who – (*He quotes.*) 'The fault, dear Brutus, is not in our stars, but in ourselves that we are underlings.'

(p. 133)

The old actor rejoices in the very sound and shape of words and, fittingly, his quotations are all from famous speeches in better-known plays – *Julius Caesar, King Lear, The Tempest* (twice). His Shakespeare is the creator, par excellence, of aphorisms and, as such, is recommended: 'You'll find it nobly said in Shakespeare'; 'You'll find everything you're trying to say in him – as you'll find everything else worth saying', and, in exasperation, 'That damned library of yours . . . When I've *three* good sets of Shakespeare you could read.' In Tyrone,

O'Neill presents the enigma of the man for whom issues must be clear cut and who, despite his own experience, accepts that the universe has a fixed moral law. The quotation enables the dramatist to do this without didacticism. The cruelty of Tyrone's position is brought sharply before us in act IV when we realize that the writer with whom we have come to associate him is the symbol of the youthful dream that was betrayed and not of the lifetime's work. Indeed, no-one in the family quotes from the 'god-damned play' which is not even graced with a name. The only direct reference to any melodrama is Jamie's laboured Old Gaspard joke, and the linking of that with *The Bells* is inaccurate.

Like the attitudes to Ireland, quotation is a means of projecting the father-son relationship. Tyrone quotes Shakespeare straight. His sons deliberately distort although, in much the same way as in *Desire Under the Elms*, O'Neill can quietly demonstrate the influence of the old man on the young rebels through the very fact of their familiarity with Shakespeare and the relish with which they quote. Edmund's distortion of Shakespeare is gauche, as we have seen. Jamie's is impressive. He quotes stage directions and asides and, when he quotes from the text itself, he has spied out another meaning for the accurately quoted words. Early in the play his jokes are mild; Othello's trumpet, for example, stands for Tyrone's snoring; but they darken as the play proceeds, culminating in the terrifying flippancy imposed on the normally neutral stage direction, 'The mad scene. Enter Ophelia' with which Jamie breaks the silence at Mary's final entrance. The audience must accommodate both the inhumanity of the distortion and the haunting aptness. For the association Jamie makes brings with it a strange, unspoken resonance, best indicated through this description of Ophelia's speech given by the gentleman in Shakespeare's play:

> her speech is nothing,
> Yet the unshaped use of it doth move,
> The hearers to collection; they aim at it,
> And botch the words up fit to their own thoughts;
> Which, as her winks, and nods, and gestures yield them,
> Indeed would make one think there might be thought,
> Though nothing sure, yet much unhappily.

> (*Hamlet* IV. v)

The second current of quotation – of *fin de siècle* poetry – is not shared by Tyrone, which in itself is revealing. More subtly, the literary consciousness of the two brothers, though similar, does not entirely coincide. O'Neill uses the difference to show the younger supplanting the elder. Jamie, we are told, wanted to become a writer but Edmund has actually become one, however flawed. The difference is made real in Jamie's only direct personal attack on his brother, which is couched in literary terms:

Your poetry isn't very cheery. Nor the stuff you read and claim you admire. (*He indicates the smart bookcase at rear.*) Your pet with the unpronounceable name, for example.
EDMUND. Nietzsche. You don't know what you're talking about. You haven't read him.
JAMIE. Enough to know it's a lot of bunk!   (p. 66)

It is one of the rare instances when Edmund's words are stronger than his brother's, and it prepares the audience for Jamie's subsequent boast and Edmund's calm acceptance of it:

And who steered you onto reading poetry first? Swinburne, for example? I did! And because I once wanted to write, I planted it in your mind that someday you'd write! Hell, you're more than my brother. I made you! You're my Frankenstein!
EDMUND. All right, I'm your Frankenstein. So let's have a drink. (*He laughs.*) You crazy nut.

(p. 144)

It prepares the audience, too, for the terrible warning that follows. The areas of overlap in the brothers' literary consciousness are used as effectively. Jamie quotes self-indulgently, identifying himself with the poet's persona in justification of his wastrel life. But for all their statements about futility, the writers he quotes did set down their thoughts for publication, did image deeds in words, whereas even Jamie's words are borrowed. The audience's response to both the poetry and the man who quotes it is made more ambivalent by Edmund, who seems to use other men's words to stimulate his own. He quotes Dowson's 'Days of Wine and Roses' before exploring the experience of his walk in the fog (p. 113) and Baudelaire's 'Epilogue', as an introduction to his description of Jamie (pp. 115–16). We might say that whereas Jamie adopts the role implied by the poetry, Edmund uses it to seek out and comprehend his own experience of the world. Jamie, who takes over the attitude of these poems most completely, is most damaged by the family situation; Edmund, whose response is more ambiguous, seems to have some beliefs which reach beyond the private turmoil and Tyrone, who most determinedly avoids looking closely at his situation, dismisses these poets angrily, as 'morbid' purveyors of 'filth, despair and pessimism' (pp. 115–16) but is the one who makes their thematic relevance apparent when he says, in unthinking fury, 'Don't compare [Shakespeare] with the pack you've got there (. . .) Your dirty Zola! And your Dante Gabriel Rossetti who was a dope fiend. (*He starts and looks guilty*)' (p. 117). The quotation thus helps to make even the very individual afflictions of this family signify a more general pattern of human suffering and mischance.

George Steiner has written of O'Neill's use of quotation:

Interspersed in the sodden morass of *A Long Day's Journey Into Night* there are passages from Swinburne. The lines are flamboyant, romantic verbiage. They are meant to show up the adolescent inadequacies of those who recite them. But, in fact, when the play is performed, the contrary occurs. The energy and glitter of Swinburne's language burn a hole in the surrounding fabric. They elevate the action above its paltry level and instead of showing up the character show up the playwright. Modern writers rarely quote their authors with impunity.

(*Language and Silence* (Penguin edition), p . 52)

Although, as we have seen, the role of quotation is rather more complex in this play than Steiner suggests, he is half-way towards the truth. Prose cannot speak to the auditory imagination in quite the way that verse does, lingering in the mind when no longer heard, and O'Neill needed this quality of sound, particularly towards the end of the play. In *Moon of the Carribbees*, O'Neill used the sound of a haunting creole lament; in *The Emperor Jones*, the beat of African drums; in *Dynamo*, the hum of the electric generator, and he wrote to the Theatre Guild directors before the production of *Dynamo*, stressing the importance to him of sound in the theatre and saying, 'It must be realized that these are not incidental noises but significant dramatic overtones that are an integral part of the composition in the theatre which is the whole play' (Cargill, p. 454). The foghorn, which sounds during the last act of *Long Day's Journey Into Night*, is a sound effect of this kind but the important sound pattern is, appropriately in this play in which language is so deftly structured, a verbal one. The quotations O'Neill uses are unusually melodious and the actors are directed to deliver them sonorously. Swinburne's words do burn and nowhere more so than in the final sequence of the play, which is the one Steiner seems to have had in mind. Here, three stanzas of Swinburne's poem 'A Leave-taking' are interwoven with the dialogue of the play. What Steiner does not admit is that the words burn *because* of the context O'Neill has created for them. A comment of Eliot's about the poet is enlightening. 'Swinburne's words', he writes, 'are all suggestion and no denotation; if they suggest nothing it is because they suggest too much.' O'Neill gives direction to their suggestiveness and so makes the denotation possible. He achieves the kind of re-creation that we found lacking in the references to Nietzsche in *Lazarus Laughed*.

Because the dialogue is shaped around the poem, Swinburne's words are at once impersonal and dreadfully appropriate: more dread-ful because impersonal, set apart from the idiosyncratic prose of the appeals spoken, in turn, by the men. Originally, O'Neill included some commentary on the poem in the dialogue and Edmund's voice alternated with Jamie's (see illustration 5). In the final draft, the quotation is not absorbed into the dialogue in this way. The links between the poem and the dialogue are many but they must be made by the audience:

... She will not know.	You know something in her does it deliberately – to get beyond our
... She will not hear.	reach, to be rid of us, to forget we're alive! It's as if in spite of loving us,
... She will not see.	she hated us.
	(p. 121)

... surely she, She too, remembering days and words that were, Will turn a little toward us ...	You must not try to touch me. You must not try to hold me. (p. 154)

Let us go seaward as the great winds go, Full of blown sand and foam.	The fog was where I wanted to be ... to be alone with myself ... Out beyond the harbour, where the road runs along the beach ... (p. 113)

The intervening dialogue, with its single words and brief sentences, has its own pattern – three times Mary speaks to herself, three times one of the men attempts to penetrate her consciousness and Jamie says the attempt is futile – but, with its rhythm and rhyme and internal verbal echoes, the poem has a more formal pattern which establishes continuity between the stanzas even though they are separated by dialogue, so that Jamie's voice, speaking it, appears to bind the whole sequence and the four individual voices together. Throughout the play we have been made aware of the part verbal deception and self-deception play in the relationships and we have seen human beings deriving comfort from the very structuring of the words spoken. Now, at the end of the play, when we have comprehended the desolation of the Tyrones, O'Neill permits to characters and to

"Let us rise up and part; she will not know,
Let us go seaward as the great winds go,
Full of blown sand and foam; what help is here?
There is no help, for all these things are so,
And all the world is bitter as a tear.
And how these things are, though ye strove to show,
She would not know."

Mary: ~~(as if she had heard this from a great distance, as something unrelated to any person's voice) That is true, but it's very sad.~~ (~~When dreamily again~~ looking around her ~~vaguely~~) Something I miss terribly. It can't be altogether lost. (She starts to move around in back of Jamie's chair)

Jamie: (turns to look up into her face, ~~with the same anguished pleading as his father~~) Mama! (She ~~remains unaware of him,~~ does not seem to hear. He ~~turns back~~ hopelessly ~~and mutters dully~~) Hell! What's the use! ~~She won't hear.~~

~~Edmund: (quoting bitterly from the same poem of Swinburne's)~~
"Let us go hence, my songs; she will not hear,
Let us go hence together without fear;
Keep silence now, for singing-time is over.
And over all old things and all things dear.
She loves not you nor me as all we love her.
Yes, though we sang as angels in her ear,
She would not hear."

Mary: (~~again as if she heard this from a great distance, as a verse detached, spoken from the air - nods her head slowly) Yes, that is only too true. It is too bad it has to be so sorrowful. (When dreamily again~~ looking around her ~~vaguely~~) Something I need terribly, ~~because~~ I remember when I had it, I was never lonely nor afraid. I can't have lost it forever. I would die if I thought that. (She moves like a sleep-walker, around the back of Jamie's chair, then forward toward left-front, passing behind Edmund)

Edmund: (turns impulsively and grabs her arm. As he pleads ~~desperately~~ he has the quality of a bewilderedly hurt little boy) Mama! ~~Won't you see!~~ It isn't a summer cold! I've got consumption!

Mary: (for a second he seems to have broken through to her. She ~~begins to~~ trembles and her expression becomes terrified ~~and grief-stricken.~~ She calls distractedly, as if giving a command to herself) No! (And instantly she ~~retreats into herself and~~ is far away again. She murmurs gently but impersonally) You must not try to touch me. You must not try to hold me. It isn't right, when I am ~~going~~ to audience the comfort that artistic ordering of experience can give: the minimal comfort of an elegy. An elegy fittingly spoken by the character for whom, of all the Tyrones, there is the least comfort possible.

The mysterious effectiveness of the final scene of the play

I have suggested that the ending of *Mourning Becomes Electra* was one of the most convincing signs of the imaginative control which O'Neill would achieve in the late plays. It was in many ways a tour de force imposing order on the play. The unfolding action of *Long Day's Journey Into Night* has a greater coherence and the dialogue is more absorbingly complex than that of the earlier play. The ending, when it comes, comes as the culmination of the meanings, the undertones and overtones we have absorbed during the play, and it is couched in words and images made potent by their use within the play. In concluding this discussion of the language of the play, it is important to look at the final sequence (pp. 150–6) which, in its quiet and stillness, is so different from that of *The Iceman Cometh*. The sequence has been praised repeatedly:[15] the method of this study should enable us to put into words some, at least, of the reasons for its extraordinary power.

O'Neill altered act IV in its second draft to keep Mary off-stage until the last few minutes of the play.[16] In doing so, he increased the suspense of the act and the subsequent impact of Mary's appearance. Throughout the act her entrance is anticipated, by the listening attitude of the men, by their comments on her restless pacing above them and by their very presence on the stage, since we recognize that their vigil must continue until she has become still. If we catch it, the reference to Ibsen's *John Gabriel Borkman* is an appropriate one with its memory of that other familial relationship, its tortured, listening women and its intimacy and destructiveness. The underlying pattern of the action demands Mary's presence for its completion. Edmund and Tyrone have moved three times from hostility to understanding, reaching a deeper level of mutual confidence at each stage. Then, the relationship between the two brothers has been presented with comparable intensification as Jamie has moved from bonhomie to threat, to self-revelation. Each of the three men having in turn exposed his secret thought to one of the others, there is a hiatus. Exhausted, they drowse. The balance in which the characters have been held until now makes Mary's entrance inevitable. But it is also startling because of the way in which it takes place. There is a moment of silence and then Edmund jerks up, listening intently. A burst of light at the back of the stage, when all five bulbs of the chandelier flash on, is followed by a burst of sound, when a Chopin waltz is played on the piano. When Mary appears in the doorway, her hair is long and braided girlishly, she wears a sky blue night gown, and carries a wedding dress. O'Neill succeeds in creating a poetry of theatre here where he failed in *Dynamo*, for all the elaborate machinery of that play, because each visual and aural impression arouses in the audience some memory of the dialogue. Things which through repeated naming have become emblems of the private mythology of the family are suddenly present before us in solid form. Jamie's words, which break the silence, have the force of words which should not have been spoken but, having been, cannot be expunged from the mind and Mary's failure to react to them signifies how dissociated from the present she has become. When she speaks she uses the schoolgirlish register entirely, 'I play *so* badly now. I'm *all* out of practice. Sister Theresa will give me a *dreadful* scolding ...' She is no longer speaking in the present and looking back to the past but, as the verb tenses show, has moved into that past time which has become her present. There follows the highly patterned passage containing the poem after which Mary speaks her final monologue.

Here, as throughout the play, the verbal and visual level are integrated with each other, so that when words leave off the stage image speaks. Once we have absorbed the impact of Mary's final entrance, the stage picture has significance not because, like that, it is startling or spectacular, but because of the way it complements the dialogue. Watching the final moments of the play, we are scarcely aware of how carefully movement and gesture have been organized and how much they contribute to the feeling of the scene. As can be seen from O'Neill's sketch of this sequence (illustration 6), the men remain still so that our eyes follow Mary as she crosses from the door to the front of the stage. Mary's seemingly aimless movement, in fact takes her past each of the men in turn, taking our attention with her from one to the other of them. In the single other movement, shortly after Mary's entrance, Tyrone approaches Mary who carries her wedding dress that has lain in the old trunk in the attic and that, described with delight by Mary earlier in the play, had become an emblem of her lost girlhood and her reproach to Tyrone. Because we have experienced this, Tyrone's simple gesture of taking the dress from her and holding it protectively is remarkably moving. When

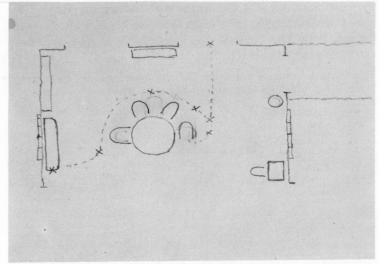

6. *Long Day's Journey Into Night*: an unlabelled sketch by O'Neill found amongst his notes. The sketch plots the final movements of the characters.

Mary comes to rest it is, as the sketch shows, at the front left corner of the stage which leaves the silent characters at the focal point in the centre. This divides the audience's attention during Mary's final speech and so acts as preparation for the last line of the play.

Whilst Mary speaks her monologue, the audience, listening to her words, observe the speaking silence of the listening men and hear, perhaps, the lingering echo of the poem, 'There is no help for all these things are so.' They recognize that Mary has given herself over to the past, obliterating her men-folk with her colloquialisms, her girlish intensifiers, her manner of discussing the interview as if it had just taken place. Her naïve and trusting words, 'I knew She heard my prayer and would always love me and see no harm ever came to me as long as I never lost my faith in her', are almost unbearable for the stage listeners, and for the audience observing the stage listeners and knowing that their perspective is from a different point in time from hers.

The overwhelming effect of the last four lines of the play comes, I think, because, just when it appears that the play has drawn to its conclusion and has reached some kind of resting place, however dismal, the sentence, '*That was* in the winter of senior year', pushes the interview back into the distant past and returns Mary to the present and the family, from which there can be, after all, no escape for any of the four Tyrones. The quiet ending of the play is not a conclusion but another relentless beginning:

That was in the winter of senior year. Then in the spring something happened to me. Yes, I remember, I fell in love with James Tyrone and was so happy for a time.

Conclusion

O'Neill's contemporaneity: real realism

O'Neill's drama found an audience in the late 1950s. At first sight, it seems remote from the dominant serious drama of this period, the post-realist drama that stemmed from Beckett's *Waiting for Godot*. A further wave of successful revivals of the late plays early in the 1970s[1] suggests that O'Neill's appeal in 1956 was not, as might have been supposed, that of a voice from the past briefly resuscitated, but that of a voice speaking directly to audiences now. It is not a quaint voice but an urgent one that we hear, one that sounds both of and outside of its own time and presents us with pressing questions about our own being. O'Neill's writing differs from the ephemeral writing of those contemporaries of his who might seem to share his conventions because, in his drama, word and word, word and stage image, interact within a developing pattern of meaning, startling us, as members of the audience, with their echoic quality, informing us with their mutual suggestiveness, compelling us to see contrasts and new relationships. The dramatist whose plays continue to live on the stage in a period in which stage conditions have altered is not one who has merely satisfied the expectations of his audience and cast events and characters into a preconceived form. He is one who, whilst acknowledging the conventions of the contemporary theatre, has given those characters and events significance within the action of a play whose form is a necessary part of its meaning. The context for the action, which is normally supplied by the audience themselves from theatrical habit and their sense of matters of current discussion, is incorporated into the verbal and visual sequence of the play itself. It is this density of internal reference and association and the demands that the play, therefore, makes on those who watch it, to take references and make associations, that enables the play to continue to weld a heterogeneous crowd into an audience and to retain meaning in an alien time and society.

I have shown, particularly in the last two chapters of this study, how fully O'Neill incorporates the context into the play. There is, in Primo Levi's book, *The Truce*, a description of a theatrical performance which was remarkably of one time and place and whose effectiveness depended, by contrast with what I have been describing, on the collective experience of a most unusual audience who, prompted by the vestigial nature of the words and gesture, supplied the context from its shared knowledge. Whilst we cannot share this response, Levi's description, both here and in the book as a whole, in part supplies the context for the reader and allows us to understand something of the kind of experience that audiences in that theatre must have had. The description, and this is its relevance here, helps us to perceive how much the dramatist himself must supply who would draw a similarly deep response to enigmas of human existence, whether we choose to label him a 'realist' or a 'post-realist', whether he writes an *Iceman Cometh* or a *Waiting for Godot*.

Levi, one of only six Italian Jews who survived Auschwitz, describes a long period of free but purposeless existence after the release from that camp, passed in the no man's land of a Russian transit camp. He tells of an entertainment improvised in the transit camp's amphitheatre by the people waiting – Italian prisoners of war, Jewish survivors, and other refugees. Some Rumanians sing a non-sense rhyme in which a word is suppressed at each repetition and replaced by a gesture:

My hat has got three corners –
Three corners has my hat.
If it did not have three corners
It would not be my hat.

This 'infant whimsicality', Levi writes, 'turned into a sinister, obscurely allegorical pantomime, full of symbolic and disquieting echoes':

A small orchestra, whose instruments had been provided by the Russians, began its tired motif in low, muted tones. Slowly, swaying to the rhythm, three nightmare figures came onto the stage; they were wrapped in black cloaks, with black hoods on their heads, and from the hoods emerged three faces, of corpse-like decrepit pallor, marked by deep, livid lines. They entered with a hesitant dance step, holding three unlighted candles in their hands. When they reached the centre of the stage, always in time to the rhythm, they bowed towards the public with senile difficulty, slowly bending their stiff joints, with small worrying wrenches; they took two full minutes to bend down and rise again, minutes which were full of anguish for all the spectators. They painfully regained an erect position, the orchestra stopped, and the three phantoms began to sing the stupid strophe in a tremulous broken voice. They sang, and at every repeat, with the accumulation of gaps replaced by uncertain gestures, it seemed as if life, as well as voice, would drain from them. With the rhythm accentuated by the hypnotic pulsation of a single muted drum, the paralysis proceeded slowly and ineluctably. The final repetition, with absolute silence from orchestra, singers and public was an excruciating agony, a death throe.

When the song ended, the orchestra began again lugubriously; the three figures, with a final effort, trembling in every limb, repeated their bow. Unbelievably, they once more managed to straighten themselves, and with their candles wavering, with a horrible and macabre hesitation, but always in time to the rhythm, they disappeared forever behind the scenes.

The 'Three Cornered Hat' number took away one's breath, and every evening was greeted with a silence more eloquent than applause. Why? Perhaps because, under the grotesque appearance, one perceived the heavy breath of a collective dream, of the dream emanating from exile and idleness, when work and troubles have ceased, and nothing acts as a screen between man and himself; perhaps because we saw the impotence and nullity of our lives and of life itself, and the hunch-backed, crooked profiles of the monsters generated by the sleep of reason.

(*The Truce*, Torino, 1963, translated S. Woolf (London, 1965), pp. 158–9)

One striking aspect of this account, I think, is that we recognize instantly what kind of experience it is that Levi describes. Our wonder is less that this 'infant whimsicality' could have had the effect it did, than that Levi's description of this brief performance should seem so familiar. Reading it, we are in the world of the post-war theatre. Here, as there, implication arises out of seeming nonsense or, rather, out of a crazy, solipsistic logic, and out of the suggestive juxtaposition of word, gesture and silence. The connections which make up a meaning must be made in the mind of each member of the audience. But there are marked differences, too. Whilst the 'Three Cornered Hat' is a brief song, a 'number' performed amongst other songs and sketches, *Waiting for Godot* is a two-act play. Since then, Beckett has written plays which are briefer than his first, even an 'Act Without Words', but these sparser plays carry implication because their audiences watch them partly in the light of what has gone before: *Waiting for Godot* and *Endgame* are part of the implicit context which helps us to assimilate *Lessness* or *Not I*. The audience Levi described did not have a theatrical context of this kind. Because of the limbo of their present and the searing and untellable experience of their recent past in the camp, they shared a common consciousness which led to a shared openness to the suggestiveness of images, in the context of which, the minimal words and action of the 'Three Cornered Hat' number could generate 'symbolic and disquieting echoes'. Such homogeneity is not to be encountered in any theatre audience. The dramatist must himself create such a context within his play if he is to lead his audience into a state of alert awareness in which they can make connections of the sort Levi describes. He must stir our memory of things we have known or half encountered and have let lie buried; he must awaken in us the capacity to take symbolic value from the action we see on the stage; he must disrupt our complacency by making unexpected associations between things we thought we knew to be apart.

Inevitably, this context must derive from the conventions of the theatre of his time and from the ways in which both dramatist and audience are accustomed to respond to and to interpret images in the theatre, although, in exploring his particular meaning in dramatic terms, any major dramatist will inevitably also startle his audience and disturb some of their preconceptions even whilst satisfying others. His private struggle with form will in this way extend the previous limits and play a part in changing the accepted conventions.

I do not wish to present an argument that O'Neill is an absurdist dramatist, but would suggest that in his insistence that his realistic manner must also be expressive, must be 'real realism', he did play a part in extending the limits and did assimilate into his form means of exploring areas of human experience which continue to be of pressing interest to us today. Retention of the realistic framework seems to have been essential to the functioning of his creative imagination. He did experiment with expressionist and symbolist techniques but, as we saw in chapter 1, even within such experiments he constantly veered towards sets and situations in which the familiar and human, as opposed to the remote or metaphysical, could be recreated and explored.

And yet whilst O'Neill never does break the illusion he does go to the edge, does threaten it. Within the conventional performing of the play itself, his characters perform for each other and adopt a succession of different roles. The characters in *Long Day's Journey Into Night* introduce their quotations or passages of heightened prose with a self-conscious gesture, they praise each other's performance and comment on the quality of each recitation; Con Melody strikes poses before a mirror, into which he also performs his recitations of Byron's poetry; Don Parritt's final exit in *The Iceman Cometh* is accompanied by a consciously histrionic 'curtain line', whilst in *A Moon for the Misbegotten*, Jamie gestures to the sunrise with the words 'Rise of Curtain, Act Four stuff'. Such speeches contribute to the ongoing action. They are 'in character', notably so in the case of the Tyrones who are presented as being professional actors. And yet, they also bring consciousness of performance and playing into the audience's minds, in much the same way as does the reiterated play metaphor in Shakespeare's drama.[2]

Similarly, although in the late plays O'Neill does appear to keep to a sequential time span, there is, co-existent with the realistic rhythm of linear time, a different temporal rhythm: a strange recurrence and circularity of the kind that would be explicit in the drama of the post-war period. In concluding this study of O'Neill's dramatic method, I should like, by looking briefly at the play of time in the late plays, to underline what is already apparent in the detailed discussion of O'Neill's language in the body of this book, that, in his fully achieved 'real realism', O'Neill gains the capacity to speak with a voice that is at once familiar and original, of the paradoxes that beset our human existence.

The fictional time span of each of O'Neill's late plays occupies only a day or a day and a half of fictional time, and each is limited to a single set. (See Appendix 3 for an account of O'Neill's handling of time in the early and middle years.) In each, a linear plot drives the action forwards. *The Iceman Cometh*, with its revelations, act by act, about the death of Evelyn and the betrayal of Rosa, is modelled on the detective mystery; *Long Day's Journey Into Night*, with its hints, its anticipated telephone calls, its trips to the doctor and drug store, its ominous predictions about the return of the fog, on the well-made play. *A Touch of the Poet* and *Moon for the Misbegotten*, the one with its duel, the other its intrigue over the old homestead and both with seduction plots, follow the course of the old melodrama. The linear plot is used in each case to hold the audience and stimulate their curiosity, whilst other elements slowly take possession at a deeper level, and meaning accrues to seemingly neutral words and images. Time and space are extended in these plays, within the firm structure of the linear plot, by a succession of vignettes of off-stage characters and events which are integrated into the dialogue in jokes, tall stories, reminiscences and involuntary memories. At their simplest, these present people or events from outside the stage setting but inside the play's fictional time span. Shaughnessey, Macguire; Simon, Mr Harford; Jamie weeping at Mamie Burns'; Hickey standing at a street corner, Hope's roomers confronting the world; Jim Tyrone and Hogan at the inn; Sara visiting Simon's room – they increase the range of the action without dissipating its concentration. In other sequences, people or events from *outside* the time-span of the play are presented. Recalled

from the past, these are the women with whom Hope's roomers failed
to establish relationships; the man through whose admiration Erie
Smith had been able to summon self-respect, and, most poignantly,
they are the characters themselves at another stage of their lives. The
events that are recalled, no longer important in themselves, have
become self-restorative or self-tormenting fictions in which the
characters seek for their own identities. Absorbed now into the
dialogue, they are often those 'strong' situations which would once
have dominated O'Neill's plot – attempted suicide, murder, betrayal,
a child discovering his mother's drug addiction, a crazy performance
at a grave-side, a ghoulish debauch. Filtered through individual
memories, constantly presenting themselves for re-examination,
altered slightly at each telling, told by one and then another character,
never actually witnessed by the audience, they are not fixed in the way
that the stage events are. By the end of the plays they have taken on the
quality of myth. The past which increasingly fills our consciousness is
shown to be always shifting, and our perception of the present which
so clearly grows from that past is made correspondingly tentative.

In *The Iceman Cometh*, the relationship with the past is bound up
with the nature of the lives represented in the present. In Hope's bar,
time has stopped. The roomers live in an eternal present, of their own
creation. The past has made them what they are yet, despite their very
different backgrounds, they have all come to the same thing. The
past, except for alcohol, is their only topic of conversation, the only
thing which stirs their thought, but the conversation and thought is
not vital, it consists of variations on the already known possibilities,
told in order to fill the time. It is no longer a deep relationship. Even
the awareness of a lost future is neutralized by being made into a
pipe-dream and by having become public territory. The past has
become a fiction, characterized by songs, slogans and tales. The
individual is lost in the community and the community has no purpose
and no future. It exists and, so long as it does, its members will
exercise mutual tolerance, will protect each other in order to protect
themselves by maintaining the status quo. Hickey disturbs the
equilibrium because he challenges the roomers to make that petrified
past with its dream of a future regain its life. Each man can see the
pointlessness of the others attempting such a transfer but each
nevertheless hopes anxiously that the others will succeed, because the
old order is being shaken and they must have something with which to
replace it. Hickey's attempt to help them forget the past and future
and free them from guilt and hope, is misguided because the game of

past and future, guilt and hope they all play is a screen to protect them from recognizing their own pointlessness. The roomers in their drifting existence 'Before Hickey' still hang on to the idea of purpose, because they are able to construct an artificial version of the progressive, linear view of time that Hickey holds. What gives the play its remarkable force is that the context O'Neill creates leads us to recognize that behind the façade of claims to purpose, made ingenuously by Hickey and self-blindingly by the roomers, there exists a universe without any purpose, and that the drifting, passive time filled by a game, is the real model of human existence. In *Long Day's Journey Into Night*, the verbal organization of Mary Tyrone's final speech leads us to perceive the character and the occasion she evokes from two different points in time. At the very last moment of this speech, and of the play, the moment to which various elements in the plot and the very title have been propelling us, we are asked to return again to the opening of the play, to the ground which has been worked over and over since the play began and to all the statements about the circularity of events which we have absorbed during the course of the play. Such an effect could only have been achieved in the drama, where visual image and spoken word interact, where we have before us not only the listeners who are tormented by the words, but the very room in which their stage life has been passed and the objects which have become identified with them. A word, therefore, a gesture, even a position on the stage, can activate our memory of those other moments contrasting with, complementing, extending the immediate image.

The far more difficult art of prose

In this study, I have explored the distinctly dramatic as opposed to the purely literary or rhetorical elements in O'Neill's language and, in doing so, have attempted to extend the discussion of why some plays entertain us pleasantly in the theatre for a couple of hours before they are forgotten, whilst others, O'Neill's amongst them, have the power to make more stringent demands on our experiencing faculties and, thereby, to become a vital part of our imaginative lives.

I do not present this study as the definitive account of O'Neill's drama, but as a working inquiry into it, which I would hope would help to stimulate further investigation of how particular arrangements of words coalesce to create dramatic meaning. Although I have tested my ideas about O'Neill's language extensively, I have inevitably had to be selective in deciding which areas I should explore and which examples of them I should present here. My selection must have been directed by my own private response to the plays, which will not have been exactly that of any other person in O'Neill's audience. My examples might look convincing, taken as they are here, out of context, but how well do they stand up to probing? Is the pattern which I have suggested as the norm for James Tyrone's speech, for example, really the norm? Are my claims about the monotony of rhythm in *Lazarus Laughed* borne out by a reading of the full text, which Stanislavski, for one, was eager to produce? Does the dialogue always interact with the movements which the stage directions demand of Tyrone, as I have shown it to do in the excerpts discussed, or does the movement and gesture relapse into mere behaviour for much of the action? Are the words of *Lazarus Laughed* always as much weaker than the choreography as they are in the examples I have given? I would hope that my method would not quell such questioning but would invite the reader to examine my claims repeatedly against the plays O'Neill has written.

What is shown by my exploration to be beyond question, I would think, is that the language of O'Neill's plays is not 'transparent', as the language of realistic drama is often felt to be, nor are the gesture, costume and set merely arbitrary, there to please the eye and fill the stage – rather, the dramatist's competence in composing the language of the play, his imaginative organization of the elements of theatre and his interrelating of the two, are shown to be as central and as inextricably intertwined in vital drama of the realist manner as they are in that of any other manner. O'Neill, like all writers of significance who might be labelled 'realist', does not, even were it possible, merely reproduce what is immediately available to sensory experience, nor do we have in any single speech, direct access to the full meaning of what is being said. His words take on a charge of meaning in the interaction and accumulation of the parts of a scene or the parts of a whole play, in the use of repetition and anticlimax, in the creation of and subsequent reward or denial of expectation, in changes in the syntactic pattern and in the echoing of keywords, in emphasizing or undercutting the spoken word with gesture, or stance, or tone of voice, and in a host of other linguistic and gestural elements, to which the audience, even without consciously recognizing how and when, gradually become attuned.

O'Neill, as I have shown, eventually achieved a fully dramatic language. Its rhythms are those of prose, certainly, but it is prose which is as complex, delicate and untranslatable, in its way, as poetry. There have been very few studies of dramatic language, but what there have been suggest strongly that we could come nearer to understanding the 'power' and 'force' and 'dramatic effectiveness' of the drama of our own time if we were to give more careful attention to the language in which it is written. Such investigation would help us to perceive the differences between contemporary writing which is complex and contemporary writing which is merely complicated or obscure, between dialogue which is casual and dialogue which is organically related to action although it gives an impression of being casual.

However nostalgically we might look to the Elizabethan and Jacobean period when both verse and prose were available, verse now seems to be an alien medium for both playwrights and audiences. To ask why verse no longer seems fully appropriate to the drama would seem to be much the same kind of question as to ask why the novel has superseded the epic or the long narrative poem, why verse has not, for a long time, seemed an appropriate medium for historical or philosophical writing, or, indeed, to ask why rhyme and regular metre have virtually ceased to figure in contemporary poetry itself. It is, arguably, the same kind of question as why it now seems necessary to celebrate the Mass in the vernacular or why incantation and ritual in public life still have the power to stir us, but always with the recognition intermingled of them as other, as things past, and of ourselves as observers, not participators. Even Eliot, the great advocate of verse in the theatre, sought to disguise its presence from his audience, saying:

Too many people, on the other hand, approach a play which they know to be in verse, with the consciousness of the difference. It is unfortunate when they are repelled by verse, but can also be deplorable when they are attracted by it – if that means that they are prepared to enjoy the play and the language of the play as two separate things. The chief effect of style and rhythm in dramatic speech, whether in prose or verse, should be unconscious.

(*Selected Prose*, p. 66)

Yeats was more confident in his use of verse, but, whilst we may admire his attempt to create a theatre of kings and peasants, delighting in *Deirdre* or in the *Plays for Dancers*, we know, even whilst watching them, that these works are precious but also remote from us: strange, archaic jewels.

The search for answers to the questions of why we are not quite at ease with verse, why we have separated literature from music, would spread beyond the scope of this study into inquiry into the social and psychological springs and direction of our culture.

But to acknowledge that verse is no longer a natural medium for drama is clearly not to have said all that needs to be said about poetic drama. The language of prose drama certainly can be, and often is, thin-blooded, and the attempt to revive verse in the theatre, not only on the part of Eliot and Yeats, but of Hugo von Hofmannsthal and of Auden and Isherwood, as well as a host of courageous, if less well-equipped, poets from Maeterlinck and Rostand to Maxwell Anderson and Christopher Fry, stems from a just realization that the language of drama must be dense and flexible, must be, in Synge's familiar words, 'as fully flavoured as a nut or an apple', capable of giving expression to what is mysterious in human existence as well as what is readily comprehended. The verse drama experiment was an attempt to incorporate one principal element from the drama of the past into the dramatic mode of the present and, as such, it was bound to fail. What was necessary was that a dialogue should be created which acknowledged its own time and the literary developments that had taken place since the seventeenth century, which caught the accents of the common speech, but ordered them more expressively. One of the really exciting aspects of the drama from Ibsen onwards has been the variety of ways and the self-consciousness with which, one after another, dramatists have engaged in a search for an appropriate language.

One mode which has emerged from this search is O'Neill's, and it stems from Ibsen. In it, as we have seen, the *illusion* that the characters are using everyday speech is retained whilst the dialogue is, in fact, being patterned by the dramatist into a language that is more evocative and suggestive, as well as more concentrated, than any comparable stretch of everyday speech could be. By referring to the original Norwegian of Ibsen's texts, or to sensitive translations of them, Inga-Stina Ewbank and John Northam have both demonstrated that Ibsen, making particular use of certain visual images and key-words used by one and then another character, created 'highly structured patterns of unified dramatic imagery' in his plays.[3] Synge, too, worked in this mode taking the peasant speech of rural Ireland and the Aran Islands as his base, as O'Neill was later to take New York slang, and Tennessee Williams the speech rhythms of America's deep south.

Another and very different mode has been that developed by Brecht and, following him in England, by John Arden. Here, the artifice of the stage is brought into the open and investigated as part of the action of the play. Far from concealing the verse and allowing its rhythms to blend into those of prose, as Eliot had tried to do, Brecht relishes the alien aspect of verse and deliberately juxtaposes prose and verse rhythms. As he says in his notes to *The Threepenny Opera*:

The three levels – plain speech, heightened speech and singing – must always remain separate from one another. Therefore, in no circumstances will singing take over where words fail for excess of emotion. The actor must not only sing but show a man singing.

(Penguin edition, p. 234)

This juxtaposition not only enables him to compose a drama which has a surface liveliness, but allows him, by a sudden shift in style, to move his audience from one way of perceiving the action to another different way. In *Mother Courage*, for example, there are sequences which offer the audience the pattern of traditional drama, in which the dialogue is derived from idiomatic German and the characters speaking it are distinguished from each other by accent and verbal idiosyncracy which contribute to our impression of them as real people. In certain of these sequences, the dramatic tension is raised by Brecht in traditional ways – the prediction of an event; the postponement of a crucial word or deed; the refusal of one character to act as another wishes; the overhearing by one character of words another would not have had him know had been uttered – and an emotional response is elicited from the audience. One example would be the scene in which Mother Courage denies Swiss Cheese; another, that in which Kattryn overhears the Cook's proposal that Mother Courage should abandon her. The intervention into these sequences of song, or of recitatives which use ballad metre and rhyme and are phrased in that strangely timeless language of traditional ballads – the Chaplain's 'Song of the Hours' in the Swiss Cheese incident, the Cook's 'Song of Solomon' in the Kattryn incident – forces us to stand back from the emotion we have experienced. The changes from action to narrative, from specific interchange to generalized comment, draw the audience's attention to the means of expression and invite them to exercise their critical faculties. Changes in distance, which interrupt or redirect the flow of attention, are of course present, as I have shown in earlier chapters of this study, in all kinds of drama. What is different in Brecht's form is the deliberateness with which such changes are introduced, and the insistence that the audience should be conscious of the changes and of the response the action elicits from them.

The language of certain post-Second World War dramatists is related to the Ibsen mode in which the illusion of speech is retained, in that the same style is used consistently through the play and the figures remain 'in character' throughout. It is, however, a language far more obviously abstracted from everyday speech than imitative of it. Sometimes grotesquely playful, it derives rather from Strindberg's

Chamber Plays or, even more, from Jarry's *Ubu* plays than from Ibsen. The dialogue may fragment into lists, contain crazy repetitions and long silences, or it may fall into patterns usually connected with non-dramatic theatre – such as those of the circus, the music hall, the stand-up comic turn – or with non-theatrical discourse – such as those of philosophical argument or biblical text. Its audiences are invited to accept that this is the way these figures speak and yet, at the same time, to be conscious of the distortions, the exaggerations and the linguistic parodies the language contains. Individual writers within this mode remain as stylistically distinct from each other as the writers of any other period. Beckett's language, for example, makes much more play with non-theatrical discourse than Pinter's does, it is barer than everyday speech and, hearing it, we are made conscious, through the echoes we catch, of how partial and fragmented our experience is. Pinter, on the other hand, locates his speech in a place and time, through frequent references to homely articles, and through the repetition of idiomatic phrases which we recognize as common in our own speech. These differences reflect and are reflected in other important differences. Beckett's stage world is timeless and unparticularized. He prevents us from making his figures into characters. References outside the present action are haphazard and lack the implication that there is a past which might be pieced together. The existence of a figure who leaves the stage is suspended until his return. Pinter, on the other hand, by a complicated pattern of clues and suggestions, leads us to believe that there could be an explanation for the strange events that we witness. The very mystification leads us to attempt to find order and explanation. The detail encourages us to recognize a particular time and place for the action and, if we cannot always identify cause and effect, or see why one event should follow another, the assumption on the part of the characters that things are proceeding normally leads us to accept that the action is sequential and that the crisis or denouement, when it comes, and it invariably does in Pinter's drama, has followed inevitably from previous events even if we cannot quite see how.

The cry, 'the silence!', 'the pause', 'the subtext', has gone up as an explanation of the effectiveness of post-realist language, but detailed stylistic studies by Andrew Kennedy and by John Russell Brown have made it clear that the expressive subtext can be identified by the audience only because of the complex organization of the text itself. Once we become accustomed, as members of a theatre audience, to a new linguistic pattern, to the idea that words will fail, for example, the shock effect of the novelty goes, we no longer find those silences threatening in themselves and we see how essential it is that the words and the interaction of the words with the visual images, should have activated the audience's own imaginations, for only, thereby, will images fill those silences.

Even a survey as brief as this will remind us of the number and variety of the writers from Ibsen and Strindberg to Brecht and Arden, from Chekhov and Jarry to Beckett and Pinter who have, in the last hundred years, been drawn to the idea of figures 'moving about on a stage and using words.'[4] It will help to make apparent, too, the truth of Edmund Wilson's comment:

In art the same things are not done again or are not done again except as copies. The point is that literary techniques are tools, which the masters of the craft have to alter in adapting them to fresh uses. To be too much attached to the traditional tools may be sometimes to ignore the new masters.

('Is Verse a Dying Technique?' *The Triple Thinkers* (London, 1952), p. 39)

A director's theatre has come into being in this century. There have been repeated attacks on the very idea of written texts in the theatre from Paul Fort's theatre of ephemeral sensory images, constructed out of light, sound, colour and even smell, at the Théâtre d'Art in the 1890s, to the theatre groups in the 1960s, who have improvised words and gestures around a theme, or have staged 'happenings', those unscheduled moments of theatre. But, despite predictions to the contrary and despite the loneliness of the struggle to achieve dramatic form, a score or more texts of extraordinary dramatic power, two of O'Neill's amongst them, have been produced, ensuring that the imaging and organizing consciousness of the individual dramatist has remained the vital centre of the drama.

APPENDIX 1

O'Neill's literary biography

In this compilation, the plays are listed chronologically and beside each is a note of works which may have been influential and then a note of books O'Neill is known to have been reading at the time and works from which he quotes directly. Both are select lists. Only books whose value to him was remarked in letters or conversation are included. (A much fuller list of the contents of O'Neill's library is held by the C. W. Post Centre and the Beinecke Library.) I have drawn heavily on the major biographies for this information. The information about influence is vast and has had to be approached tentatively. I have included only those suggestions about sources, echoes and half-quotations which were subjected to thorough discussion in the original article and seem to me to bear further examination. Frequently, whilst reading such articles, I have felt that the author had sensed something of another writer in O'Neill's theme, plot or style and has attempted to take the comparison further than the work will bear, in order to clarify the original sensation or give it credence in discussion.[1] Similarly, a writer has sometimes attempted to identify an individual work as source material – London's *Call of the Wild* is identified with *The Emperor Jones*, Wharton's *Ethan Frome* with *Desire Under the Elms* – when all that can really be claimed is that O'Neill has developed an idea that was 'in the air' as, in these two cases, were primitivism and the distortion of puritanism in New England. More important than any single example is that so many writers have found literary reminiscences in O'Neill's plays.

For reasons of space and clarity, I have not noted the source of individual items when that is apparent from the title of the appropriate article in the bibliography pp. 230–2 nor where the information is common to two or more of the full length studies all of which, with the exception of Boulton's account, *Part of a Long Story (1917–19)*, carry efficient indices. The most helpful of the full-length studies are the books by Tiusanen, *Eugene O'Neill's Scenic Images*, Törnqvist, *A Drama of Souls*, Raleigh, *The Plays of Eugene O'Neill*, Engel, *The Haunted Heroes of Eugene O'Neill*, and, most recently and most comprehensively, Bogard, *Contour in Time*.

I have grouped together, at the outset, those books read by O'Neill before he began writing plays. These include many of the works that were most important to him and which he reread frequently. I have marked with a symbol (J) those books later included amongst the books listed as belonging to Edmund Tyrone in *Long Day's Journey Into Night*, since this seems to indicate a deliberate tribute by O'Neill. Where I have made suggestions of my own about influence, I note the chapter in which my suggestion is discussed.

Books and authors read by O'Neill before 1914

a. *At school and college* (up to 1912)

Every summer read and reread James O'Neill's books: Dumas; Victor Hugo; Charles Lever; Kipling; Dickens; Scott's poetry (E. S. Sergeant, 'Eugene O'Neill: The Man with a Mask', p. 90) and 'rare acting editions of old plays' (Gelbs, *O'Neill*, p. 84).

Jack London; Melville, stories, *Moby Dick*; Poe, stories (J); Richard Dana, *Two Years Before The Mast*; Conrad, particularly 'Nigger of the Narcissus' (Alexander, *Tempering of Eugene O'Neill*, p. 139).

Conrad; Walt Whitman, *Leaves of Grass* (J); Oscar Wilde, 'The Ballad of Reading Gaol', 'The Picture of Dorian Gray': this 'left an indelible impression' (Sheaffer, *O'Neill, Son and Playwright*), the poetry of Baudelaire (J); Dowson (J); Verlaine; Rossetti (J); Kipling (J); Byron, *Don Juan*, *Childe Harold*; Fitzgerald, *The Rubáiyát of Omar Khayyam*; Zola (J).

1905, Shaw (J), *The Quintessence of Ibsenism*.

By 1907, O'Neill was frequenting Benjamin Tucker's anarchist bookshop. Tucker published Shaw, Zola, Wilde, and introduced O'Neill to the writing of Nietzsche (Gelbs, *O'Neill*, pp. 119–21).

1908, Nietzsche (J), *Thus Spake Zarathustra*, *The Birth of Tragedy* – O'Neill learnt German in order to understand Nietzsche more fully.

Dostoevski; Tolstoi; Schopenhauer (J); Max Stirner (J), *The Ego and its Own*. Plays which O'Neill saw performed on stage: 1900, Yeats, *The Land of Heart's Desire* (Sheaffer, *O'Neill, Son and Playwright*, p. 83). 1906, Nazimova's Ibsen season which included *A Doll's House*; *The Master Builder* and *Hedda Gabler* which O'Neill saw ten times (Sheaffer, *O'Neill, Son and Playwright*, p. 122).

b. *At Gaylord Sanatorium* and up until the production of the first play in 1914.

The plays of Ibsen (J): Shaw (J); Strindberg (J); Gorki; Wedekind; Hauptmann; Yeats; Lady Gregory; Brieux; Greek drama; 'The Elizabethans'; Sheldon, *Salvation Nell*.

Ibsen's *Brand* and *Peer Gynt*, Gorki and the Greek drama 'seemed to open new worlds to O'Neill' (– report of a friend: Gelbs, *O'Neill*, p. 277).

Thompson, *The Hound of Heaven* (letter to Mary Clark, 5 August 1923) – learnt by heart (Alexander, *Tempering of Eugene O'Neill*, p. 176).

Zola, *La Terre*, *L'Assommoir*, *Germinal* (Alexander, *Tempering of Eugene O'Neill*, p. 162).

Dostoevski, *The Idiot*; Strindberg, *The Dance of Death* – O'Neill was impressed by the ability of these two books to 'communicate a powerful emotional ecstasy' (Gelbs, *O'Neill*, p. 233).

Plays which O'Neill saw performed on stage, 1911: The Irish Players in T. C. Murray, *The Birthrite*; Lady Gregory, *The Workhouse Ward*, *The Rising of the Moon*, *The Goal Gate*, *Hyacinth Harvey*, *The Jackdaw*, *The Image*, *Spreading the News*; W. B. Yeats, *Cathleen Ni Houlihan*; Synge, *Playboy of the Western World*, *Riders to the Sea*; *Well of the Saints*, *The Shadow of the Glen*.

Plays up to 1918

	Influences and echoes noticed by commentators	Current reading or direct quotation
Ten Lost Plays	Strindberg (*Before Breakfast*); Zola (*The Web*); Coleridge, *The Ancient Mariner*: scenic effects in *Fog* and *Thirst* (Bogard, *Contour in Time*, p. 30). Melville, *Moby Dick* (*Ile*), *White Jacket* (*Bound East*).	Strindberg, *Son of a Servant*, *The Red Room*, *Inferno* (Boulton, *Part of a Long Story* (*1917–19*), p. 76).
Caribbees	Conrad, 'Children of the Sea', 'Nigger of the Narcissus'. In both, we find 'men moving in the pattern established by an elemental force to which they belong' (Bogard, *Contour in Time*, p. 39); O'Neill, like Conrad is 'realist and romanticist' (Winther, *Eugene O'Neill: A Critical Study*, p. 17).	Cheney, *The New Movement in the Theatre* (Bogard, p. 172). *Saturday Evening Post*, short stories: for plots (Bogard, *Contour in Time*, p. 204).

1918–24

Horizon	T. C. Murray, *The Birthrite*: plot and character (Sheaffer, *O'Neill, Son and Playwright*, p. 206). Sheldon, *The High Road*, in which one character demands to know what is beyond the horizon. (Quinn, *A History of American Drama*, p. 90.) Wharton, *Ethan Frome*: Raleigh finds close similarity in 'the cast and setting' (*Plays of Eugene O'Neill*, p. 241). A Hardyesque view of fate. Neith Boyce, *The Two Sons*, *Provincetown Plays 3*: O'Neill's is a more sophisticated reworking of Boyce's plot (my suggestion).	O'Neill used to talk of 'White Nights' [Dostoevski] (Boulton, *Part of a Long Story* (*1917–19*), p. 52).

The Straw
Gold
Anna Christie   Synge, *Riders to the Sea*:
Chris's philosophy.
Caldwell, *Tobacco Road*:
goodhearted prostitute
figure, Dostoevski also
suggested as model.
Anderson, *Winesburg, Ohio*:
Christ symbolism.

Macgowan and Rosse,
Masks and Demons. Bought
new copy of Strindberg,
Dance of Death, Dream Play
(Boulton, *Part of a Long
Story (1917–19)*, p. 76).
Tolstoi, *Power of Darkness*
(at Theatre Guild, 1920).
Isaac Goldberg, *The Drama
of Transition*.

Jones   Conrad, *The Heart of
Darkness* (Scott Fitzgerald,
see ch. 2). London, *The
Call of the Wild*.
Hauptmann, *Drayman
Henschel*. Ibsen, *Peer Gynt*
(Bogard. *Contour in Time*,
p. 136; Törnqvist, *A Drama
of Souls*, p. 221). Austin
Strong, *Drums of Oude*
(Clark, *Eugene O'Neill, The
Man and His Plays*).
Strindberg's dream plays.
Ridgely Terrence, *Three
Plays for a Negro Theatre*
(1913). Macgowan, *Masks
and Demons*: witch doctor.
Boucicault, *The Octoroon*:
situation (ch. 2).

'Wonderful illustrated
pamphlets of the German
Theatre' (to Macgowan, 1
July 1921). Macgowan,
Theatre of Tomorrow.

Diff'rent   *Moby Dick* (O'Neill's
suggestion): Nantucket
whaling community, and
obsessions it breeds.
Sherwood Anderson,
Winesburg, Ohio:
characterization of Emma.

The First Man
Ape   Strindberg's expressionistic
plays. Synge, *Riders to the
Sea*: Paddy's lament.
Kaiser, *From Morn to
Midnight, Gas*: stokehole
scenes modelled on 'Corral'.
Sandburg, *Smoke and Steel*:
sped 'the crystallization' of

Sandburg, *Smoke and Steel*.
Kaiser, *Morn to Midnight*
(Sheaffer, *O'Neill, Son and
Playwright*, p. 76;
Tiusanen, *Eugene O'Neill's
Scenic Images*, p. 130).
Fraser, *The Golden Bough*.
Fiske, *The Discovery of*

	Ape (Sheaffer, *O'Neill, Son and Artist*, p. 73).	*America* (to Macgowan, 29 March 1921).
Fountain	Dante [dubious]; George Cram Cook, *The Spring*: resemblance of scene (Bogard, *Contour in Time*, p. 234); Macgowan, *Theatre of Tomorrow*; Nietzsche, *Thus Spake Zarathustra*: style echoes that of the English translation (chap. 4).	Macgowan, *Continental Stagecraft*. 'I've read all the Dunsany and Synge things' (to Macgowan, 29 March 1921). *Back to Methuselah* (*Theatre Guild*, 1921).
Chillun Welded	Ridgely Torrence; *Masks and Demons* (Tiusanen, *Eugene O'Neill's Scenic Images*, p. 178); Strindberg, *Comrades, Dance of Death*.	Readings of Stanislavski, *My Life in Art* at Provincetown. Howard's play in hands of Exp. Theatre directors. (Bogard, *Contour in Time*, p. 202.) Bogard suggests plagiarism, unconscious or otherwise.
Desire	T. C. Murray, *The Birthrite, Autumn Fire*; Howard, *They Knew What They Wanted*; Euripides, *The Hippolytus*; Denham Thompson, *The Old Homestead* (Falk, *Eugene O'Neill and the Tragic Tension*, p. 161): all suggested as sources for the plot. Zola, *La Terre*; Ibsen, *Rosmersholm*; Tolstoi, *The Power of Darkness*: all suggestive of mood, atmosphere. Removable walls used in Victorian melodrama (Leech, *Eugene O'Neill*, p. 54). Set modelled on sketch by Yegoroff for Maeterlinck, *The Blue Bird* (ch. 1).	O'Neill recommends to Macgowan: Andreyev, *Black Maskers*: for use of masks, *King Hunger*; Wedekind, *Erdgeist*; Gorki; Strindberg, *Spook Sonata* and *Dance of Death* (Autumn 1923). Takes Wedekind's *Lulu* (combination of *Erdgeist* and *Pandora's Box*) from Library of Congress and complains programme of Exp. Theatre lacks, 'the "Big Men" we recognize as Masters of the Modern Drama' (to Macgowan, 19 August 1921).
1925–34		
Marco Millions	Sinclair Lewis, *Babbitt*: for satire on American businessman. Marco Polo, *The Travels*. Don Byrne,	Quotation from Nietzsche among ms. notes: 'Do I then strive after happiness? I strive after my own work'.

Messer Marco Polo –
novelette, published 1921,
about Marco's romance
with the daughter of Kublai
(Bogard, *Contour in Time*,
p. 254). Waley, *Chinese Poems*.

Read and very impressed by
Ulysses (Sheaffer, *O'Neill,
Son and Artist*, p. 199).
O'Neill champions Hart
Crane (*ibid*, p. 207). Freud,
*Group Psychology and the
Analysis of the Ego, Beyond
the Pleasure Principle*.
Nietzsche, *Joyful Wisdom,
The Birth of Tragedy* (*ibid*,
p. 174). Quotation from
Thomas à Kempis (II. ii).

Brown

Theatre of Tomorrow.
Nietzsche. Wilde, 'The
Picture of Dorian Gray'.
(Sheaffer, *O'Neill, Son and
Playwright*, p. 117.) Kaiser,
'The Corral': comparable
plot (Blackburn,
'Continental influence', p.
123). 'It is a heap of literary
reminiscences, unorganized,
undigested' (Tiusanen,
*Eugene O'Neill's Scenic
Images*, p. 192).

Lazarus

Nietzsche, *Thus Spake
Zarathustra, The Birth of
Tragedy*: plot, philosophy.
Reinhardt, *The Miracle*;
Macgowan: use of groups
and of marionette-like
central figure. Salmi Morse,
Passion Play (my
suggestion).

Praises Werfel's *Goat Song*
in letter *N.Y. Times* (7
March 1926, VIII, 2:8).
Jonson, the *Alchemist*.
Quotation from New
Testament, and from
Nietzsche. Quotation from
Nietzsche among MS notes.
Bergson, *Laughter*; Freud,
Wit and the Unconscious.

Interlude

Alice Gerstenburg,
Overtones; Woolf; Joyce,
Ulysses: interior monologue.
Wedekind, *Pandora's Box,
Erdgeist*: for
characterization of Nina
Leeds. Shaw, *Back to
Methuselah*: length.

Dudley Fitts' translation of
Alcestes. Noted
dissatisfaction with way
'Electra' ends in Greek
drama (Sheaffer, *O'Neill,
Son and Artist*, p. 336).
Proust (Sergeant, 'Eugene
O'Neill: The Man with a
Mask', p. 87).
Hofmannsthal's *Elektra*: 'I
find it the only modern play

in verse that is both true
poetry and true drama' (4
April 1926, to Macgowan).
Admires Paul Green,
Abraham's Bosom. Asked if
had literary idol, replied
'Nietzsche' (Sheaffer,
O'Neill, Son and Artist, p.
122).

Dynamo	Henry Adams, *The Dynamo* (Koischwitz, *O'Neill*, p. 45). Kaiser, '*Gas*: Modern Science as God', (Blackburn 'Continental influence', p. 132).	Aristotle, *Poetics* (O'Neill's copy in Beinecke, heavily underlined). Saw Lenormand's *Mixture* (Sheaffer, *O'Neill, Son and Artist*, p. 350).
Electra	Sophocles, Aeschylus, Euripides. Melville: sea images; escapism of South Sea Islands. G. V. Hamilton and Kenneth Macgowan, *What's Wrong with Marriage?* – a Freudian account of human relationships. Freud: dramatization of 'Oedipus complex'. Stephen Crane, '*The Red Badge of Courage*: Orin's memories of the civil war' (ch. 4).	Discussion, by characters in the play, of Melville's *Typee*.
Wilderness	Booth Tarkington, *The Magnificent Ambersons*: nostalgic portrayal of American small-town family life.	Quotation of *Rubáiyát*, by nostalgic character, Lily. Quotation or discussion by rebel-poet adolescent of Wilde; Shaw, *The Quintessence*; Carlyle; Swinburne.
Days		T. S. Eliot, *Ash Wednesday*. Quotation from and reference to Thompson, *The Hound of Heaven*; Nietzsche, *Thus Spake Zarathustra*.

1934–39		
O'Neill preparing and writing his Cycle of plays	Zola, *Rougon-Macquart* novels (Appendix 3).	Makes notes in C. R. Fish, *The Rise of the Common Man* (1929). O'Neill reading nineteenth-century history of America and novelists, for background material. (Notes, *BEINECKE*.) Early 1936, O'Neill thought Nobel prize should go to Dreiser. (Sheaffer, *O'Neill, Son and Artist*, p. 458.) 1936, tribute to Nietzsche and to Strindberg in Nobel prize acceptance speech. 1938, wrote to *Nordiske Tidende* that had recently reread Ibsen completely.
1939–43 Hughie		Nichols describes O'Neill as valuing Zola highly in this period (letter 5 November 1959, Nichols to Yale Univ. Library).
Iceman	Gorki, *The Lower Depths*; Ibsen, *The Wild Duck*; Saroyan, *The Time of Your Life*; Strindberg, *The Red Room*. Nietzschean philosophy: Larry.	O'Neill saw *Time of Your Life*, and later suggested principal actor, Eddie Dowling, to play Hickey. Anarchist writings of Emma Goldman and colleagues; Hyppolite Havel, *The Flame*.
Journey	Strindberg, *The Dance of Death*. Ibsen, *Ghosts* (treatment of time). Richard Dana (ch.6).	Quotation from Nietzsche; Kipling; Shakespeare; Baudelaire; Swinburne; Dowson.
Poet	Thoreau, *Walden*: Simon modelled on Thoreau's persona. Charles Lever, *Charles O'Malley*: Alexander demonstrates in her article that Lever is the	Quotation of Byron, *Childe Harold*. Extensive quotation in ms. notes of Thoreau. Quotation in ms. notes from Emerson, *Journal*; Whitman, *Leaves of Grass*.

source of O'Neill's Irish dialect, military slang and battle descriptions. O'Casey, *Juno and the Paycock*.	Notes taken from *Charles O'Malley*.
Moon	Quotation from Shakespeare; Dowson, *Cynara*: this is brief but in first draft was extensive, the poem being the central motif of the original act IV (ms. notes for *Moon*).1948, Basso, 'The Tragic Sense', describes O'Neill's room – sets of Zola, Victor Hugo and Balzac. Two shelves of English and American Poets. (13 March 1948, p. 46.)

In addition to the specific references given here, commentators are in agreement that there is a pervasive influence of Conrad on the early sea plays (see Bogard, *Contour in Time*, pp. 39–42), and of Nietzsche and Strindberg throughout. Engel (*Haunted Heroes*, p. 89) finds a general influence in O'Neill's work of Thoreau, Wagner, Freud, Mallarmé and Maeterlinck, although there is little biographical evidence that O'Neill was much interested in any of these writers except Thoreau.

Van Wyck Brooks (*The Confident Years*, p. 243) suggests that O'Neill was particularly receptive to American concerns of the day and finds themes in the plays that are shared with Norris, Dreiser, London, Hemingway, Steinbeck and Faulkner. Raleigh (*The Plays of Eugene O'Neill*, pp. 239–85) investigates the connection with Emerson, Henry Adams and Melville, and the 'complex tortuousness of classical American Literature of the 19th Century' (p. 241).

APPENDIX 2

Irish dialect and artifice in
the two last plays

A confusion has arisen about O'Neill's use of Irish dialect in the late plays. In these plays, he looks directly to his own autobiography for his material and he also, for the first time, creates a large number of serious characters who are Irish in origin. He also makes use of Irish brogue and this had led some commentators to explain the effectiveness of the late plays by likening O'Neill's language to Synge's. Brustein, for example, has written:

And in writing these plays, he stammers no more. In the lilting speech of predominantly Irish Catholic characters, O'Neill finally discovers a language congenial to him, and he even begins to create a music very much like Synge's, while his humour bubbles more and more to the surface.

(The Theatre of Revolt, London, 1965, p. 358)

And Rudolph Stamm is even more explicit:

He was never more successful . . . than in depicting people of his own Irish origin. When he wrote speeches for them, he could draw on the inexhaustible source of language that had fed the works of John Millington Synge, Lady Gregory, Sean O'Casey and many another writer of the dramatic revival in Ireland. O'Neill was one of the Tyrones himself, and he was connected in a special way with Larry Slade and Pat Macgloin, with the Hogans and the Melodys. Among them, there existed no linguistic perplexities for him.

(The Shaping Powers at Work, Heidelberg, 1967, pp. 275–6)

There is a curious sentimentality about the Irish language evident here. The writing of Synge, Lady Gregory and O'Casey is very different and, after the first moment of recognition that each does have an Irish basis, it is the difference which is interesting. The comparison with Synge is too easy: it is one which comes readily whenever a writer uses Irish dialect effectively, regardless of how he uses it. But as anything more than a loose compliment it is not helpful.

This is not to deny that the Irishness of the characters was intensely important to O'Neill. It does look as though he deliberately avoided using Irish dialect on several occasions in the early plays and Brustein is right, if we except *The Iceman Cometh*, in noting that the characters of the late plays are predominantly Irish Catholic, at least in origin. But that is an important qualification. We need to be clear which characters normally use Irish dialect, or even an Irish lilt and, again importantly, when. The Tyrone sons speak General American; the speech of their parents, as of Larry Slade in *The Iceman Cometh*, is also General American, but it occasionally contains a suggestive lilt. Cathleen, the brogue-speaking maid in *Long Day's Journey Into Night*, plays only a minor part in the play, as we have seen, and Macgloin's New York Irish is simply part of the medley, one ethnic speech mode among many. The Irish dialect, in these plays, is never O'Neill's general medium but is used by him, like New York slang or Mary Tyrone's girlish effusiveness, on particular occasions, for particular purposes.

The brogue is used by major characters in *A Moon for the Misbegotten* and *A Touch of the Poet*. So it is in connection with these plays that we must consider O'Neill's use of Irish dialect. It is quite removed from anything that Synge wrote.

Nicholas Grene, in a study of Synge's language, has noted that the writers of the Irish Dramatic Movement consciously rejected stage Irishry. Unlike the melodramatists, neither Synge nor Lady Gregory attempted to indicate pronunciation through divergent orthography and, in the later drafts of his plays, Synge deleted markers like 'Sure ...'. The markers which do appear in Synge's dialect are certain recurrent words, 'queer'; 'the like of'; 'his like'; 'what way' and 'And ...' to begin a sentence, and some syntactical features which Synge had observed in Gaelic and had translated into English. These include the suppression of the relative 'which' and the use of the progressive form of the verb, 'I am going' for 'I go'.[1] In O'Neill's brogue we meet the very elements that Synge rejected – the orthography, the traditional stage Irishisms: 'destroyed entirely', 'divel a ...', 'Sure ...', 'acushla', 'faix'. Indeed, Doris Alexander, in a piece of scholarly detective work, has shown that O'Neill took many of his phrases and Irish idioms ready-made from Charles Lever's romance, *Charles O'Malley*.[2] I found, in support of Alexander's theory, that the numbers beside the dialect phrases O'Neill has recorded coincide with the numbers of the pages of my copy of *Charles O'Malley* on which the same phrases occur. (And see the reference to Lever in Appendix 1.) O'Neill, moreover, makes little use of the poetic period, so characteristic of Synge's dialogue.

O'Neill's language is quite different in form from Synge's. It is as essential a part of his dramatic context but that context, too, is different. O'Neill is not writing about the kings and peasants of Ireland. His characters are Irish immigrants to America and first or second generation Americans of Irish extraction. This is not a quibble; the cultural change involved was a significant one[3] and O'Neill was sensitive enough to time and place to reflect that change in the language. The Irish cadences we heard occasionally in the speech of Mary Tyrone or Larry Slade shadowed their loss and their longing. The brogue used in *Touch of the Poet* and *A Moon for the Misbegotten*, represents another aspect of the immigrant experience. Using it, the Hogans and the Melodys play the role of Irishman: they fit themselves to a model of Irishness created by an alien culture.

In *A Moon for the Misbegotten*, the brogue is used humorously although, as always in O'Neill, the humour has serious implications. Like slang, its use can separate insiders from outsiders: in their discomforting of Harder, Phil and Josie Hogan, who usually speak low-colloquial American with a sprinkling of Irishisms, adopt a heavy brogue and, with it, the fluency, quick wit, confidential manner and tone of total self-belief traditional in the stage Irishman. Throughout the play, Phil can resort to his Irish role to mask embarrassment or avert another's anger so that the very use of the brogue, whilst it amuses the audience, signals these emotions to them. The use is more complicated in *A Touch of the Poet*. Indicating a former life style that has been shrugged off in the act of emigrating, the brogue is a despised idiom. It marks out those who have not succeeded from those who have. The riff-raff who flock to Melody's inn for free liquor use it habitually, revelling in their role as Irishmen. The first time the brogue is mentioned, as opposed to used, is when Melody reproaches Nora, saying 'you won't even cure yourself of that damned peasant's brogue' (p. 19). Nora's speech acts as a constant reminder to Melody, and to the audience, of his antecedents and his precarious position in the present. The deliberate adoption of the brogue by first one and, eventually, the other, is used by O'Neill to project the relationship of Sara and Melody. The daughter, resenting her father's pose, mocks him by adopting the brogue and he reveals himself vulnerable to the mockery, in exchanges such as this, which follows a gallant compliment from Melody:

SARA. Musha, but it's you have the blarneyin' tongue, God forgive you!
MELODY. Be quiet. How dare you talk to me like a common, ignorant – You're my daughter, damn you. (*He controls himself and forces a laugh*.) A fair hit! You're a great tease, Sara.

(p. 35)

As Nora says, 'She only puts on the brogue to tease you. She can speak as fine as any lady in the land if she wants' (p. 32). Sara's role-playing serves as a preparation for the end of the play. Melody's adoption of a heavy brogue replete with stage-Irish phrases – 'begorrah'; 'bejaysus' – after he has publicly disgraced himself, tells us clearly that he has still not found the truth about himself but has substituted one pose, that of Irish shebeen-keeper, for that of gentleman and hero of Talavera. O'Neill is as much concerned with questions of identity and self-deception in this play as in *The Iceman Cometh* and here, as there, the linguistic structure of the play and the interaction in it of different kinds of language is an essential element in our response to the play and our recognition of its meanings.[4]

A note on 'A Tale of Possessors, Self-Dispossessed', O'Neill's cycle of American history plays

Several commentators have bitterly lamented the fact that O'Neill was never able to complete his projected cycle of plays, 'A Tale of Possessors, Self-Dispossessed'. Travis Bogard, for example, introducing his scholarly reconstruction of the material, has written:

> That Eugene O'Neill could not complete the historical cycle as it was designed is one of the greatest losses the drama in any time has sustained. Goethe's comment on Marlowe's *Dr. Faustus*, 'How greatly it was planned', has more relevance to 'A Tale of Possessors Self-Dispossessed'. It was a work of astonishing scope and scale. Theresa Helburn rightly called it a *comedie humaine*. Nothing in the drama, except Shakespeare's two cycles on British history could have been set beside it. The two plays that survived reveal something of the power of life that beat in it, but they show only vestiges of what its full plan realised could have provided: a prophetic epitome for the course of American destiny.[1]

But in the light of what we have seen of O'Neill's late plays, such comments seem inappropriate. *A Touch of the Poet*, which has many features in common with the late plays, did not 'survive': it was detached from the cycle by O'Neill and completely rewritten in 1942, after he had written *The Iceman Cometh* and *Long Day's Journey Into Night*. It cannot, therefore, be considered to be properly representative of the cycle plays which O'Neill deliberately destroyed. *More Stately Mansions* does seem to have been a genuine 'survival' but the only version currently available was drastically cut by Karl Gierow for production from approximately the length of *Strange Interlude*, and is therefore hardly the text that O'Neill wrote.[2] It is difficult, for this reason, to discuss O'Neill's form or method with any certainty although some observations do seem to be possible. The play is written wholly in General American and there seems to be little of the internal density of reference that was apparent in the late plays. Some of the devices present in the middle plays, but not subsequently, are found in *More Stately Mansions*, the most notable being the use of lengthy spoken-thoughts or thought-asides. Equally telling in deciding where in O'Neill's writing the cycle must be located, is the dramatist's handling of the passage of time. In this area, moreover, information from Gierow's published text can be reinforced from the extant plans and notes for the cycle, which refer to the organization of the plays which O'Neill either failed to write or chose to destroy. I think that it would be helpful to investigate this in some detail.

In the early plays, O'Neill used the traditional quarter-hour interval break in the action to mark the passage of time. Several months or years would be understood to have passed between each of the two or three parts of the play. In *Beyond the Horizon*, visible decay, shown by changes in make-up, costume and set, from scene to scene, images the spiritual decay of the characters. *Diff'rent* falls into two parts, separated by a period of twenty years, and, indeed, a major flaw in the play is that the effects we see in act II derive too directly from causes twenty years past, whilst the motivation for the changes that take place in the space between the first and the second half of the play has had to be too explicit in act I. In the middle years, as we saw in chapter 7, O'Neill attempted to make the passage of time seem more realistic by increasing the sheer bulk of the play.[3] The episodes of *Strange Interlude*, span a fictional period of twenty-eight years: again, physical ageing is used to give objective form to the spiritual alteration of the characters. The change here is that the ageing takes place gradually over the nine acts of the play so that, although the characters have quite changed between the first and the final acts, they can be identified as themselves by the audience who have witnessed several stages in the process of falling away and accretion.

The appeal to O'Neill of a cycle of plays in which such a process could be developed over a number of plays, can well be imagined. Causes and sources could be traced but most of the expository material dropped since the background for each play would be formed by the events of other plays in the cycle. A character could be gradually shown whole because different facets could be revealed in different plays, his appearance and characteristics could be shown as recurring in his descendants and the long term effects of decisions and actions could be demonstrated. When the plays were performed in sequence, the immediacy of the dramatic experience in each individual play would coexist with an impression of evolution normally only possible in an unusually extended work.[4]

The evidence of the cycle material that remains makes it clear that, as with the middle plays, the passing of time is to be demonstrated on the stage. This is not true of *A Touch of the Poet*, whose time span is of a piece with the other late plays, although it is unclear whether this was the case before the play was rewritten, in 1942. With the possible exception of *A Touch of the Poet*, then, each cycle play was planned to cover at least one year of fictional time, and some were to span twenty. They were to move, too, in space: 'The Man on the Iron Horseback', for example, was to be set in New York, Paris, Shanghai and the Mid-West. The action of *More Stately Mansions* spans ten years and moves between a log cabin on a lake near a Massachusetts village, the garden and the parlour of the Harford home in the city, the sitting room of Sara's home in a neighbouring mill town, and Simon Harford's city office.

A letter from O'Neill to Sisk, written in July 1935, reinforces the impression which O'Neill's notes and plans give, that the cycle has more in common with the middle than the late plays. O'Neill continually thinks of the cycle plays in relation to the middle plays:

it's a cycle of seven plays portraying the history of the inter-relationships of a family over a period of approximately a century. The first play begins in 1829, the last ends in 1932. Five generations of this family appear in the Cycle. Two of the plays take place in New England, one almost entirely in a clipper ship . . . Each play will be concentrated around the final fate of one member of the family but will also carry on the story of the family as a whole ... In short, it is a broadening of the *Electra* idea – but, of course, not based on any classical theme. It will be less realistic than *Electra* in method, probably – more poetical in general, I hope – more of *The Great God Brown* over and undertones, more symbolical and complicated (in that it will have to deal with intermingling relationships) – and deeper probing. There is a general spiritual undertheme for the whole Cycle and the separate plays make this manifest in different aspects.

Despite O'Neill's initial enthusiasm for the project, there were problems from almost the beginning. In 1936, he wrote to the Theatre Guild, that he was hoping for 'a surge of creative energy' (7 April 1936) and, at the end of the year, noted in his diary, 'cannot figure out a way of ending "Greed of the Meek"'. In 1937, he noted that his new play was 'psychologically too complicated' and, the following year, wrote of the fourth play to Macgowan, 'It is, I think – and hope! – the most difficult of the lot. Psychologically extremely involved and hard to keep from running wild and boiling over the play mould' (28 December 1938). In 1939, he wrote to Lawrence Langner:

I made myself put it aside for the past seven months. Had gone terribly stale, as I told you when we talked on the phone, and did not start the fifth play beyond getting it ready to start. Since then I have been working on other things.

(Quoted Gelbs, *O'Neill*, p. 834)

The 'other things' were, of course, *The Iceman Cometh* and the scenario of *Long Day's Journey Into Night*. The cycle is subsequently referred to in letters to both Sisk (3 August 1940) and Clark (27 March 1941) as 'on the shelf' and, in 1941, O'Neill, again writing to Clark, said, 'the vision of life that binds it into a whole has bogged down in shifting uncertainties'.

Terrible as it was, O'Neill's physical paralysis seems to have played only a part, if even a part, in his abandoning of the cycle. Perhaps we might best think of the cycle as O'Neill's last missionary activity – his last work in which the form was partially dictated by his idea of what ought to be written for a serious American theatre. Alternatively, O'Neill's insistence on size and scope might be seen as deriving from a more private need: the writing of the cycle being an experience he had to undergo before he could write the late plays – his *Emperor and Galilean*. Rothenburg, in his article, demonstrates convincingly that Deborah of *More Stately Mansions* is an earlier version of Mary Tyrone, her retreat into dream prefiguring Mary's retreat into drug addiction. He suggests that the writing of this portrait and probably of others in the cycle, in which O'Neill explores relationships from his own past, but sets them in situations and amongst characters which were not recognizably of that past, enabled O'Neill to face his private self more directly than he had yet been able to do and so made possible the writing of the late plays.

Since the cycle was destroyed[5] such judgements can only be tentative, but it seems to me to be likely that the vital role of the cycle in O'Neill's writing was that it prepared and freed him to write the late plays. These may appear smaller in conception. They do not directly link private fictions to actual events in American history, as the cycle would have done, but their actual felt presence is much larger than what we have of the one surviving cycle play. They are wholly dramatic and seem to transmit the essence of the American – indeed, the Western – experience: the restlessness of the mobile society, the tensions within the nuclear family, the isolation of the individual.

Notes

I have shortened the title of each of O'Neill's plays to a single prominent word when I mention it in these notes: *The Hairy Ape*, for example, appears as *Ape*, *Lazarus Laughed* as *Lazarus*. The place of publication of all books cited is New York, unless stated otherwise, and all letters or manuscript material quoted is held in the Beinecke Library of Yale University, unless otherwise stated.

Introduction

1 Some of the many sources here are: Ibsen, *Letters and Speeches*, ed. E. Sprinchorn (1965); Strindberg, 'The Preface to *Lady Julie*', *Letters to the Intimate Theatre*; Shaw, *Letters*. See bibliography, pp. 234–6, for details and for further sources.

2 Such writers are, Inga-Stina Ewbank and John Northam on Ibsen, and Andrew Kennedy and John Russell Brown on post-war English dramatists. More general studies of drama, which include some discussion of dramatic language are, M. C. Bradbrook, *English Dramatic Form* (London, 1966), and Raymond Williams, *Drama in Performance* (revised edn, 1968). Pierre Larthomas in *Le Langage Dramatique* (Paris, 1972) attempts a poetics of drama and makes detailed reference to the writing of three French dramatists.

3 Notable exceptions are Larthomas' discussion of Molière in the work cited above and Jonas Barish's exploration of Ben Jonson's language, *Ben Jonson and the Language of Prose Comedy* (Cambridge, Mass., 1960). For details of the writings mentioned here and in note 2, see bibliography, pp. 234–6.

4 Letter to Lucie Wolf (May 1883) collected in Ibsen, *Letters*, p. 218.

5 But see John Russell Brown, *Shakespeare's Plays in Performance* (1969). The book by Raymond Williams mentioned in note 2, includes a brief account of conditions of performance in the theatre for which the plays under consideration were written. See, too, Arthur Colby Sprague, *Shakespeare and the Audience* (Cambridge, Mass., 1935).

6 See, 'A Short Organum for the Theatre' and *The Messingkauf Dialogues* (trans. John Willett, London, 1960 and 1965), particularly.

7 Constantin Stanislavski, *Building a Character* (London, 1949), p. 113.

8 There is an account of the work of the Survey in D. Crystal and D. Davy, *Investigating English Style* (London, 1969). See, too, Randolph Quirk, *The English Language and Images of Matter* (London, 1972), p. 114. In *The Use*

of English (London, 1968), Quirk distinguishes 'believed usage' from 'actual usage'.

9 Crystal and Davy, *Investigating English Style*, p. 106.

10 Of the three examples given we may be most reluctant to allow that our contemporary, Pinter, does not *reproduce* real speech. Andrew Kennedy, *Six Dramatists in Search of a Language* (Cambridge, 1975), pp. 165–91, shows that Pinter's language is a carefully ordered *parody* of contemporary speech.

11 See, the studies of O'Neill by John Henry Raleigh, Timo Tiusanen, Egil Törnqvist, Travis Bogard and Clifford Leech. (Leech's is the only English study of O'Neill's work.) Details of the work of these writers will be found in the bibliography, pp. 228–30.

12 Note accompanying the reprinting of a 1926 review of *Chillun* in *O'Neill and his Plays*, ed. O. Cargill, N. Bryllion Fagin, William J. Fisher (paper edn, 1966). Hereafter cited as 'Cargill'.

13 The quotations in this sentence are from, Mary McCarthy, 'Dry Ice', *Partisan Review*, no. 1189, reprinted, *Sights and Spectacles* (London, 1959), p. 80; J. H. Raleigh, *The Plays of Eugene O'Neill* (S. Illinois, 1965), p. 209; Ruby Cohn, *Dialogue in the American Drama* (Indiana, 1971), p. 66; and Edwin Engel, *The Haunted Heroes of Eugene O'Neill* (Cambridge, Mass., 1953), p. 299.

14 The quotations, here, are from Francis Fergusson, 'Eugene O'Neill', *Hound and Horn*, no. 3 (Jan.–March 1930), reprinted Cargill, p. 275; Ronald Peacock, *The Poet in the Theatre* (1946, reprinted 1960), p. 5, and Lionel Trilling, 'Eugene O'Neill', *New Republic*, no. 88 (Sept. 1936), p. 176. See also, the drama columns of the British press for 22 December 1971, following the opening of the National Theatre production of *Long Day's Journey*, and the New York press for December 1973, following the opening of the most recent Broadway production of *Iceman*, for a remarkable testament to the 'power' of O'Neill's writing.

15 See, for example, the work of Törnqvist and Tiusanen. Tiusanen has the advantage of practical experience in the theatre in his discussion of O'Neill's 'scenic images'. See, too, Alan Downer, 'Eugene O'Neill as Poet of the Theatre', *Theatre Arts*, no. 35 (Feb. 1951), pp. 22–3.

16 A noteworthy exception, here, is Raymond Williams, who completely revised his discussion of O'Neill for the new edition (1968) of *Drama from Ibsen to Brecht*. See, too, Rudolph Stamm's account of O'Neill's work in *English Studies*, 40 (1959), which is much warmer than his earlier essay, in *English Studies*, 28 (1947).

17 See, Daniel Boorstin, *The Image* (London, 1962); Lionel Trilling, *Sincerity and Authenticity* (London, 1972); Harold Rosenberg, *The Tradition of the New* (Paladin paperback, 1970), and Edgar Wind's Reith Lectures, 1960, published as *Art and Anarchy* (London, 1963).

18 Rosenberg, *Tradition of the New*, pp. 23–4.

19 I will not repeat the arguments. The best discussions of O'Neill's *Electra* and Greek Tragedy are, Rudolph Stamm's in *English Studies*, 30 (1949), pp. 244–55 and Raymond Williams, *Drama from Ibsen to Brecht*, p. 222 and *Modern Tragedy*, pp. 118–19. The two earliest discussions of monologue are Kenneth Macgowan, 'The O'Neill Soliloquy', *Theatre Guild*

Magazine (1929), reprinted, Cargill, p. 449 and Dorothy Kaucher, 'Modern Dramatic Structure' (Missouri, 1928), pp. 125–58. See, also, Tiusanen's thorough account, *Eugene O'Neill's Scenic Images*, pp. 45–8, 78–80, 225ff.

1. *O'Neill and the American theatre*

1 *The Smart Set*, no. 55, p. 72.
2 From an article included in O'Neill's album of press-cuttings (vol. II).
3 1922, from *Selected Letters*, ed. Elizabeth Nowell (1958), p. 11.
4 *Life*, 8 March 1929. Reprinted Cargill, p. 187.
5 Letter to Macgowan, 3 June 1926. The phrase 'shooting at a star' recurs: to Macgowan, 21 January 1922; to Robert Sisk, 28 August 1930. (In subsequent quotations from letters in the Beinecke Library collection, in the text and in notes, the date will be cited immediately after the extract.)
6 20 June 1920. Published in Isaac Goldberg, *The Theatre of George Jean Nathan* (1926, reprinted 1968), pp. 120–1.
7 Doris Alexander, *The Tempering of Eugene O'Neill* (1962), p. 64.
8 Barrett H. Clark, *Eugene O'Neill, The Man and His Plays* (Dover Paperback, 1967), p. 17.
9 Letter to the *New York Times*, 13 January 1935. Reprinted in Wisner Payne Kinne, *George Pierce Baker and the American Theatre* (Cambridge, Mass., 1954), pp. 287–8.
10 *The Oxford Companion to the Theatre*, ed. Phyllis Hartnoll (London, 1967), p. 945.
11 Frank Rahill, *The World of Melodrama* (Penn., 1967), chapter 7.
12 Hamsun's editor, B. G. Morgridge, notes that the chronicle is often embellished and that he had been unable to find record of the verse appendage described by Hamsun. That the spirit of Hamsun's account is accurate is not doubted.
13 David Belasco, *The Theatre Through Its Stage Door* (1919), pp. 53–61.
14 Mordecai Gorelik, *New Theatres for Old* (London, 1947), p. 163. Rahill makes the same point, *World of Melodrama*, p. 26.
15 *Arena* (1897). Reprinted, Alan Downer, *American Drama and Its Critics* (Chicago, 1965), pp. 1–9.
16 William Dean Howells, 'Some New American Plays', *Harper's Weekly* (16 January 1904), pp. 89–90.
17 Act I. Reprinted in John Gassner (ed.), *Best Plays of the Early American Theatre* (1967), p. 53.
18 Letter, dated 13 May 1938. Published in *Nordiske Tidende* (2 June 1938).
19 Cf. *New York Times*, 14 February 1926, VIII, p. 2. In an article entitled 'Ibsen in America', the following plays are listed as having been produced in New York: 1906–7, *An Enemy of the People*; 1907, *The Vikings at Helgeland*, *Peer Gynt*; 1907–8, *Rosmersholm*; 1908, *Love's Comedy*; 1911, *Little Eyolf*.
20 Excepting *The Ghost Sonata*, published 1916, and *To Damascus*, published 1933, in *Poet Lore*; 1939, in book form.
21 My information about publication dates comes from the Library of Congress catalogue and acquisition lists.

22 For example, Robert Edmond Jones, *Drawings for the Theatre* (1925), *The Dramatic Imagination* (1941); Lee Simonson, *The Stage is Set* (1932); Lawrence Langner, *The Magic Curtain* (1931).

23 Helen Deutsch and Stella Hanau, *The Provincetown* (1931), p. 92. Travis Bogard's discussion of the Provincetown Players is good, see *Contour in Time* (1972), pp. 66–80. See also, *The Provincetown Plays*, ed. George Cram Cook and Frank Shay (Cincinnati, 1921). For comments on the importance to O'Neill of the Provincetown subscription list, see Edna Kenton's unpublished ms. on 'The Provincetown', quoted in Cargill, pp. 33–4 and Clark, *Eugene O'Neill, The Man and His Plays*, p. 31.

24 See the introduction by Kathleen Herne to *Shore Acres and Other Plays* (1928).

25 The most accessible sources here, are J. Henderson, *The First Avant-Garde* (London, 1971); A. Veinstein, *Du Théâtre Libre au Théâtre Louis Jouvet* (Paris, 1955); A. Antoine, *Mes Souvenirs sur le Théâtre Libre* (Paris, 1921).

26 Interview with Carol Bird, *Theatre Magazine* (June 1924, pp. 9, 60).

27 One might note, however, that throughout his life O'Neill followed Baker's advice about making a detailed initial scenario.

28 Interview with *New York Tribune*, 16 March 1924. Reprinted, Cargill, p. 110.

29 Author's introduction to *The Wilderness Edition* of the play, vol. III, p. xii.

30 Letter to the *New York Tribune*, 13 February 1921. Reprinted Cargill, pp. 104–6.

31 Letter to the *New York Times*, 18 December 1921.

32 Letter to A. H. Quinn, published in Quinn, *A History of the American Drama*, vol. II (1927), p. 199.

33 'Om Modernt Drama och Modernt Teater', *Samlade Skrifter* (Stockholm, 1913). Translated Børge Gedsø Madsen in Toby Cole, *Playwrights on Playwriting* (London, 1960) p. 19.

34 In O'Neill's article, 'Strindberg and our Theatre', reprinted, 'Deutsch and Hanau', pp. 191–2. See, also, O'Neill's Nobel prize acceptance speech, A. and B. Gelb, *O'Neill* (1962), p. 234.

35 Gelbs, *O'Neill*, p. 520. No source given. Compare Lukács' comment: 'True art thus aspires to maximum profundity and comprehensiveness, at grasping life in its all-embracing totality. That is, it examines in as much depth as possible the reality behind appearance', *Writer and Critic*, trans. A. Kahn (London, 1970), p. 77. Lukács is one of the few major contemporary critics to have written seriously about O'Neill. See, too, *Writer and Critic*, pp. 17–18; *The Meaning of Contemporary Realism* (London, 1962), pp. 84–5.

36 Tiusanen's discussion of O'Neill's use of masks includes a detailed account of their role in O'Neill's *mise en scène* for *The Ancient Mariner* (*Eugene O'Neill's Scenic Images*, pp. 168–78).

37 Copies of *The Mask* are listed amongst items formerly belonging to O'Neill, donated to the Beinecke Library by Agnes Boulton.

38 'Memoranda on Masks', *The American Spectator* (November 1932), p. 3.

39 Introduction, *The Hairy Ape, The Emperor Jones and Anna Christie*, Modern Library Edition (1937), p. vii.

40 See, for example, O'Neill's letter to the *New York Tribune*, 16 November 1924. Quoted in Clark, *Eugene O'Neill, The Man and His Plays*, pp. 84–5.

41 See, Engel, *Haunted Heroes*, pp. 68–74; Bogard, *Contour in Time*, p. 59, and Tiusanen, *Eugene O'Neill's Scenic Images*, pp. 129ff.

42 See, particularly, *New York Globe*, 4 November 1920, '*The Emperor Jones*: an extraordinary drama of imagination'; 10 May 1922, 'Eugene O'Neill sets a new mark in *The Hairy Ape*'. In the second article, Macgowan describes the play as having an 'extraordinarily challenging' new dramatic form.

43 See, for example, a disgruntled letter from O'Neill, dated 7 August 1926, after which he left the Experimental Theatre and signed a contract with the Theatre Guild for subsequent productions of his plays. See, also, letters of 1 August 1924 and 28 September 1925.

44 Page 73, sketch, p. 70. O'Neill's sketches are reproduced from the *Provincetown Playbill*, no. 5 (1924–5). They are also published in Clark, *Eugene O'Neill, The Man and His Plays*, p. 183.

45 See papers in the Beinecke Library. These are discussed in some detail by Doris Falk in *Eugene O'Neill and the Tragic Tension* (New Brunswick, 1958), pp. 15ff. See, also, O'Neill's letters to Clark, 15 November 1932 and to Sisk, 6–10 March 1933, about his difficulties with the play.

46 O'Neill's notebook, entitled, 'List of all the plays ever written by me, including those later destroyed' (Beinecke [restricted]).

2. *O'Neill's literary biography*

1 Interestingly, according to recent biographies of Malcolm Lowry, O'Neill's writing seems to have played much this kind of role in Lowry's life. (See, e.g. Douglas Day, *Malcolm Lowry* (Dell paperback, 1973), p. 89.)

2 For examples, see Appendix 1. Where the source of the information given in this chapter is obvious from references in the Appendix I do not repeat it in the notes to the chapter.

3 The play is published in A. H Quinn, *Representative American Plays* (1938), p. 396. [Extracts from plays in this anthology are hereafter noted as *American Plays*.]

4 The most detailed account is chapter four of an unpublished thesis, Stein, 'O'Neill and the Philosophers' (Yale, 1967). O'Neill's most direct paraphrase of Nietzsche's account of the idea of Eternal Recurrence (LVII), occurs in act IV, sc. i, p. 133.

5 *Thus Spake Zarathustra*, trans. Thomas Common, *The Complete Works of Friedrich Nietzsche*, ed. Oscar Levy, volume IV (London, 1909), p. 266. [Hereafter noted by section number beside the quotation in my text.] This is the translation which would have been available to O'Neill.

6 Compare O'Neill's *mise en scène* for *The Ancient Mariner*. The poem was to be recited in its entirety and the action on stage to illustrate it through gesture, sound, lighting effect and choreographed movement (published in *Yale University Library Gazette*, vol. 35, pp. 61–86).

7 *Modern Drama*, IX (1966–7), pp. 127–35. See, also, Bogard, *Contour in Time*, pp. 37; 434.

8 Collected in R. Sanborn and B. H. Clark, *A Bibliography of the Work of Eugene O'Neill* (1931), p. 111.
9 Tiusanen, also, points out that these 'two plays of reminiscence' are pivotal in O'Neill's career (*Eugene O'Neill's Scenic Images*, p. 241). For discussion of the autobiographical evidence in *Wilderness*, see Gelbs, *O'Neill*, pp. 81–7; in *Days*, see L. S. Sheaffer, *O'Neill, Son and Artist* (London, 1974), p. 410.

3. The American vernacular in the early plays

1 'The Druid' nos 5, 6, 7, *Pennsylvania Journal* (May 1781). Collected M. M. Mathews, *The Beginnings of American English* (Chicago, 1931), pp. 13–30.
2 For a general discussion see, Randolph Quirk, 'Philology, Politics and American English' in *The English Language and Images of Matter* (London, 1972), pp. 1–13.
3 Walt Whitman, 'An American Primer', undelivered lecture (1850), published in *The Atlantic Monthly* (April 1904), pp. 460–70, p. 466.
4 Walt Whitman, *Leaves of Grass*. Reprint of the first edition, edited Malcolm Cowley (1959), line 63, p. 90.
5 (February 1881), collected in Walt Whitman, *Complete Prose* (1910), p. 286.
6 See, Mark Twain, 'Concerning the American Language', in *The Stolen White Elephant* (1888); William Archer, 'America and the English Language', *Pall Mall Magazine* (1898), reprinted, *America Today* (London, 1900), pp. 168–81.
7 'The Editor's Study', no. 4, *Harper's*, LXXII (January 1886), p. 324.
8 *The New Republic*, 13 February 1929, collected in Edmund Wilson, *The Shores of Light* (London, 1952), pp. 421–9.
9 'America Today', *Scribner's* (February 1899), p. 251. The comparison between slang and poetic metaphor has become commonplace. I question it in my discussion of the slang of *The Iceman Cometh*, chapter 5.
10 *Hawthorne* (1879), Macmillan paperback edition (1967), p. 142.
11 Quoted in Malcolm Cowley, *After the Genteel Tradition* (Cambridge, Mass., 1959), p. 14.
12 'Talking United States' (15 July 1936), collected Wilson (see note 8 above), p. 632.
13 Editor's Introduction (October 1916), p. 1.
14 William Wordsworth, *Poetical Works* (London, 1950), p. 735.
15 Address at Washington University (1953), collected in T. S. Eliot, *To Criticize The Critic* (London, 1965), p. 54.
16 *The Collected Works of Geoffrey Chaucer* (London, 1966), p. xxx.
17 See the account in Francis Hodge, *Yankee Theatre, The Image of America on the Stage, 1825–1850* (Texas, 1964).
18 *The Lion of the West, or, The Raw Kentuckian*: an extract from the play, now lost, which was quoted in the *Daily Louisville Public Advertiser* (17 October 1831), collected in Mathews, *The Beginnings of American English*, p. 117.
19 Published in *Best Plays of the Early American Theatre*, ed. Gassner (1967), p. 562.

20 E. N. Barnes, *The High Room* (London, 1953), p. 49.
21 See, for example, the plays of Odets, Miller, Williams and Albee, for New York City, immigrant and southern dialects.
22 Gelbs, *O'Neill*, p. 159.
23 'Poetry and Drama' (Harvard, 1950), collected in T. S. Eliot, *Selected Prose* (London, 1963), p. 65.
24 My information in this paragraph comes from E. Partridge and J. W. Clark, *British and American English Since 1900* (London, 1951), chapter four, and from J. S. Kenyon and T. A. Knott, *A Pronouncing Dictionary of American English* (Cambridge, Mass., 1953), p. xxxli. For further reading, see also, the bibliography.
25 In the 1840s, New York had sixteen daily newspapers serving a population of 400,000, and, in 1919, there were 2,600 daily papers in America (Max Lerner, *America as Civilization* (London, 1958), p. 759).
26 Between 1800 and 1914, thirty-five million people emigrated from Europe to the United States. In 1905–14, the flow of immigrants averaged one million a year (D. S. Lloyd and H. R. Warfel, *American English in its Cultural Setting* (1956), p. 22).
27 Lloyd and Warfel, *American English in its Cultural Setting*, p. 22. Lerner, *America as Civilization*, p. 35.
28 See Lerner, *America as Civilization*, p. 59.
29 By 1890, eighty per cent of the population of New York City were of foreign parentage (N. Glazer and D. P. Moynihan, *Beyond the Melting Pot* (Cambridge, Mass., 1963, my edn 1970), p. 219).
30 This is discussed cogently by Raleigh, *The Plays of Eugene O'Neill*, pp. 219–20.
31 The occurrence of this sound in New York speech, and the literary habit of representing it by 'oi', as in 'choich', 'skoit', is discussed by Kenyon and Knott, *Pronouncing Dictionary*, p. xl, and by H. Wentworth in his *American Dialect Dictionary* (1944), p. 217.
32 G. P. Krapp, *The English Language in America*, vol. I (1925, republished 1960): the discussion of Harte is on p. 236; of Harris, p. 251.
33 See Wentworth for discussion of 'purty', *American Dialect Dictionary*, p. 475; 'lonesome', p. 367. 'Plumb', which was used by Crane in 1894, was in fact not from New England but from Tennessee.
34 David Humphreys, *A Yankey in England* (Boston, 1815). The glossary follows the text, no pagination.
35 H. Wentworth and S. B. Flexner, *A Dictionary of American Slang* (London, 1960): see, for example, the quotation of 'nix on de loud noise', p. 356.

4. *The failure of language in the middle years*

1 A. H. Quinn, *A History of the American Drama* (1927), p. 198.
2 Ruby Cohn, *Dialogue in the American Drama* (Indiana, 1971), p. 26.
3 See for example, the letter explaining the meaning of *Brown* printed in several New York papers, including the *New York Times*, 14 February 1926, VIII, p. 2.
4 See Gordon Craig, *On The Art of the Theatre* (London, 1911, Mercury paperback, 1962), pp. vi–xii. See, also, chapter 1, above.

5 Antonin Artaud, *The Theatre and its Double*, originally published in *Metamorphoses*, no. IV (Paris, 1938). English translation by M. C. Richards (Grove Press, 1958), p. 61.

6 See letters 1929–30, especially to Clark, 29 May 1929, and a letter from Dudley Nichols to Yale University Library, 5 November 1959.

7 *Lazarus* notes – the sketches are pp. 1–6.

8 See Una Ellis Fermor's discussion of O'Neill's choruses in *The Frontiers of Drama* (London, 1948), p. 102.

9 Published 1935; my edition, Faber paperback (1965).

10 T. S. Eliot, 'The Music of Poetry' (1942), collected in *On Poetry and Poets* (London, 1957), p. 28.

11 See, also, Margaret Anderson's introduction to *The Little Review Anthology* (1953). She describes a series of articles on Nietzsche and says, 'Since we were a revolutionary magazine, Nietzsche was naturally our prophet.' See also, H. L. Mencken's tribute in *The Philosophy of Friedrich Nietzsche* (Boston, 1908): Nietzsche was fiercely admired by many of the literati in America in the early decades of this century.

12 First produced January 1921, the play is published in *Contemporary American Dramatists*, no. 5 (London, 1925), p. 48.

13 Compare Stark Young, 'I had the curious experience with *Great God Brown* of being moved by something that I felt behind the play but almost always untouched by the play itself,' 23 January 1926, quoted F. I. Hoffmann, *The Twenties* (paper edn, 1965), p. 249.

14 Letter to Macgowan, 21 February 1927.

15 To Clark, 30 March 1930.

16 To Clark, 22 February 1944.

17 To Macgowan, 21 January 1927.

18 To Clark, 27 April 1930.

19 To Macgowan, 14 May 1926.

20 To Macgowan, 21 January 1927.

21 To Macgowan, 28 March 1930; to Clark, 27 April 1930.

22 Work Diary, May 1929, p. 2. The note was not included in the published version of the diary.

23 John Anderson, 'Eugene O'Neill', *Theatre Arts* (November 1931), pp. 38–42, p. 39.

5. *The late plays and the development of 'significant form':* The Iceman Cometh

1 The frustration is expressed in letters written throughout the period to Macgowan, Clark and Sisk. The cycle is discussed in Appendix 3. *Poet* was detached from the cycle in 1942.

2 In a letter to Sisk, 26 January 1941, he writes: 'I have no plans whatever for the "Iceman" production, and I'm not letting the Guild make any. With war crisis preoccupying every mind and the immediate future so uncertain, I don't want to commit myself to anything except keeping on writing.' *Iceman* was first produced in 1946 and published in 1947; *Moon* failed on a provincial tour in 1947 and was published in 1952, whilst the three other plays were all produced and published posthumously.

3 To Clayton Hamilton, 1939, quoted in *Congress Record* (2 April 1970, no. PS 4843).
4 29 August 1943. A slightly altered version is published in Clark, *Eugene O'Neill, The Man and His Plays*, p. 147. O'Neill makes essentially the same point in letters to Macgowan, 29 November 1940; 15 December 1940.
5 There is a description of these notes in the Beinecke catalogue. See, also, letters to and from Dudley Nichols, 1943–50. Nichols suggested that O'Neill should dictate the play to him when the writer was no longer able to hold a pen, but O'Neill found it impossible to compose in this way (Nichols to Yale University Library, 5 November 1959).
6 Letter to Joseph Wood Krutch, written three months after O'Neill had completed *Interlude*, 1926. Quoted Gelbs, *O'Neill*, p. 630.
7 I have borrowed the phrase from R. P. Blackmur's *Language as Gesture* (London, 1954). Blackmur's discussion of the problems of language in the poetry of Whitman and Emily Dickinson was helpful in my thinking about O'Neill's style.
8 See letters, 1939–45, especially that to Sisk, mentioned in note 2, above, and letters to Macgowan, 10 September 1939; 21 July 1940, and to Nichols, 2 May 1940 and 7 July 1940.
9 See Alexander, *Tempering of Eugene O'Neill*, p. 149.
10 O'Neill's one-act play *Hughie*, is a *tour de force* of this robust slang. Erie Smith's speech is notable for its hyperbole: 'When you call her plain, you give her all the breaks' (p. 27), 'feeling lower than a snake's belly' (p. 31) and, also, for its use of fantastic elaboration: the slang phrase for delirium tremens is 'The Brooklyn Boys will get you', which is, in fact, used in *The Iceman Cometh*. In *Hughie*, this becomes, 'the Brooklyn Boys march over the bridge with bloodhounds to hunt you down' (p. 18). Raleigh gives a list of colourful expressions used by Erie Smith, *The Plays of Eugene O'Neill* (p. 228).
11 In, for example, Maurice H. Weseen, *A Dictionary of American Slang* (1934); and Wentworth and Flexner, *A Dictionary of American Slang*. Page references to these are noted in my text: Weseen is the fuller on O'Neill's period, Wentworth and Flexner is the most recent and authoritative dictionary of American slang. Other dictionaries are noted in the bibliography.
12 Scenario, *Jimmy the P–H.H. play*.
13 'Hugo of *The Iceman Cometh*: realism and O'Neill', *American Quarterly*, V (Winter, 1953), pp. 357–66. For other accounts of prototypes amongst O'Neill's acquaintance, see Alexander, *Tempering of Eugene O'Neill*, passim and Tiusanen, *Eugene O'Neill's Scenic Images*, pp. 225; 264; 267, and Gelbs, *O'Neill*, pp. 170; 187; 286; 298; 361.
14 I don't think that the biographical scholars have pointed out that whilst the roomers in Hope's bar are based on acquaintances of O'Neill, the more fully rounded characters, the Tyrones and Larry Slade, are derived from his own family and a very close friend. The contrast is telling.
15 The quotation is also used in *Ah, Wilderness!* where it is quoted with fondness by the semi-autobiographical character, Richard Miller – see Appendix 1.

16 Rudolph Stamm, *The Shaping Powers at Work* (Heidelberg, 1967), p. 242.
17 One of the most effective sequences in Albee's *The Zoo Story* comes when Albee adapts O'Neill's method and one character tells 'The Story of Jerry and the Dog'. The relationship between *Hughie* and Albee's play is notable.
18 Ruby Cohn, *Dialogue in the American Drama*, p. 52, gives a detailed list of examples of animal and death imagery in O'Neill's play and shows that both occur repeatedly in the roomers' slang. She does not, however, make the further point that one of these two threads remains latent whilst the other exists in lively relationship to the meaning of the play, is brought into focus by the stage action and has an essential role in the play's structure.
19 As a help to the biographical scholars, several of the characters in these notes had the names of the people on whom they were modelled. 'Terry' was Terry Carlin who had a strong influence on O'Neill in the Provincetown days, and with whom O'Neill shared a room. O'Neill helped to support Carlin in the 1940s when the old anarchist was dying.
20 See note 7, above. Blackmur wrote: 'gesture is made of language – made of the language beneath, or beyond, or alongside of the language of words. When the language of words fails we resort to the language of gesture,' p. 3.
21 J. L. Styan, *Chekhov in Performance* (Cambridge, 1971), pp. 239–337.

6. *Significant form:* Long Day's Journey Into Night

1 The term 'register' has been debated by linguists. I have in mind the idea that any speaker is capable of different kinds of speech, according to situation. The term is discussed by Ullman in Seymour Chatman, *Literary Style: A Symposium* (Oxford, 1971), pp. 141–2; in R. Quirk *et al.*, *A Grammar of Contemporary English* (London, 1972), pp. 20–1, and in M. A. K. Halliday, A. McIntosh and P. Strevens, *The Linguistic Sciences and Language Teaching* (London, 1964), p. 87, in which register is regarded as being classifiable according to field, mode and tenor of discourse.
2 In 'Ben Jonson' (1919), also collected in *Elizabethan Dramatists* (1963), p. 79.
3 On 'flat' and 'round' characters, see E. M. Forster, *Aspects of the Novel* (1927), pp. 103–4. Compare, too, R. Peacock in *The Art of Drama* (London, 1957), pp. 178–9; Peacock stresses the centrality of characterization.
4 See, Engels, *Haunted Heroes*, Falk, *Eugene O'Neill and the Tragic Tension*, Alexander, *Tempering of Eugene O'Neill*, Sheaffer, *O'Neill, Son and Playwright* (London, 1969). Sheaffer, in the most recent biography, supplements his information with details derived from the plays and the Gelbs offer as evidence of O'Neill's identity crisis, the fact that a character labelled autobiographical by them turns out not to be wholly so, *O'Neill*, p. 579. The most bizarre piece of such criticism is, perhaps, an article by A. A. Nethercot, 'The Psychoanalysing of Eugene O'Neill', *MD*, 3 (December 1960; February 1961). The best are C. Leech, *Eugene O'Neill*, (London, 1963), chapter one; the final pages of Bogard, *Contour in Time*

and a short article by A. Rothenburg, 'Autobiographical Drama: Strindberg and O'Neill', *Literature and Psychology*, no. 17 (1967), pp. 95–114, in which the psychoanalysis is tentative and the discussion of the relationship between the personal life and the dramatic form, penetrating.

5 Compare W. H. Auden: 'I do not believe that the knowledge of writers' private lives sheds any *significant* light upon their works. For example, the scene between Wotan and Fricka in *Die Walküre* is no doubt based upon Wagner's reminiscences of marital rows with Minna, but this does not explain why it is, musically, one of the greatest scenes in all opera.' *Forewords and Afterwards*, edited Edward Mendelson (1973), p. 244.

6 There is a discussion of more recent trends in Jonathan Culler, *Structuralist Poetics* (1975), pp. 230–8. See, too, Virginia Woolf, *Mr. Bennett and Mrs. Brown* (Hogarth Press, 1924).

7 Quirk, *The English Language and Images of Matter*, pp. 102–7. Quirk reports on tests on students of the effects of introducing and removing 'redundancies' of speech such as intimacy markers ('you know', 'you see', etc.) and disjunction of the type we find here. When such redundancies were used, the students' concentration on and understanding of the subject matter was noticeably increased.

8 Yeats, 'The Play of Modern Manners', in *Discoveries, Collected Works*, vol. VIII (London, 1908), p. 20.

9 O'Neill's first experiment with the device is *Before Breakfast* (1916), a monologue modelled on Strindberg's *The Stronger*. In both plays the audience becomes increasingly sensitive to the silent listener and to the modifying effect he has on the speaker. There are several piercing examples in the words Ella speaks before Jim in *Chillun*.

10 In *Moon*, the delight of Josie Hogan in her somewhat commonplace poeticism about the dawn, draws our sympathy to her and diffuses our irritation with the words uttered.

11 Richard H. Dana, *Two Years Before the Mast* (1840, my edn, Glasgow, 1924). Compare: 'One night ... I ... lay over the boom for a long time admiring the beauty of the sight before me ... There rose up from the water, supported only by the small black hull, a pyramid of canvas, spreading out far beyond the hull and towering up almost, as it seemed in the indistinct night air, to the clouds. The sea was still as an island lake ... there was no sound but the rippling of the water under the stern ... and highest of all, the little sky sail, the apex of the pyramid, seeming actually to touch the stars ... I was so lost in the sight that I forgot the presence of the man who came out with me until he said (for he, too, rough old man-of-wars-man as he was, had been gazing at the show) half to himself still looking at the marble sails – How quietly they do their work!' (p. 327).

12 See also, *The Iceman Cometh*, where the dominant relationship is friendship and all the marital relationships are a part of the past and *Hughie*, where we find the same thing in a more tenuous form. In *A Moon for the Misbegotten*, where sexual love seems all important at the outset, it eventually gives way to the trusting relationship between Confessor and Confessed. In *A Touch of the Poet*, Simon, the young lover, is kept off-stage, and the dominant relationship is that between father and daughter.

13 For comparisons with Strindberg see the articles noted in the bibliography. The best discussion is Rothenburg's (see note 4 above). The influence on Albee is discussed by Albee himself in 'An Interview with Edward Albee' in A. S. Downer, *American Theatre Today* (1967); and by M. Valgemae in an article, 'Albee's Great God Alice', *MD*, 10, pp. 267–73.

14 The interweaving of two or more monologues for tragi-comic contrast has become a familiar device in the drama written in English since the mid-1950s. We find it in the work of Albee, Orton, Mercer, among others. Only Pinter, in *Landscape* and *Silence*, particularly, but also in his earlier work, seems to me to have used it as effectively as O'Neill.

15 See, for example, Raleigh, *Plays of Eugene O'Neill*, p. 238; Tiusanen, *Eugene O'Neill's Scenic Images*, p. 299.

16 Ms. act IV, pp. 9–10.

Conclusion

1 Especially notable amongst recent productions which I have been able to see, have been, *Long Day's Journey Into Night* at the National Theatre (1971/2); *The Iceman Cometh* at the Aldwych (1976); *The Iceman Cometh*, at the Circle in the Square, New York (1973/4); *A Moon for the Misbegotten*, Broadway (1974), and a production of *Moon* performed with an expressionist set, in Paris by the Comédie Française, as *Une Lune pour les Déshérités* (1975). In 1980, the National Theatre staged an O'Neill season playing *S. S. Glencairn*; *The Iceman Cometh* and *Hughie*.

2 See Ann Righter, *Shakespeare and the Idea of the Play* (London, 1962).

3 John Northam, *Ibsen* (Cambridge, 1973), p. 7.

4 This is the way Pound describes drama in *The ABC of Reading* (London, 1931), p. 6.

Appendix 1

1 An extreme example is Winifred Frazer's 'Love as Death in *The Iceman Cometh*', where just a faint echo has been pursued through a whole monograph. 'Love as Death in *The Iceman Cometh*', University of Florida Monograph, *Humanities*, 27 (Florida, 1967).

Appendix 2

1 Nicholas Grene, *Synge* (London, 1975), pp. 65–9.

2 'Eugene O'Neill and Charles Lever', *MD*, 6 (1963), pp. 415–20.

3 See, for example, the account in Nathan Glazer and Daniel P. Moynihan, *Beyond the Melting Pot*, pp. 17; 246.

4 See, too, the ending of *Hughie*, where the adoption by Hughes of Erie's argot puts the seal on Erie's reconstitution of identity and faith in himself:
ERIE. I shoot two bits.
CLERK. Four's my point. (p. 41)

Appendix 3

1 p. 369. The cycle material is described in Bogard, *Contour in Time*, pp. 368–75; Sheaffer, *O'Neill, Son and Artist*, pp. 470–1; Miller, *Eugene*

O'Neill and the American Critic, pp. 130–1, and Fitzgerald, 'The Bitter Harvest of O'Neill's Projected Cycle', *New English Quarterly*, no. 40 (1967), pp. 367–70.

2 *More Stately Mansions*, ed. Karl Gierow and Donald Gallup (London, 1964). Donald Gallup describes the original in the introduction.

3 There is a great deal of underlining in O'Neill's copy of Aristotle's *Poetics* (ed. S. H. Butcher, 1925, and dated '1929' by O'Neill). This includes the sentence, 'the greater the length, the more beautiful will the piece be by reason of its size, provided that the whole be perspicuous' (vii. 7).

4 O'Neill himself compared the idea with *War and Peace*; both Raleigh and Bogard liken it to Shakespeare's History Plays. I would see Zola's *Rougon-Macquart* sequence as a closer model, both as regards the author's conception and his method of work – see O'Neill's description of the cycle in his letter quoted pp. 211–12.

5 'Greed of the Meek' and 'Or Give Me Death', in 1944, since they were, 'too complicated ... too many interwoven themes and motives, psychological and spiritual'. The rest were destroyed in 1952–3. Sheaffer, *O'Neill, Son and Artist*, pp. 454; 666.

Select Bibliography

I *Primary sources*

The Standard English edition of O'Neill's plays is published by Jonathan Cape. All references to the plays are to this edition unless otherwise stated. The first and principal American editions of the plays are listed in *O'Neill and his Plays*, edited by O. Cargill, N. Bryllion Fagin and William J. Fisher (1961, paperback edition, 1966). Other editions of the plays which should be noted are:

The Wilderness edition (1934), which contains brief prefaces to each play written by O'Neill

Nine Plays by Eugene O'Neill (Modern Library edition, 1932). The plays were selected by O'Neill

There are also two pirate editions of O'Neill's first plays:

Ten 'Lost' Plays (1950, London, 1965)

'Children of the Sea' and Three Other Unpublished Plays, ed. J. M. Atkinson (NCR Microcard editions, Washington, 1972). Besides the title play, this includes 'Bread and Butter' (1914); 'Now I Ask You' (1917), and 'Shell Shock' (1918)

These plays were discovered in the Library of Congress. In 1942, O'Neill renewed the copyright on 'Thirst', 'The Web', 'Warnings' and 'Restlessness'. These were reprinted in the Standard edition as *'Thirst' and Other One Act Plays*. O'Neill seems to have believed that all copies of the other early plays had been destroyed. The publication of the 'Lost' plays in 1950, without his consent, was bitterly resented by him

'Tomorrow', a short story, published in the *Seven Arts Magazine* (June 1917), pp. 147-70

The most significant amongst the unpublished letters held in the Beinecke Library are those to Sisk, 1928-34; to Macgowan, 1921-50; to Barrett H. Clark, 1919-45; and to Dudley Nichols, 1932-52

'Collected Poems by O'Neill', in Ralph Sanborn and Barrett H. Clark, *A Bibliography of the Works of Eugene O'Neill* (1931), pp. 109-61

'Notes to a Fragmentary Work Diary', of *Mourning Becomes Electra* (Spring 1926-November 1931) are held in the Beinecke Library. They are reprinted, almost complete, in B. H. Clark, *European Theories of the Drama* (1947), pp. 530-6.

'The Ancient Mariner', presented in the 1923-4 season of the Experimental

Theatre, with *mise en scène* by O'Neill, is published in the *Yale University Library Gazette*, vol. 35 (Oct. 1960), pp. 61–86

There is a detailed list of O'Neill's published letters and articles in Cargill *et al.* (eds), *O'Neill and his Plays*

Eugene O'Neill, A Descriptive Bibliography, by J. McCabe Atkinson (Pittsburg, 1974), lists published books, interviews in newspapers and periodicals and O'Neill's contributions to pamphlets and books

Manuscripts of the plays

There are notes for and early drafts of the plays in the Museum of the City of New York (the early sea plays and *Ah Wilderness!*); in Princeton University Library (see M. L. McAneny, 'Eleven Manuscripts of Eugene O'Neill', *Princeton University Library Chronicle*, no. 4 (April 1943), pp. 86–9), and in the Beinecke Library of Yale University.

Walter Pritchard Eaton's account, 'The Eugene O'Neill Collection', *Yale University Library Gazette*, vol. 18 (July 1943), pp. 5–8, is brief, and now sadly out of date.

In order to give an impression of the extent of the holdings in the Beinecke Library, Yale University, I include here a list of the Yale material connected with *The Iceman Cometh* and *Long Day's Journey Into Night*.

The Iceman Cometh material includes a holograph and two successive typewritten versions of the play with manuscript corrections. There is also a very interesting typewritten copy of the final (as published) version of the play which contains swingeing cuts and corrections in O'Neill's hand. These were not included in any published version of the play and were presumably made by O'Neill after publication of the play. There is a file of notes about the play and preparatory to the writing of it. These include a list of characters and brief descriptions of them; a list of possible names for various characters, and a list of songs of the period. There are some detailed factual notes, of events and dates of fighting in South Africa from the Zulu War of 1875 to the end of the Boer War (1902) [for Wetjoen and Lewis]; of facts about Al Adams and policy rackets [for Willie Oban], and a note about the dynamiting of trains, 1 October 1910 [for Parritt]. There are four drawings of stage plans, two of which are reproduced on p. 139 of this book, and eleven pages of close-written notes entitled *Jimmy the P. – H. H. play, Scenario*.

The *Long Day's Journey Into Night* material includes a pencil manuscript version and a typewritten copy of the first draft of the play with major alterations in O'Neill's hand. There is a summary of the plot which runs to six pages of manuscript and includes a good deal of dialogue, subsequently included in the play. A page of this scenario is reproduced on p. 141 of this book. Amongst O'Neill's notes for this play are an outline of the action of act I; various working notes for revision of different acts and of ideas for inclusion in certain scenes and snatches of dialogue. There are lists of 'recurrent items'; of the ages of the characters, at marriage, at the time of the play etc.; of Irish names, and of quotations from Shakespeare to be checked for accuracy. There are notes of the clock-time of scenes; of 'shifting alliances in battle'; of the 'weather progression' of the play and of 'scene progression' for acts IV and V [e.g. 'Mother and Maid'; 'Mother alone'; 'Mother, Father and Younger

Son']. There is a two-page description of a wedding dress in Carlotta Monterey's hand and there is a detailed diagram of the ground floor of the house on which the set of the play is based. This includes parts of the house (presumably O'Neill's New London home) not shown on the stage. There is also a movement plan for Mary Tyrone at her final entrance. This is reproduced on p. 183.

II *Secondary sources*

I list here the biographies and book-length critical studies of O'Neill (biographies are indicated by*). I also list articles concerned with influences of other writers on O'Neill, the works I have consulted which deal with the American theatre, dramatic language, dramatic form, and the American language and additional books on language referred to in the discussion. Unless otherwise stated the place of publication in each case is New York.

Critical studies and biographies

*Alexander, Doris, *The Tempering of Eugene O'Neill* (1962)

Anderson, John, 'Eugene O'Neill', *Theatre Arts* (November 1931)

Anonymous [St John Ervine], 'Counsels of Despair', *Times Literary Supplement*, 2410 (10 April 1948), 197–9

*Basso, Hamilton, 'The Tragic Sense', *The New Yorker* (28 February 1948), 34–45; (6 March 1948), 34–49; (13 March 1948), 37–40

Bentley, Eric, 'Trying to Like O'Neill', *Kenyon Review*, XIV (July 1952), 476–92

Biese, Y. M., *Eugene O'Neill's Strange Interlude and the Linguistic Presentation of Interior Monologue* (Helsinki, 1963)

*Bogard, Travis, *Contour in Time* (1972)

*Boulton, Agnes, *Part of a Long Story (1917–19)* (1958)

*Bowen, Crosswell, with Shane O'Neill, *The Curse of the Misbegotten* (1959)

Carpenter, F., *Eugene O'Neill* (1964)

Chiaromonte, Nicola, 'Eugene O'Neill', *Sewanee Review*, 68 (Summer 1960), 494–501

*Clark, Barrett H., *Eugene O'Neill, The Man and His Plays* (1929; revised 1947; Dover Paperback, 1967)

Dahlstrom, Carl, '*Dynamo* and *Lazarus Laughed*: Some Limitations', *Modern Drama (MD)*, 3 (December 1960), 224–30

Daiches, David, 'Mourning Becomes O'Neill', *Encounter*, XVI (June 1961), 74–8

Day, Cyrus, 'The Iceman and the Bridegroom', *MD*, I (May 1958), 3–9

Dobree, Bonamy, 'The Plays of Eugene O'Neill', *Southern Review*, 2 (Winter 1937), 435–46

—— 'Mr O'Neill's Latest Play', *Sewanee Review*, 56 (Winter 1948), 118–26

Downer, Alan S., 'Eugene O'Neill as Poet of the Theatre', *Theatre Arts*, 35 (February 1951), 22–3

Driver, Tom F., 'On the Late Plays of Eugene O'Neill', *Tulane Drama Review*, 3 (December 1958), 8–20

Engel, Edwin A., *The Haunted Heroes of Eugene O'Neill* (Cambridge, Mass., 1953)

—— 'O'Neill 1960', *MD*, 3 (December 1960), 219–23

Ervine, St John, Introduction to *The Moon of the Caribbees* (London 1923), 7–17
—— 'Is O'Neill's power in Decline?', *Theatre Magazine*, 43 (May 1926), 15, 58
Falk, Doris, *Eugene O'Neill and the Tragic Tension* (New Brunswick, 1958)
Falk, Signi, 'Dialogue in the Plays of Eugene O'Neill', *MD*, 3 (Dec. 1960),
Fergusson, Francis, 'Eugene O'Neill', *Hound and Horn*, 3 (January–March 1930), 145–60
Fitch, P.M., 'The Language of the Last Three Plays of Eugene O'Neill' (unpublished doctoral dissertation, Stanford, 1966)
Fitzgerald, J. J., 'The Bitter Harvest of O'Neill's Projected Cycle', *New English Quarterly*, 40 (1967), 367–70
Frenz, Horst, *Eugene O'Neill* (1971)
Gassner, John (ed.), *O'Neill in Twentieth Century Views* (1964)
Geddes, Virgil, 'The Melodramadness of Eugene O'Neill', *Brookfield Players Pamphlet* (Conn., 1934)
Gelb, A., 'On Stage he played the Novelist', *New York Times* book review, 30 August 1964
Gelb, A. and Gelb, B., *O'Neill* (1962)
Gierow, Karl-Ragner, 'Eugene O'Neill's Posthumous Plays', *World Theatre*, 7 (Spring 1958), 46–52
Hays, P. L., 'Biblical Perversions in *Desire Under the Elms*', *MD*, 11 (1968–9), 423–8
Hofmannsthal, Hugo von, 'Eugene O'Neill', translated Barrett Clark, *Freeman*, 7 (March 1923), 39–41
Itkin, Bella, 'The Patterns of Verbal Imagery as found in Ten Major Works of Eugene O'Neill' (unpublished doctoral dissertation, Western Reserve, 1954)
Jackson, Bryer (ed.), 'Forty Years of O'Neill Criticism', *MD*, 4 (1961–2), 196–216
Kaucher, Dorothy, 'Modern Dramatic Structure', *University of Missouri Studies*, 3 (October 1928), 125–58
Koischwitz, Otto, *O'Neill* (Berlin, 1938)
Lee, Robert C., 'The Lonely Dream', *MD*, 9 (1966–7), 127–35
Leech, Clifford, 'Eugene O'Neill and his Plays', *Critical Quarterly*, III (1961), 242–56; 339–53
—— *Eugene O'Neill* (London, 1963)
Long, C. C., *The Role of Nemesis in the Structure of Selected Plays of Eugene O'Neill* (1968)
McCarthy, Mary, 'Dry Ice', *Partisan Review*, 1189 (reprinted *Sights and Spectacles*, London, 1959)
Macgowan, Kenneth, 'The O'Neill Soliloquy', *Theatre Guild Magazine*, 6 (February 1929), 23–5
Miller, J. Y., *Eugene O'Neill and the American Critic* (Hamden, Conn., 1962)
Modern Drama (MD), no. 3, is devoted to studies of O'Neill
Nathan, George Jean, 'Eugene O'Neill after Twelve Years', *American Mercury*, 63 (October 1946), 462–6
—— 'O'Neill: A Critical Summation', *American Mercury*, 63 (December 1946), 713–19

Quintero, Jose, 'Postscript to a Journey', *Theatre Arts*, 41 (April 1957), 27–9; 88 (reprinted Raleigh (ed.), *Twentieth Century Interpretations of 'The Iceman Cometh'*)

Raleigh, John Henry, *The Plays of Eugene O'Neill* (South Illinois, 1965; Forum House Paperback, 1969)

—— (ed.), *Twentieth Century Interpretations of 'The Iceman Cometh'* (New Jersey, 1968)

Rothenburg, A., 'Autobiographical Drama: Strindberg and O'Neill', *Literature and Psychology*, 17 (1967), 95–114

Rust, R. D., 'The Unity of O'Neill's S.S. Glencairn', *American Literature (Am. Lit.)*, 37 (November 1965), 280–90

Sergeant, Elizabeth S., 'Eugene O'Neill: The Man with a Mask', *New Republic*, 50 (16 March 1927), 91–5

*Sheaffer, Louis S., *O'Neill, Son and Playwright* (London, 1969)

—— *O'Neill, Son and Artist* (London, 1974)

Shipley, Joseph T., *The Art of Eugene O'Neill* (Seattle, 1928)

Skinner, R. D., *Eugene O'Neill: A Poet's Quest* (1935)

Stamm, Rudolph, 'The Dramatic Experiments of Eugene O'Neill', *English Studies*, 28 (February 1947), 1–15

—— 'A New Play by Eugene O'Neill', *English Studies*, 29 (October 1949), 244–55

—— 'Faithful Realism: Eugene O'Neill and the problem of Style', *English Studies*, 40 (August 1959), 242–50. (These two essays are reprinted in Rudolph Stamm, *The Shaping Powers at Work*, Heidelberg, 1967)

Tiusanen, Timo, *Eugene O'Neill's Scenic Images* (Princeton, 1968)

Törnqvist, E., 'Personal Nomenclature in the Plays of Eugene O'Neill', *MD*, 8 (1965–6), 363–73

—— *A Drama of Souls* (Uppsala, 1968)

Trilling, Lionel, 'Eugene O'Neill', *New Republic*, 88 (September 1936) 176–9

—— Introduction to *The Emperor Jones, Anna Christie, The Hairy Ape* (Modern Library edn, 1937), vi–xix

Voto, Bernard De, 'Minority Report', *Saturday Review of Literature*, 15 (21 November 1936), 3–4, 16

Weissmann, P., 'Conscious and Unconscious Autobiographical Dramas of Eugene O'Neill', *Journal of Am. Psychoanalytical Association* (July 1957), 432–60

Winther, S. K., '*The Iceman Cometh*: A Study in Technique', *Arizona Quarterly*, 3 (Winter 1947), 293–300

—— 'O'Neill's Tragic Themes: *Long Day's Journey Into Night*', *Arizona Quarterly*, 13 (Winter 1957), 295–307

—— *Eugene O'Neill: A Critical Study* (1934)

Young, Stark, 'Eugene O'Neill: Notes from a Critic's Diary', *Harper's*, 214 (June 1957), 66–74

Influences on O'Neill

Alexander, Doris, '*Strange Interlude* and Schopenhauer', *Am. Lit.* 25, no. 2 (May 1953), 213–28

—— 'Psychological Fate in *Mourning Becomes Electra*', *PMLA*, LXVIII

(December 1953), 923 (discussion of G. V. Hamilton and Kenneth Mac-
gowan, *What's Wrong with Marriage*, 1929)
—— 'O'Neill, *The Hound of Heaven* and the Hell Hole', *Modern Language
Quarterly*, xx, no. 4 (December 1959), 307–14
—— 'O'Neill and *The Light on the Path*' (theosophical pamphlet) *MD*, 3
(1960–1), 260–7
—— 'Eugene O'Neill and Charles Lever', *MD*, 6 (1963), 415–20
Andreach, Robert, 'The use of Dante in *The Fountain* and *The Hairy Ape*',
MD, 10 (1967–8), 48–56
Arested, Sverre, 'The Wild Duck and The Iceman Cometh', *Scandinavian
Studies*, xx (February 1948), 1–11
Baum, Bernard, '*The Tempest* and *The Hairy Ape*', *Modern Language Quar-
terly*, xiv (September 1953), 258–73
Blackburn, Clare, 'Continental Influence on O'Neill's Expressionist Drama',
Am. Lit. 13 (1941), 109–33
Brashear, W. R., 'The Wisdom of Silenus in O'Neill's *The Iceman Cometh*',
Am. Lit. 34 (1964–5), 180–8
—— 'O'Neill and Conrad', *Renascence*, no. 2 (1966–7)
Bridgwater, W. P., *Nietzsche in Anglosaxony* (Leicester, 1972) (chapter 14,
pp. 184–90 on O'Neill)
Brown, R. M., 'An Analysis of Conflict in the Plays of August Strindberg and
Eugene O'Neill' (unpublished M.A. thesis, Sussex, 1963)
Chabrowe, L., 'Dionysus in *The Iceman Cometh*', *MD*, 4 (1961–2), 377–88
Cohn, Ruby, 'Absurdity in English: Joyce and O'Neill', *Comparative Drama*,
iii (1969)
Conlin, H. T., 'Tragic effect in *Autumn Fire* and *Desire Under The Elms*', *MD*,
1 (1958–9), 228–35
Falk, Doris, 'That Paradox O'Neill', *MD*, 6 (1963–4), 30–5 [*The Old Home-
stead* parodied]
Fleischer, F. 'Strindberg and O'Neill', *Symposium*, x (Spring 1956), 84–94
Frenz, H., 'O'Neill's *Desire* and Ibsen's *Rosmersholm*', *Jahrbuch für Amerika
Studien*, ix (1963–4)
Hastings, W. H., and Richard F. Weeks, 'Undergraduate Days at Princeton',
Princeton University Library Chronicle, xxix (1965), 208–15
Hayward, Ira M., 'Strindberg's Influence on O'Neill', *Poet Lore*, xxxix
(December 1928), 596–604
Hilton, J., 'The Short Plays of Eugene O'Neill', *The Bookman*, 84 (September
1933), 288–9 [Conrad]
Hopkins, V. C., '*The Iceman* seen through the Lower Depths', *College
English*, 11 (November 1949), 81–7
Muchnic, H., 'Circe's Swine: Plays by Gorki and O'Neill', *Comparative
Literature*, iii (Spring 1951), 119–228
O'Casey, Sean, 'Dramatis Personae Ibseniensis', *American Spectator* (July
1933)
Olson, Esther, 'An Analysis of the Nietzschean Elements in the Plays of
Eugene O'Neill' (unpublished thesis, Missouri, 1956)
Racey, E. F., 'Myth as Tragic Structure in Desire Under the Elms', *MD*, 5
(1962–3), 42–6 [The Hyppolytus]
Sergeant, Elizabeth, *Fire under the Andes* (1927) [pp. 81–104 on O'Neill]

Stamm, Rudolph, 'The Orestes Theme in three plays by O'Neill, T. S. Eliot and Jean P. Sartre', *English Studies*, 30 (1949), 244–55
Stein, Daniel, 'O'Neill and the Philosophers' (unpublished thesis, Yale, 1967)
Törnqvist, Egil, 'Ibsen and O'Neill – a study in influence', *Scandinavian Studies*, XXXVII (August 1965), 211–35
—— 'Nietzsche and O'Neill – a study in affinity', *Orbis Litterarum*, 23 (1968), 97–126
Winther, S. K., 'Strindberg and O'Neill – a study in influence', *Scandinavian Studies*, XXXI (August 1959), 103–20

The American theatre

Alexander, Doris, 'The Passion Play in America', *American Quarterly*, XI, no. 3 (1959), 351–71
Anderson, Annette, 'Ibsen and America', *Scandinavian Studies*, XIV (1935), 115–55
Anderson, Margaret, *The Little Review Anthology* (1953)
Archer, William, *America Today* (London, 1900)
—— 'O'Neill's First Decade', *Yale Review*, XV (July 1926), 789–92
Baker, George Pierce, *Dramatic Technique* (Boston, 1919)
Barnes, E. N., *The High Room* (London, 1953). [A biography of Edward Sheldon]
Bechhofer, G. E., *The Literary Renaissance in America* (London, 1923)
Belasco, David, 'My Life Story', *Hearst's Magazine*, XXVI (November 1914), 601–15
—— *The Theatre through its Stage Door* (1919)
Bewley, M., *The Complex Fate* (London, 1952, reprinted 1968)
Boorstin, Daniel, *The Image* (London, 1962)
Boyd, A. K., *The Interchange of Plays Between London and New York 1910–39* (1948)
Brooks, Van Wyck, *The Confident Years, 1885–1915* (London, 1952)
Broussard, L., *American Drama* (Oklahoma, 1962)
Brown, John Mason, *Upstage* (1930, reprinted Kennicat Press, 1969)
Cargill, Oscar, *Intellectual America* (1941)
Cerf, Bennet Alfred (ed.), *The Most Successful Plays in the History of the American Stage* (1946)
Cheney, Sheldon, *The New Movement in the Theatre* (1914)
Clark, Barrett H. (ed.), *'Lost' Plays of the American Theatre* (20 volumes) (Princeton, 1940, reissued, Indiana, 1963–5)
Cohn, Albert, *'Salvation Nell*: An Overlooked Milestone in American Theatre', *Educational Theatre Journal*, IX (March 1957), 11–22
Cook, George Cram, *The Spring: Contemporary American Dramatists*, vol. 5 (London, 1925)
Cook, George Cram and Shay, Frank (eds), *The Provincetown Plays* (Cincinnati, 1921
Cordell, Kattryn, *Pulitzer Prize Plays* (1940)
Count of Monte Cristo (Fechter version) – the script as produced by James O'Neill (New York City Museum; copy, Beinecke)

Cowley, M., *After the Genteel Tradition: American Writers* (Cambridge, Mass., 1959)
Coyle, W. and Damaser, H. G. (eds), *Six Early American Plays* (Ohio, 1968)
Deutsch, Helen and Hanau, Stella, *The Provincetown: A Story of the Theatre* (1931)
Dickenson, T. H., *Playwrights of the New American Theatre* (1925)
Downer, Alan, *Fifty Years of American Drama 1900–1950* (Chicago, 1951)
—— (ed.), *American Drama and its Critics* (Chicago, 1965)
Dunlap, William, *A History of the American Theatre* (1832)
Eaton, W. P., *The Theatre Guild: The First Ten Years; with articles by the directors* (1925)
Edwards, H., 'Zola and the American Critics', *Am. Lit.* 4 (May 1932), 114–29
Evans, James Roose, *Experimental Theatre from Stanislavski to Today* (London, 1970)
Fuerst, Walter Rene and Hume, Samuel J., *Twentieth Century Stage Decoration*, vols. I and II (1929, republished, Dover paperback, 1967)
Gassner, John (ed.), *Best Plays of the Early American Theatre: to 1916* (1967)
Gilder, Rosamund, 'A Picture Book of Plays and Players, 1916–41', *Theatre Arts Monthly* (August 1941), 563–5
Glaspell, Susan, *The Road to the Temple* (London, 1926)
Glazer, Nathan and Moynihan, Daniel P., *Beyond the Melting Pot* (Cambridge, Mass., 1963, my edn 1970)
Goldberg, Isaac, *The Drama of Transition* (1922)
—— *The Theatre of George Jean Nathan* (1926, republished 1968)
Gorelik, Mordecai, *New Theatres for Old* (London, 1947)
Hamsun, Knut, *The Cultural Life of Modern America* (Copenhagen, 1889), ed. and trans. B. G. Morgridge (Harvard, 1969)
Helburn, Theresa, *A Wayward Quest* (1960)
Herne, James, *Shore Acres and Other Plays*, ed. Kathleen Herne (1928)
Hilfer, A. C., *The Revolt from the Village, 1915–1930* (N. Carolina, 1969)
Hodge, Francis, *Yankee Theatre: The Image of America on the Stage, 1825–1850* (Texas, 1964)
Hoffman, Frederick, *The Twenties* (1962, Freepress paperback, 1965)
Hornblow, Arthur, *A History of the Theatre in America* (Philadelphia and London, 1919)
Howells, William Dean, 'Some New American Plays', *Harper's Weekly* (16 January 1904)
Humphreys, David, *A Yankey in England* (Boston, 1815)
Jones, Robert Edmond, *Drawings for the Theatre* (1925)
—— *The Dramatic Imagination* (1941)
—— Catalogue of designs in 'Three Designers for the Contemporary Theatre', *Fogg Art Museum Pamphlet* (1950)
Jones, Robert Edmond and Macgowan, Kenneth, *Continental Stagecraft* (1922)
Kinne, Wisner Payne, *George Pierce Baker and the American Theatre* (Cambridge, Mass., 1954)
Langner, Lawrence, *The Magic Curtain* (1931, republished London, 1952)
Lerner, Max, *America as a Civilization* (London, 1958)

Macgowan, Kenneth, *The Theatre of Tomorrow* (1921; London, 1923)
Macgowan, Kenneth and Rosse, Herman, *Masks and Demons* (1923)
Mackaye, Constance D., *The Little Theatre in the United States* (1917)
Moses, Montrose J., *The American Dramatist* (1925, reissued 1964)
Moses, M. J. and Brown, J. M., *The American Theatre as seen by its Critics* (1934)
Nathan, George Jean, *The Intimate Notebooks of George Jean Nathan* (1932)
Quinn, A. H., *A History of the American Drama from the Civil War to the Present Day* (1927, revised edn 1936)
—— (ed.), *Representative American Plays from 1767 to the Present Day* (1938)
Rahill, Frank, *The World of Melodrama* (Penn. State U.P., 1967)
Reed, P. I., *The Realistic Presentation of American Characters in Native American Plays* (Ohio, 1918)
Salvan, A. J., *Zola Aux États Unis* (Providence, R.I., 1943)
Saylor, Oliver, *Our American Theatre* (1923)
Sheldon, Edward, *Salvation Nell* (1908)
Simonson, Lee, *The Stage is Set* (1932)
Tocqueville, Alexis de, *Democracy in America* (1835), trans. G. Lawrence, ed. J. P. Meyer and Max Lerner (Fontana Paperback, London, 1968)
Tyler, Royal, *The Contrast* (1790), ed. James B. Wilbur (1920)
Wilson, Edmund, *The Shores of Light* (London, 1952)
Zangwill, Israel, *The Melting Pot* (1913)

Language and form

(a) *Dramatic language and dramatic form*

Arden, John, 'Verse in the Theatre', *New Theatre Magazine*, vol. II, no. iii (April 1961)
Artaud, Antonin, *Le Théâtre et Son Double* (Paris, 1938), translated M. C. Richards (Grove Press, 1958)
Barish, Jonas A., *Ben Jonson and the Language of Prose Comedy* (Cambridge, Mass., 1960)
Beckett, Samuel, *Proust* (1931)
Bentley, Eric, *The Playwright as Thinker* (1946)
—— *The Dramatic Event* (1954)
—— *The Life of the Drama* (London, 1965)
Bradbrook, M. C., *English Dramatic Form* (London, 1966)
Brecht, Bertold, *The Messingkauf Dialogues*, trans. John Willett (London, 1965)
Brook, Peter, *The Empty Space* (London, 1968)
Brown, John Russell, *Theatre Language* (London, 1972)
—— *Shakespeare's Dramatic Style* (London, 1970)
Brustein, Robert, *The Theatre of Revolt* (London, 1965)
Chekhov, A., *Letters*, ed. Avraham Yarmolinsky (London, 1974)
Clark, Barrett H., *European Theories of the Drama* (1947)
Clemen, Wolfgang, *Shakespeare's Dramatic Art* (London, 1972)
Cohn, Ruby, *Dialogue in the American Drama* (Indiana, 1971)
Cole, Toby (ed.), *Playwrights on Playwriting* (London, 1960)

Craig, Gordon, *On the Art of the Theatre* (London, 1911, Mercury paper edn, 1962)

Donoghue, Denis, *The Third Voice* (Princeton, 1966)

T. S. Eliot, *Selected Prose*, ed. John Hayward (1953, my edn Peregrine 1963)

—— *Elizabethan Dramatists* (London, 1963)

Ewbank, Inga-Stina, 'Ibsen's Dramatic Language as a link between his realism and his symbolism' in *Contemporary Approaches to Ibsen*, vol. I (Oslo, 1965)

—— 'Ibsen and the Far More Difficult Art of Prose' in *Contemporary Approaches to Ibsen*, vol. II (Oslo, 1970)

Fergusson, Francis, *The Idea of a Theatre* (Princeton, 1949)

Fermor, Una Ellis, *The Frontiers of Drama* (London, 1948)

Goldmann, Lucien, *Situation de la Critique Racinienne* (Paris, 1971)

Grene, Nicholas, *Synge* (London, 1975)

Hinchliffe, Arnold P., *Modern Verse Drama* (London, 1977)

Hofmannsthal, Hugo von, *Selected Prose* (London, 1953)

Hugo, Victor, 'Preface de *Cromwell*' (Paris, 1827)

Ibsen, H., *Letters and Speeches*, ed. Evert Sprinchorn (1965)

Ionesco, E., *Notes et Contre Notes* (Paris, 1962)

Kennedy, Andrew, *Six Dramatists in Search of a Language* (Cambridge, 1975)

Knauf, D. M. (ed.), *Papers in Dramatic Theory and Criticism* (Iowa, 1967)

Laan, Thomas F. Van, *The Idiom of Drama* (Cornell, 1970)

Lamm, Martin, *Modern Drama*, trans. Karin Elliott (Oxford, 1952)

Langer, Suzanne, *Feeling and Form* (London, 1959)

Larthomas, Pierre, *Le Langage Dramatique* (Paris, 1972)

Leech, Clifford, *The Dramatist's Experience* (London, 1970)

Mincoff, M., 'The Structural Pattern of Shakespeare's Tragedies', *Shakespeare Survey* 3 (1950), 59ff

Muir, Kenneth, 'Verse and Prose', *Contemporary Theatre, Stratford on Avon Studies*, 4 (London, 1967)

Northam, John, *Ibsen's Dramatic Method* (London, 1953)

—— *Ibsen, A Critical Study* (Cambridge, 1973)

Peacock, Ronald, *The Poet in the Theatre* (London, 1946; Hill and Wang, 1960)

—— *The Art of Drama* (London, 1957)

Raysor, T. M., 'The Aesthetic Significance of Shakespeare's Handling of Time', *Studies in Philology*, XXXII (1935), 197–209

Righter, Ann, *Shakespeare and the Idea of the Play* (London, 1962)

Sprague, A. C., *Shakespeare and the Audience* (Cambridge, Mass., 1935)

Shaw, George Bernard, *Major Critical Essays* (London, 1932)

—— *Shaw on Theatre*, ed. E. J. West (London, 1958)

Stanislavski, Constantin, *Building a Character*, trans. E. R. Hapwood (London, 1949)

—— *My Life in Art*, trans. J. J. Robbins (London, 1967)

Strindberg, A., 'The Preface to *Lady Julie*' (1888, my edn Everyman paperback, 1950)

—— *Letters to the Intimate Theatre*, translated Walter Johnson (London, 1967)

Styan, J. L., *Elements of Drama* (Cambridge, 1960)

—— *The Dark Comedy* (Cambridge, 1962)
—— *Chekhov in Performance* (Cambridge, 1971)
Synge, J. M., 'Preface to *Playboy of the Western World*'
Vannier, Jean, 'A Theatre of Language', *Tulane Drama Review*, vol. 7 (Spring 1963)
Williams, Raymond, *Drama from Ibsen to Eliot* (London, 1952)
—— *Modern Tragedy* (London, 1966)
—— *Drama from Ibsen to Brecht* (London, 1968)
—— *Drama in Performance* (Revised edn, 1968, Penguin edn, 1972)
Wilson, Edmund, 'Is Verse a Dying Technique', *The Triple Thinkers* (London, 1952, Penguin, 1962)
Yeats, W. B., *Discoveries, Complete Works*, vol. VIII (London, 1908)
—— *Plays and Controversies* (London, 1924)
—— *Essays and Introductions* (London, 1961)
—— *Explorations* (London, 1962)
Zola, Emile, 'Le Naturalisme au Théâtre', *Le Roman Expérimental* (Paris, 1880)

(b) *The American language*

Bartlett, J. R., *A Dictionary of Americanisms* (Boston, 1892)
Berrey, L. V. and Bark, Melvin van den, *The American Thesaurus of Slang* (1942, revised 1954)
Blackmur, R. P., *Language as Gesture* (London, 1954)
Chatman, Seymour, *Literary Style: A Symposium* (Oxford, 1971)
Craigie, William A., *The Growth of American English* (Oxford, 1940)
Crystal, D. and Davy, D., *Investigating English Style* (London, 1969)
Fowler, Roger, *The Languages of Literature* (London, 1971)
James, Henry, *The Question of Our Speech* (Boston, 1905)
—— 'James Russell Lowell' (1892), collected Leon Edel, *Henry James: The American Essays* (1956)
Kenyon, J. S. and Knott, T. A., *A Pronouncing Dictionary of American English* (Cambridge, Mass., 1953)
Killheffer, Marie, 'A comparison of the dialect of the Biglow Papers with the dialect of four Yankee Plays', *American Speech*, III (February 1918) 222–36
Krapp, G. P., *The English Language in America*, vol. I (1925, republished 1960)
Kurath, H., 'The American Languages', *Scientific American*, CLXXXII (January 1950), 52
Lloyd, D. J. and Warfel, H. R., *American English in its Cultural Setting* (1957)
Lodge, David, *The Language of Fiction* (London, 1966)
Lowell, James Russell, *Prefaces to The Biglow Papers*, 1st and 2nd series (Cambridge, Mass., 1848; 1866)
Mathews, M. M., *The Beginnings of American English* (Chicago, 1931)
—— *Dictionary of Americanisms on Historical Principles* (Chicago, 1951)
Mencken, H. L., *The American Language* (1919; 2nd edn, 1922; 4th, London, 1936)
Page, Norman, *Speech in the English Novel* (London, 1973)

Partridge, E. and Clark, J. W., *British and American English since 1900* (London, 1951)

Pickering, John, *Vocabulary, or, Collection of Words and Phrases* (Boston, 1816)

Quirk, Randolph, *The Use of English* (2nd edn, London, 1968)

—— *The English Language and Images of Matter* (London, 1972)

—— *The Linguist and the English Language* (London, 1974)

Quirk, R., Greenbaum, S., Leech, G., and Svartvik, J., *A Grammar of Contemporary English* (London, 1972)

Sandburg, Carl, *Abraham Lincoln: The Prairie Years*, vols 1–2 (1927)

Strevens, Peter, *British and American English* (London, 1972)

Tanner, Tony, *The Reign of Wonder* (Cambridge, 1965)

Wall, Bernard, 'Questions of Language', *Partisan Review*, IX (1948), 997–1006

Wentworth, H., *American Dialect Dictionary* (1944)

Wentworth, H. and Flexner, S. B., *A Dictionary of American Slang* (London, 1960)

Weseen, Maurice, *A Dictionary of American Slang* (1934)

Whitman, Walt, *Complete Prose* (1910)

Index